Financial Products, Markets & Services

Edition 2, June 2017

This workbook relates to syllabus version 2.0
and will cover examinations from
1 Sep 2017 to 31 Aug 2018

APPROVED WORKBOOK

CISI
CHARTERED INSTITUTE FOR
SECURITIES & INVESTMENT

Welcome to the Chartered Institute for Securities & Investment's Financial Products, Markets & Services study material.

This workbook has been written to prepare you for the Chartered Institute for Securities & Investment's Financial Products, Markets & Services examination.

Published by:
Chartered Institute for Securities & Investment
© Chartered Institute for Securities & Investment 2017
20 Fenchurch Street
London
EC3M 3BY
Tel: +44 20 7645 0600
Fax: +44 20 7645 0601

With grateful thanks to the IA

This is an educational manual only and the Chartered Institute for Securities & Investment accepts no responsibility for persons undertaking trading or investments in whatever form.

While every effort has been made to ensure its accuracy, no responsibility for loss occasioned to any person acting or refraining from action as a result of any material in this publication can be accepted by the publisher or authors.

A Learning Map, which contains the full syllabus, appears at the end of this workbook. The syllabus can also be viewed on the Institute's website at cisi.org and is also available by contacting our Customer Support Centre on +44 20 7645 0777. Please note that the exam is based on the syllabus. Candidates are reminded to check the Candidate Update area of the Institute's website (cisi.org/candidateupdate) on a regular basis for updates that could affect their exam as a result of industry change.

The questions contained in this workbook are designed as an aid to revision of different areas of the syllabus and to help you consolidate your learning chapter by chapter. They should not be seen as a 'mock' exam or necessarily indicative of the level of the questions in the corresponding exam.

Workbook version: 2.1 (June 2017)

Learning with the CISI

The CISI is the leading professional body for the financial services industry. We have over 40,000 members worldwide who benefit from our qualifications to further their careers. We hope that this exam will help you to build awareness of career opportunities and also your personal financial knowledge. If you intend to go to University, then this exam, in addition to the extended project, attracts up to 60 UCAS points and leads to the Certificate for Introduction to Securities & Investment. Students can also sit our Certificate in Finance, Risk & Decision Making in order to obtain the full Diploma in Finance, Risk & Investment and up to 120 UCAS points.

We work with schools across the UK to make the qualification available to sixth form students. When you register for the exam, you will be able to access a wide range of resources on our website (cisi.org) which will not only help with your studies, but help to broaden awareness of all aspects of the investment banking world. This workbook and the elearning product are updated annually, so please check to ensure you have the correct version for your exam. As well as using industry specialists to update and review the material, we also use students and teachers to ensure that the material is relevant to your needs and level of experience.

For teachers, we also offer a host of support for this module, including teacher training, teaching slides and recommended activities, and for the Extended Project, a Teacher-Assessor Guide as well as exemplar projects, which are available to download from the CISI website at cisi.org/mycisiteachers.

We really hope that you enjoy your studies with the CISI and that you find the learning experience a stimulating one.

It is estimated that this workbook will require approximately 70 hours of study time.

Chapter One
Putting Financial Services Into Perspective

CISI

CHARTERED INSTITUTE FOR
SECURITIES & INVESTMENT

1. Introduction

The significance of the financial services industry has been made abundantly clear since the financial crisis of 2008 was blamed on dubious practices at financial institutions and resulted in governments worldwide 'bailing out' many banks (such as Citigroup in the US and the Royal Bank of Scotland in the UK) as they were 'too big to be allowed to fail'. The activities of bankers and speculators in the financial services industry have been blamed for all manner of issues, from the high price of oil and gold, to the need for countries to seek assistance to enable them to raise finance at a reasonable price, such as Ireland, Greece and Portugal.

This workbook provides a vital introduction to the world of finance, starting with an outline of just how important it is in a developed economy like the UK.

The financial services industry is constantly evolving and it is vital for anyone working in, or aspiring to work in, the industry to keep pace with these changes by scanning the news for important developments. At the time of writing (March 2017), there are major political developments, such as the new Trump administration in the US and the decision for the UK to leave the European Union (Brexit), that will inevitably alter some aspects of financial services. In the US, there may be increased government spending with the inevitable impact on borrowing and some rules that currently restrict the activities of banks may be relaxed. Brexit may result in some financial services activities moving away from London, creating more powerful financial centres in Europe, such as Paris and Frankfurt.

As with other developed countries, the financial services industry in the UK is a major contributor to the economy. Indeed, financial services firms provide employment opportunities in all of the major cities, especially London.

Traditionally, financial services in London were centred on the City of London, although the reinvigoration of east London's docklands around Canary Wharf is equally important as the hub of the UK's financial services activity today. The firms located in and around the City of London and Docklands not only provide considerable employment, but they are also vital in that they generate considerable overseas earnings for the UK economy.

2. The Importance of Financial Services to the UK Economy

Financial and related professional services are a major part of the UK economy and make a major contribution to employment, trade, jobs and taxes.

The financial services sector employs over one million people in the UK, with another million in the related professional services industry. In total, nearly 2.2 million people across the UK work in financial and related professional services – including legal services, accounting services and management consultancy – accounting for over 7% of total UK employment. Of total financial services employment of 1 million, the majority was in banking (416,800 employees) and insurance (308,700 employees). Securities dealing (47,600) and fund management (41,600) were the other main categories, with other

Employment by Sector in UK Financial and Related Professional Services

Employment in main sectors (thousands)

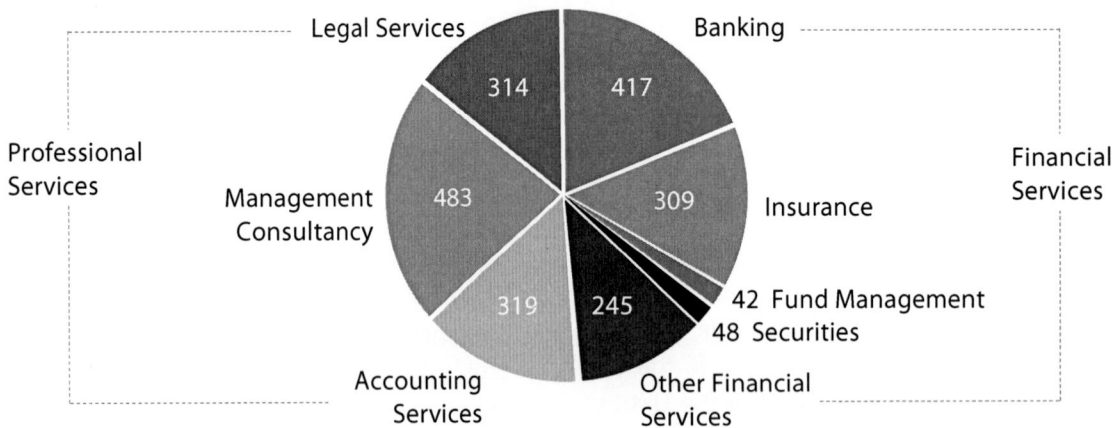

Legend: Legal Services 314; Banking 417; Professional Services; Management Consultancy 483; Insurance 309; Financial Services; Accounting Services 319; Other Financial Services 245; Fund Management 42; Securities 48

Source: ONS Business Register and Employment Survey

UK Sectors Generating Trade Surplus (£ billion)

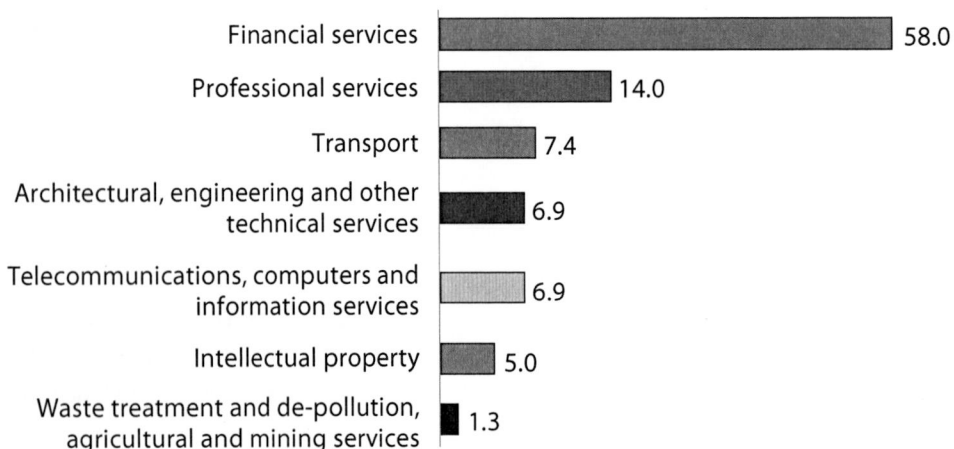

Sector	£ billion
Financial services	58.0
Professional services	14.0
Transport	7.4
Architectural, engineering and other technical services	6.9
Telecommunications, computers and information services	6.9
Intellectual property	5.0
Waste treatment and de-pollution, agricultural and mining services	1.3

Source: ONS Balance of Payments Yearbook

Employment in UK Financial and Related Professional Services

Total: 2,176,700
- ■ >11% of regional economy
- ▨ 9–11% of regional economy
- ☐ <9% of regional economy

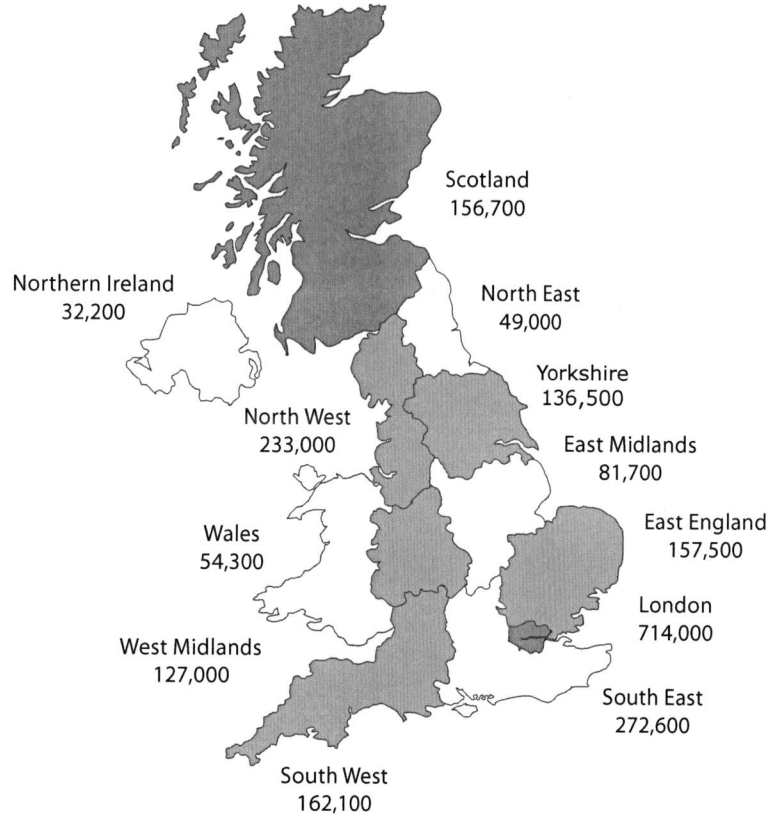

Northern Ireland
32,200

Scotland
156,700

North East
49,000

Yorkshire
136,500

North West
233,000

East Midlands
81,700

Wales
54,300

East England
157,500

London
714,000

West Midlands
127,000

South East
272,600

South West
162,100

Source: TheCityUK, 2016

financial services accounting for 245,300 employees. Professional services employment of 1.1 million people is divided between management consultancy (483,400), legal services (314,100) and accounting services (319,300).

These jobs are not just concentrated in London alone. More than two-thirds are employed outside London, including over 200,000 in the North West and South-East; around 150,000 in the East of England, Scotland and the South West; and around 130,000 in West Midlands and Yorkshire and The Humber. Over 20 towns and cities in the UK each have over 10,000 people employed in financial and related professional services.

The sector makes a major contribution to the UK economy. The UK is the leading exporter of financial services across the world and its trade surplus in financial services is larger than the combined surplus of all other net exporting industries in the UK and is double that of the next largest trade surpluses recorded by Luxembourg, Switzerland and the US. The UK's major trading partners include the US, EU member states and other advanced economies such as Switzerland, Japan, Australia and Canada. These are followed by emerging markets such as Russia, Saudi Arabia, South Africa and Turkey, as well as international financial centres such as Hong Kong and Singapore.

UK financial services are also a vital source of tax receipts, contributing £71.4 billion in tax revenue in the year to March 2016, accounting for 11.5% of total UK tax receipts.

3. Careers in Financial Services

Across the UK as a whole, business services including acting as an intermediary in financial transactions represents almost a third of employment possibilities.

This focus on services is even more pronounced in London and the South East.

A career in financial services is particularly attractive because financial services salaries are substantially higher than those elsewhere in the economy.

The following statistics provide some interesting insights:

- Average starting salaries in investment banks are between £35,000 and £40,000.
- The average graduate starting salary ranges from £20,000 to £30,000.
- The minimum starting salary of a qualified teacher is between £22,467 (England and Wales) and £28,098 (inner London).
- The average gross salary for full-time employees (who had been in the same job for at least 12 months) was £27,600.

4. Professional and Retail Business

The financial services industry can be divided into two distinct areas:

- The **professional sector** – also known as the wholesale or institutional sector. This involves transactions where both sides are businesses, and are commonly described as **business to business**.
- The **retail sector** – in the retail sector one side of the transaction is an individual 'retail customer' and the transactions are described as **business to customer**.

Certain contrasting assumptions are made about professional and retail business.

In the professional sector it is assumed that the participants know what it is they are getting involved in, so there is little need to explain the trades and the professional clients do not need to be protected from their own ignorance about finance and financial services.

Professional trades also tend to be bigger than those in the retail sector, with the result that prices will be 'wholesale' and cheaper.

Professional sector (B2B)	
Assumed to know what they are doing.	
Transactions tend to be larger.	
Cheaper 'wholesale' prices.	

In contrast, in the retail sector the customers do not always know what they are getting involved in. So they need to be given as much information as possible and are only allowed to be sold investments which are suitable for their needs. Furthermore, retail customers are often given the opportunity to pull out of financial transactions for either a particular period after the sale (known as a 'cooling-off' period) or if the products were mis-sold to them, including the provision of insufficient information.

Retail customers also tend to deal in smaller-sized transactions than professionals, so the prices tend to be higher.

Retail sector (B2C)	
Assumed to not always know what they are doing – given a 'cooling-off' period.	
Transactions tend to be smaller.	
More expensive 'retail' prices.	

4.1 Retail and Professional Business in the Foreign Exchange Market

As detailed above, prices tend to be higher for retail customers when compared to wholesale or professional customers. This can be illustrated by looking at the purchase or sale of one currency for another (the so-called **foreign exchange market**).

Exercise 1

A retail customer who is planning a day trip to France has £100 and wants to convert the money into euros. They visit a local bank and see that the bank is quoting the following:

	Bank buys GBP/ sells EUR	Bank sells GBP/buys EUR
GBP/EUR	1.15	1.32

Different currencies are described using three letters with GBP being pounds sterling (the Great British pound or £), and EUR being the euro (€). How many euros will the retail customer get for their £100?

Please try to answer the exercise and then check your response against the answer that can be found at the end of the chapter.

Now, in contrast to the foreign exchange quotes provided to retail customers in the 'high street', the foreign currency quotes provided to professional clients will be different. This is illustrated in exercise two.

Exercise 2

The following are the contrasting quotes from a bank for retail customers and professional clients:

	Bank buys GBP/sells EUR	Bank sells GBP/buys EUR
Retail customers	1.15	1.32
Professional clients	1.2301	1.2303

1. You have £30,000 which you want to convert into euros. How many euros will you get if you are:
   a. a retail customer
   b. a professional client?

2. You have €75,000 which you want to convert into pounds sterling. How many pounds will you get if you are:
   a. a retail customer
   b. a professional client?

3. In percentage terms, how much less favourable are the buy and sell quotes for the retail customer compared to the professional client?

Please try to answer the exercise and then check your responses against the answer that can be found at the end of the chapter.

As exercise 2 shows, the retail customer pays more to buy another currency than a professional client, and the retail customer gets less than a professional client when he sells one currency for another. As will be developed shortly, the reason is essentially that the professional client will be dealing in larger quantities.

This difference between the prices clients pay to buy a currency and the amount they get from the sale of that same currency can be a major source of profit to the money changing bank. This is best illustrated by developing the earlier example of a retail customer changing money in anticipation of a trip abroad.

Exercise 3

A retail customer was planning a day trip to France and converted £100 into euros. Unfortunately, due to a family bereavement, they have been forced to stay in the UK. The following exchange rates apply:

	Bank buys GBP/ sells EUR	Bank sells GBP/buys EUR
GBP/EUR	1.15	1.32

a. How much in pound sterling will they receive when selling the euros back to the bank?
b. How much has the bank made on the transaction?

Please try to answer the exercise and then check your response against the answer that can be found at the end of the chapter.

Where professional clients are involved, the percentage profit margin generated by the bank will inevitably be smaller than that generated from retail customers. However, the sums involved tend to be much more substantial.

Exercise 4

The following are the contrasting quotes from a bank for retail customers and professional clients:

	Bank buys GBP/sells EUR	Bank sells GBP/buys EUR
Retail customers	1.15	1.32
Professional clients	1.2301	1.2303

A professional client converts £30,000 into euros. The client then reverses the same transaction, exchanging the euros received back into pounds sterling.

a. How much in pounds sterling will the professional client receive when he sells his euros back to the bank?
b. How much has the bank made on the transaction?

Please try to answer the exercise and then check your responses against the answer that can be found at the end of the chapter.

Professional clients typically have to enter into transactions that meet or exceed a certain minimum quantity. For example, the minimum 'lot' size for a professional (wholesale) currency transaction might be 100,000 units of currency. So despite the bank's profit margin being a modest 0.016%, the minimum gross profit the bank will generate would be: £100,000 x 0.016% = £16 profit.

Furthermore, the typical transaction size will tend to be a lot bigger than the minimum. Indeed, most professional foreign exchange transactions are in lots of 8 to 10 million units of currency. For a £10 million deal, the bank's gross profit would be £10m x 0.016 = £1,600.

Answers to Chapter Exercises

Exercise 1

A retail customer who is planning a day trip to France has £100 and wants to convert the money into euros. They visit a local bank and see that the bank is quoting the following:

	Bank buys GBP/ sells EUR	Bank sells GBP/buys EUR
GBP/EUR	1.15	1.32

How many euros will the retail customer get for their £100?

The bank's quotes are how many euros it requires to give the retail customer £1 (the 'bank buys' quote), and how many euros it will give the customer in exchange for £1 (the 'bank sells' quote). Since this customer wants euros in exchange for pounds, the 'bank sells' quote must be used and the retail customer will get £100 x 1.15 = €115.

Exercise 2

The following are the contrasting quotes from a bank for retail customers and professional clients:

	Bank buys GBP/sells EUR	Bank sells GBP/buys EUR
Retail customers	1.15	1.32
Professional clients	1.2301	1.2303

1. You have £30,000 which you want to convert into euros. How many euros will you get if you are:
   a. a retail customer
   b. a professional client?

   You are buying euros and selling pounds, so the bank is selling euros to you and you must use the sell quote.
   a. Retail customer: £30,000 x 1.15 = €34,500
   b. Professional client: £30,000 x 1.2301 = €36,903

2. You have €75,000 which you want to convert into pounds sterling. How many pounds will you get if you are:
   a. a retail customer
   b. a professional client?

You are selling euros in order to obtain pounds. The bank is buying euros from you, so you must use the buy quote:

a. Retail customer: €75,000 ÷ 1.32 = £56,818.18

b. Professional client: €75,000 ÷ 1.2303 = £60,960.74

3. In percentage terms, how much less favourable are the buy and sell quotes for the retail customer compared to the professional client?

For the buy quotes: 1.32 − 1.2303 = 0.0897

(0.0897 ÷ 1.2303) x 100 = 7.29% less favourable

For the sell quotes: 1.2301 − 1.15 = 0.0801

(0.0801 ÷ 1.2301) x 100 = 6.51% less favourable

Exercise 3

A retail customer was planning a day trip to France and converted £100 into euros. Unfortunately, due to a family bereavement, he has been forced to stay in the UK. The following exchange rates apply:

	Bank buys GBP/ sells EUR	Bank sells GBP/buys EUR
GBP/EUR	1.15	1.32

a. How much in pound sterling will he receive when he sells his euros back to the bank?

Remember that the retail customer got £100 x 1.15 = €115 (in exercise 1). When he sells these euros back to the bank he needs to use the bank's buying rate of €1.32 for £1, so he will get €115 ÷ 1.32 = £87.12.

b. How much has the bank made on the transaction?

The bank received £100 for the €115, and then purchased the same €115 for just £87.12. So the bank has made £100 − £87.12 = £12.88. Clearly this is before considering any other costs that the bank has incurred, such as staff salaries and the like, but this is a generous margin of 12.88% (based on £12.88 ÷ £100 expressed as a percentage).

Exercise 4

The following are the contrasting quotes from a bank for retail customers and professional clients:

	Bank buys GBP/sells EUR	Bank sells GBP/buys EUR
Retail customers	1.15	1.32
Professional clients	1.2301	1.2303

A professional client converts £30,000 into euros. The client then reverses the same transaction, exchanges the euros received back into pounds sterling.

a. How much in pounds sterling will the professional client receive when he sells his euros back to the bank?

Remember that the professional client got £30,000 x 1.2301 = €36,903 (from exercise 2). When the same client sells €36,903 to the bank in exchange for pounds sterling, the client will receive €36,903 ÷ 1.2303 = £29,995.12

b. How much has the bank made on the transaction?

The bank has made £4.88 on the transaction (£30,000 – £29,995.12), which is only a 0.016% margin (£4.88 ÷ 30,000 expressed as a percentage).

Learning Objectives

Chapter One has covered 'Putting Financial Services in Perspective'.

Based on what you have learned in Chapter One, try to answer the following end of chapter questions.

End of Chapter Questions

1. Approximately what proportion of UK jobs is in the financial services sector?

   Answer Reference: Section 2

   ~~ANY~~. > 7%. /over 7%.

2. How do starting salaries for graduates in investment banks compare to other available options?

   Answer Reference: Section 3

   – average graduate stufing salary rages from 20,000 to 30,000. Average gross salary is £27,600

3. What is the difference between the professional and retail sectors?

   Answer Reference: Section 4

   Professional → "wholesale" or institutional sector. Both sides are businesses and trasactions are larger. Retail → one side is a retail "costumer" → business to costumer. Smaller Transactions and larger duty of care.

4. What is a 'cooling-off' period, and what type of client is a cooling-off period most likely to be given to?

   Answer Reference: Section 4

   a "cooling-off" period is where customers given opportunity to pull out of financial transactions for either a paticulal period or mis-sold items. Given to retail customers.

5. In the foreign exchange market, how do quotes for retail customers differ from those for professional clients?

   Answer Reference: Section 4.1

   Prices tend to be higher for retail customers when compared to wholesale or profession of Customers.

6. What is the typical size of a professional client transaction in the foreign exchange market?

Answer Reference: Section 4.1

100,000 units of currency

Chapter Two
The Financial Services Industry

1. Introduction

Mention the financial services industry and the first type of business that springs to mind is a bank. This chapter begins by exploring the traditional purpose of banks – gathering money by taking deposits from some of their customers and lending money by granting loans to other customers. It then goes on to explore how some banks specialise in particular activities and highlights whether these activities are typically provided to professional or retail clients. Finally the chapter briefly covers the ways that people can invest surplus money, in particular highlighting the so-called 'distribution channels' that are used to enable potential clients to invest.

2. Cash and Where to Keep It

Cash has to be the most basic form of financial asset, it can be spent easily, but it is also a security risk. Because cash can be spent by whoever may have it, it is important that it is kept somewhere safe and secure, and not simply stuffed under the mattress.

The more appropriate and safer place to keep cash is with some form of **savings institution**. In the UK that usually means a bank or a building society. Certain banks are well-known because they have branches on the 'high street' and their customers are individuals or, in bank jargon, 'retail clients'. These banks provide services such as enabling their clients to deposit money into bank accounts and perhaps allowing clients to borrow money in the form of loans. Holding money in a bank account allows the client to make payments by writing cheques or transferring money to others by setting up standing orders, perhaps to the providers of electricity or to the television licensing authority. These types of services are known as 'money transmission services'.

In the UK, these high street banks include the likes of HSBC, Barclays and Lloyds. Banks like these attract cash deposits from a wide variety of clients including retail customers, companies, local and national governments and other financial institutions. They are often huge organisations that have grown in size by linking up with other banks as well as with non-bank institutions such as insurance companies.

In addition to providing traditional banking services through branches over the internet and by telephone, these larger retail banks also offer other financial products such as investments, pensions and insurance.

Banks differ from building societies in that banks are themselves companies, and just like any other company they are ultimately owned and controlled by shareholders. In contrast, a building society tends to attract just retail clients and is mutually owned by those clients. In other words, building societies do not have a separate group of shareholders and are instead owned by all of their depositors and borrowers. At the time of writing, the biggest and most well-known building society in the UK is the Nationwide Building Society, or simply 'the Nationwide'.

Building societies were established in the 19th century when small numbers of people would group together and pool their savings, allowing some members to build or buy houses. As seen, building societies are jointly owned by the individuals that have deposited money with or borrowed money from them – the 'members'. It is for this reason that such savings organisations are often described as mutual societies.

Over the years, many smaller building societies have merged or been taken over by banks. Furthermore, in the late 1980s, legislation was introduced allowing building societies to become companies – a process known as **demutualisation**. However, some large building societies remain as mutuals, continuing to specialise in services for retail customers, especially the provision of deposit accounts and mortgages. Most countries have mutual savings institutions similar to the UK's building societies that started off by specialising in offering savings products to retail customers, but which now tend to offer a similar range of services to those offered by banks.

3. Bank Interest

It may not come as a surprise to know that money deposited with banks or building societies does not just sit within the bank's vaults.

The basic model of a bank is to take deposits, paying the depositor interest on their deposited funds and to lend most of the deposited funds on to borrowers, charging interest on the borrowings. Clearly, the interest charged by the bank to the borrowers will be higher than the interest paid to the depositors. The difference between the two should be sufficient to provide the bank with enough surplus to pay its operating costs and generate a profit for its shareholders.

3.1 Characteristics of Cash Deposits

Cash deposits are accounts held with banks or other savings institutions, such as building societies. They are held by a wide variety of depositors – from retail investors, through to companies, governments and financial institutions.

The main characteristics of cash deposits are:

- The return simply comprises interest income.
- The amount invested (the 'capital') is repaid in full either at the end of a set period, or when withdrawn. Other than through the addition of interest, there is no potential for capital growth (for the amount invested to become larger).

Please try the following exercise to illustrate the concepts of capital and income and highlight some of the advantages and disadvantages of cash deposits.

Exercise 1

Jack Jones has just been left £250,000 by an elderly aunt. He is considering his options and has been told he could buy a one-bedroom flat in a city centre location with the money. Alternatively he could put the money on deposit with a bank.

a. What would make the one-bedroom flat the more attractive option?
b. How much interest could he earn, if instead of buying the flat Jack placed the £250,000 on deposit with a building society paying 1.75% each year, for three years?

Please try to answer the exercise and then check your responses against the answer that can be found at the end of the chapter.

Some accounts are known as **instant access** and the money can be withdrawn at any time; other accounts are for a **fixed term**, of a year or more, while others require notice to be given before monies can be withdrawn.

The interest rate paid on deposits will vary with the amount of money deposited and the time for which the money is tied up. Large deposits are more economical for a bank or building society to process and will also earn a better rate. This is illustrated in the table below with 'notice accounts' that require a certain period of notice before the money can be withdrawn.

The rate will also vary because of competition, and in most developed markets deposit-taking institutions compete intensely with one another to attract new deposits.

In the recent past, the interest rates payable have suffered as a result of monetary policy that has kept base rates at 0.50% or lower. The result has been that the rates on offer from banks and other savings institutions are at historic lows and, in some cases, negative interest rates are in place. Some banks pay no interest to large companies and others are considering charging large companies for holding cash with them as they cannot earn enough after costs to offer a return.

In the table below, banks A and B are examples of accounts that offer instant access (ie, there is no notice period) and the rates of interest that are available.

3.2 Tax on Bank Interest

Generally, interest received by an individual is subject to income tax.

UK individuals earning income below a certain threshold pay income tax at the basic rate and are referred to as basic rate taxpayers. Those earning income above this threshold pay a higher rate of income tax and are known as higher rate taxpayers. Basic rate taxpayers are liable to pay 20% tax on interest earned.

Bank A	Instant Access	1% Variable ISA only	£100 Minimum
Bank B	Instant Access	1.05% Variable	£1,000 Minimum
Bank C	90 Days' Notice	1.1% Variable	No Minimum
Bank D	1-Year Fixed	1.05% Fixed	£1 Minimum
Bank E	1-Year Fixed	1.50% Fixed	£50,000 Minimum
Bank F	3-Year Fixed	2.0% Fixed	£100 Minimum £3,000 Maximum
Bank G	5-Year Fixed	2.25% Fixed	£25,000 Minimum

Higher rate taxpayers are liable to tax at 40%, and those with incomes over £150,000 are liable to the additional rate of tax at 45%.

Until April 2016, interest used to be paid net of tax as deposit-takers were required to deduct tax before it was paid to the depositor and then account for the tax to HM Revenue & Customs (HMRC). From April 2016, however, there has been a new personal savings allowance to remove tax on up to £1,000 of savings income for basic rate taxpayers, and up to £500 for higher rate taxpayers. As part of this change, since April 2016, banks and building societies have been required to stop automatically taking 20% in income tax from the interest earned on non-ISA savings.

Exercise 2

Mr Evans is a basic rate taxpayer. He has had £3,000 on deposit at XYZ Bank for a year, earning 4% gross interest.

How much interest does Mr Evans receive, and how much would he be left with after tax assuming he pays tax at the basic rate of 20% and no other allowances are available?

Please try to answer the exercises and then check your responses against the answers that can be found at the end of the chapter.

3.3 Bitcoin

Bitcoin is a cryptocurrency. Bitcoins are mined by computers solving fiendishly hard mathematical problems. The 'coin' does not exist physically – it is a virtual currency that exists only as a computer file. No one computer controls the currency. A network keeps track of all transactions made using Bitcoins but it does not know what they were used for – just the ID of the computer 'wallet' they move from and to.

Ownership of Bitcoins implies that a user can spend Bitcoins associated with a specific address. To do so, a payer must digitally sign the transaction using the corresponding private key. Without knowledge of the private key, the transaction cannot be signed and Bitcoins cannot be spent. The network verifies the signature using the public key. If the private key is lost, the Bitcoin network will not recognise any other evidence of ownership; the coins are then unusable, and thus effectively lost.

While major central banks are now treating Bitcoin seriously, there are concerns about its use as it is possible to make transactions anonymously which has meant that it has attracted criminals.

3.4 Risks in Relation to Cash Deposits

Although cash investments are relatively simple products, it does not follow that they are free of risks, as bank failures in 2008 so clearly demonstrated with the collapse of Northern Rock.

However, deposits are generally protected by some form of compensation scheme. These schemes will typically repay any deposited money lost, up to a set maximum, as a result of the collapse of a deposit taking institution, such as a bank. Depositors based in the UK are covered by the Financial Services Compensation Scheme (FSCS). The FSCS provides protection for the first £85,000 of deposits per person with an authorised institution.

As well as the obvious benefit of earning interest, cash deposits are also attractive because of the liquidity they offer. Liquidity is the ease and speed with which an investment can be turned into cash to meet spending needs. Most investors are likely to have a need for cash at short notice and so should plan to hold some cash on deposit to meet possible needs and emergencies before considering other less liquid forms of investment.

The risks inherent when depositing cash include:

- Deposit-taking institutions are of varying creditworthiness and there is a risk of collapse, although the FSCS does mitigate the risk for most modest depositors.
- Inflation reduces returns and could mean the real return after tax is negative. Inflation and real rates will be covered in more detail later in this manual.
- Interest rates change and so the returns from cash deposits will vary.
- If money is deposited overseas in a currency other than pound sterling, there is a risk that exchange rate movements mean it may fall in value in sterling terms, as well as the deposit taking institution being subject to a different regulatory regimes.

As a result, when comparing available deposit options it is important to consider the relevant risks as well as comparing the interest rates available.

4. Borrowing

As seen earlier, the traditional banking model is for the financial institution to take deposits and lend the majority of the deposited funds to borrowers. Individuals can borrow money from banks and building societies in three main ways:

1. Overdrafts.
2. Credit card borrowing.
3. Loans.

4.1 Overdrafts

When an individual attempts to spend more money than he holds in his bank account, for instance by writing a cheque, it is possible that the bank will refuse to honour the cheque. This is referred to as 'bouncing' the cheque, and once upon a time it was quite common as shown by the following example relating to former UK Prime Minister Gordon Brown in his college days.

In 1972, Gordon Brown tried to pay for his university lodgings with a cheque for £3.

The cheque was not honoured by the bank because Mr Brown had insufficient funds in his account. 'Refer to Drawer' is bank-speak for 'this person has insufficient funds in his account to pay the cheque'. The bounced cheque cost Mr Brown an additional 13p in charges.

Today it would be unusual for a bank to bounce a cheque for a relatively small sum, with the bank more likely to honour the cheque while charging the account holder a fee and a high rate of interest for going 'overdrawn'. The account is described as being in overdraft when the depositor owes money to the bank.

If the amount overdrawn is within a limit previously agreed with the bank, the overdraft is said to be **authorised**. If it has not been previously agreed, or exceeds the agreed limit, it is **unauthorised**. Unauthorised overdrafts are very expensive, usually incurring both a high rate of interest on the borrowed money and a fee.

Authorised overdrafts agreed with the bank in advance are charged interest at a lower rate. Some banks allow small overdrafts without charging fees to avoid infuriating a customer who might be overdrawn by a relatively low amount.

Overdrafts are a convenient but expensive way of borrowing money and borrowers should try to restrict their use to temporary periods and avoid unauthorised overdrafts as far as possible.

An acceptable and sensible way to use an overdraft is illustrated in the following example.

Example

XYZ Hot Dog ltd is due to pay its meat supplier £7,000 on 5 February but does not have enough money in its account to pay the bill. The Finance Director knows he is due to receive £8,500 from a customer on the 19 February but the gap leaves him with a cash-flow problem. He decides to arrange a £10,000 overdraft with a bank to cover that payment and any other expenses over the 14-day period. XYZ Hot Dog ltd can now pay the bill for £7,000 and not worry about the cheque 'bouncing'. Not only would bounced cheques cost the business money in bank charges but the company's relationship with its meat supplier would be

damaged. The supplier might in future refuse to offer credit to XYZ Hot Dog ltd and demand cash up front.

XYZ Hot Dog ltd will be charged interest only on the amount it actually borrows. The overdraft facility is £10,000. If the business only uses say £7,750, it will only pay interest on the £7,750, not the whole £10,000.

4.2 Credit Cards

Customers in the UK are very attached to their credit cards from savings institutions like banks and building societies, and to other cards from retail stores, known as store cards. In other countries, including much of Europe, the use is much less widespread.

A wide variety of retail goods such as food, electrical goods, petrol and cinema tickets can be paid for using a credit card. The retailer is paid by the credit card company for the goods sold; the credit card company charges the retailer a percentage fee, but this enables the store to sell goods to customers using their credit cards.

Customers are typically sent a monthly statement by the credit card company. Customers can then choose to pay all the money owed to the credit card company, or just a percentage of the total sum owed. Interest is charged on the balance owed by the customer.

XYZ Credit Card	0% 18 months 2.89% fee	0% 3 months	16.8% APR
	* Instant online decision is available * 18.9% APR on transferred balances * 10% off ABC Holidays		

Generally, the interest rate charged on credit cards is relatively high compared to other forms of borrowing, including overdrafts. However, if a credit card customer pays the full balance each month, he is borrowing interest-free. It is also common for credit card companies to offer 0% interest to new customers for balances transferred from other cards and for new purchases for a set period, often six months. However, these offers are often only available if a fee is paid, as illustrated below.

Credit card interest is so profitable to banks that they entice people to switch their outstanding balance over to a new card.

The bait is 0% interest charged on transferred balances for an extended period. The catch is there's a fee that has to be paid on the balance transferred – in this case 2.89%.

4.3 Loans

Loans can be subdivided into two groups:

* secured loans and
* unsecured loans.

Unsecured loans are typically used to purchase consumer goods, although another example is a student loan to be repaid after university. The lender will check the creditworthiness of the borrower – assessing whether he or she can afford to repay the loan and interest over the agreed term of, say, 48 months from income given existing outgoings.

The unsecured loan is not linked to the item that is purchased with the loan (in contrast to mortgages which are covered below), so if the borrower fails to meet the repayments it can be difficult for the lender to enforce the loan agreement. The usual mechanism for the unsecured lender to enforce repayment is to start legal proceedings to get the money back.

In contrast, if **secured** loans are not repaid, the lender can repossess the specific property which was the security for the loan.

Example

Jenny borrows £500,000 to buy a house.

The loan is secured on the property. Jenny loses her job and is unable to continue to meet the repayments and interest.

Because the loan is secured, the lender is able to take the house to recoup the money. If the lender takes this route, the house will be sold and the lender will take the amount owed and give the rest, if any, to Jenny.

As seen in the above example, it is common for loans made to buy property to be secured. Such loans are referred to as **mortgages** and the security provided to the lender means that the rate of interest is likely to be lower than on other forms of borrowing, like overdrafts and unsecured loans.

Exercise 3

This exercise returns to the earlier example of XYZ Hot Dog ltd utilising a £10,000 overdraft facility. XYZ Hot Dog ltd is worried that its bank might withdraw the overdraft facility without any warning. It is considering taking out a loan at 13% for £10,000 for a fixed, three-year period. What are the advantages and disadvantages of using a loan instead of an overdraft?

Please try to answer the exercise and then check your response against the answer that can be found at the end of the chapter.

4.3.1 Payday Loans

Payday lending is the provision of small-sum cash loans marketed on a short-term basis that is not secured against collateral and includes loans repayable on the customer's next payday or at the end of the month but which can be for much longer. The term 'payday loans' is not used exclusively to refer to loans linked to the borrower's payday. A range of different products come within the definition of payday loans but they have some common features:

- They are short-term unsecured loans for periods up to 12 months, although most are for periods of 31 days or less.
- They are for relatively small amounts.
- New borrowers can typically borrow between £100 and £500.
- Repeat borrowers may be able to borrow more but rarely more than £1,000.

Payday lending is an issue which attracts a large amount of political and media attention. Regulators, consumer groups, debt-advice charities and other interested parties have expressed concerns about payday lending, including the cost of borrowing, whether lenders are acting responsibly, whether advertisements are misleading or inappropriate and the approach shown to customers that get into difficulties in meeting repayments.

The UK regulator, the Financial Conduct Authority (FCA), refers to these types of loans as 'high-cost short-term credit' which brings out one of the key characteristics of these loans – the exorbitantly high costs involved. Just look at the annualised percentage rates that are regularly advertised and you will see many well in excess of 1,000% per annum! New rules have now been imposed that put a price cap on the rate of interest that can be charged at 0.8% per day but this still means that someone taking out a £100 loan for 30 days and paying it back on time may still pay £24 in fees and charges. If borrowers do not repay their loans on time, default charges must not exceed £15 and the maximum cost is capped at 100% of the original sum, which means no borrower will ever pay back more than twice what they borrowed.

4.4 Interest Rates

The costs of borrowing (mainly interest) vary depending on the form of borrowing, how long the money is required for, the security offered and the amount borrowed.

Mortgages, secured on a house, are much cheaper than credit cards and authorised overdrafts. Unauthorised overdrafts will incur even higher rates of interest plus charges.

Borrowers also have to grapple with the different rates quoted by lenders – loan companies traditionally quote flat rates that are lower than the true rate or **effective annual rate (EAR)**.

Example

The Moneybags Credit Card Company quotes its interest rate at 12% per annum, charged on a quarterly basis.

The effective annual rate can be determined by taking the quoted rate and dividing by four (to represent the quarterly charge). It is this rate that is applied to the amount borrowed on a quarterly basis; 12% ÷ by 4 = 3%.

Imagine an individual borrows £100 on his/her Moneybags credit card. Assuming he or she makes no repayments for a year, how much will be owed?

At the end of the first quarter, £100 x 3% = £3 will be added to the balance outstanding, to make it £103.

At the end of the second quarter, interest will be due on both the original borrowing and the interest. In other words there will be interest charged on the first quarter's interest of £3, as well as the £100 original borrowing. £103 x 3% = £3.09 will be added to make the outstanding balance £106.09.

At the end of the third quarter, interest will be charged at 3% on the amount outstanding (including the first and second quarters' interest). £106.09 x 3% = £3.18 will be added to make the outstanding balance £109.27.

At the end of the fourth quarter, interest will be charged at 3% on the amount outstanding (including the first, second and third quarters' interest). £109.27 x 3% = £3.28 will be added to make the outstanding balance £112.55.

In total the interest incurred on the £100 was £12.55 over the year. This is an effective annual rate of 12.55%.

There is a shortcut method to arrive at the effective annual rate seen above. It is simply to take the quoted rate, divide by the appropriate frequency (four for quarterly, two for half-yearly, 12 for monthly) and express the result as a decimal – in other words 3% will be expressed as 0.03, 6% as 0.06 and so on.

The decimal is then added to 1, and multiplied by itself by the appropriate frequency. The result minus 1, and then multiplied by 100 is the effective annual rate.

From the above example:

12% ÷ by 4 = 3%, expressed as 0.03.

1 + 0.03 = 1.03.

$1.03^4 = 1.03 \times 1.03 \times 1.03 \times 1.03 = 1.1255$.

1.1255 − 1 = 0.1255 x 100 = 12.55%.

This formula can also be applied to deposits to determine the effective rate of a deposit paying interest at regular intervals.

To make comparisons easier, lenders must quote the true cost of borrowing, embracing the effective annual rate and including certain fees that are required to be paid by the borrower. This is known as the Annual Percentage Rate (APR). The additional fees that the lender adds to the cost of borrowing might be loan arrangement fees.

Exercise 4

Company A is offering:

- Minimum agreement period of two years.
- 0% introductory rate for 14 months on all balance transfers.
- 2.98% fee payable upon transfer of balance.
- 16.6% APR on the balance from month 15 onwards.

Company B is offering:

- Minimum agreement period of two years.
- 3.5% monthly introductory rate for first 12 months on all balance transfers.
- No fee payable upon transfer of balance.
- 12% on the balance from month 13 onwards.

You have a credit card balance of £1,800. You want to switch to a new credit card company. You are determined not to put any more spending on your new card at all. You just want the cheapest cost over the life of the two year deal. Which offer do you choose?

Please try to answer the exercise and then check your response against the answer that can be found at the end of the chapter.

5. Other Types of Financial Institution

Banks have evolved beyond the 'high street bank' and the building society's traditional purpose of deposit taking and lending. They have specialised, sometimes as a result of regulatory developments, and today there is a wide range of both types of bank and other financial institutions. The services they provide generally revolve around investments such as shares issued by companies, bonds issued by companies and governments and derivatives. All of these investments will be looked at in more detail later in this manual. In this section, these financial institutions are explored in a little more detail.

5.1 Investment Banks

Confusingly, investment banks do not take deposits and grant loans. Instead, they provide advice and arrange finance for companies that want to make their shares available to the investing public (known as 'floating' on the stock market), that want to raise additional finance by issuing further shares or bonds, or carry out mergers and acquisitions. Many investment banks also provide services for those who might want to invest in shares and bonds, for example, pension funds and asset managers. All of this will be considered in greater detail later in this workbook.

The financial crisis of 2008 saw the disappearance of many of the larger independent investment banks. They were either taken over by other banks or converted into bank holding companies. For example, Merrill Lynch was taken over by Bank of America.

Typically, an investment banking group provides some or all of the following services, either in divisions of the bank or in associated companies within the group:

- **Corporate finance and advisory work**, normally in connection with new issues of securities for raising finance, takeovers, mergers and acquisitions.
- **Treasury dealing** for corporate clients in international currencies, with financial engineering services to protect them from interest rate and exchange rate fluctuations.
- **Investment management** for sizeable investors such as corporate pension funds, charities and private clients. They may do this either via direct investment for the wealthier, private clients or by way of collective investment schemes (or 'investment funds'). In larger firms, the value of funds under management runs into many billions of pounds.
- **Securities trading** in equities, bonds and derivatives and the provision of broking and distribution facilities.

Only the largest few investment banks provide services in all these areas. Most others tend to specialise to some degree and concentrate on only a few product lines. A number of banks have diversified their range of activities by developing businesses such as proprietary trading, servicing hedge funds, or making private equity investments.

5.2 International Banks

International banking refers to banking activities that involve cross-border transactions, and its growth reflects the increasingly global nature of trade and the associated banking activities.

Typical activities involved in this sector relate to the financing of trade between parties in different countries. Trade finance involves the bank acting as an intermediary between an exporter who prefers an importer to pay in advance for goods before they are shipped, while the importer wants documentary evidence from the exporter that the goods have been shipped before payment is made. Traditionally, this involved the importer's bank providing a letter of credit to the exporter that guaranteed payment upon presentation of documentation which proved the goods had been shipped. More recently, this has developed to utilise the international payment systems provided by the Society of Worldwide Interbank Financial Telecommunication (SWIFT) to facilitate the payment for goods and speed up the flow of trade.

5.3 Peer-to-Peer (P2P) and Crowdfunding

A more recent development in the banking industry has been the emergence of competitors to the traditional role of banks in the form of peer-to-peer lending (P2P) or crowdfunding.

In the traditional banking model, banks take in deposits on which they pay interest and then lend out at a higher rate. The spread between the two is where they earn their profit. P2P lending cuts out the banks so borrowers often get slightly lower rates, while savers get far improved headline rates, with the P2P firms themselves profiting via a fee.

In exchange for accepting greater risk, savers can earn higher returns which can be very useful in periods of low interest rates. Available rates vary depending on the type of borrower that the P2P site lends to and the risk the lender is prepared to accept. The deposit is lent out to individuals and businesses, but it may take time before all of a large deposit is lent out and earning interest. No interest is paid while it is waiting to be lent out. Immediate withdrawals are not always possible and, where they are, may take time and incur a charge or a reduced interest rate.

Since April 2016, an Innovative Finance ISA has been available as an investment option so that the P2P deposit can be sheltered in a tax-free wrapper.

5.4 Pension Funds

Most individuals hope that, in later life, they will be able to stop working and retire. However, in order to save enough money to enjoy this period of retirement, the individuals will inevitably need income. This is where pension schemes come in. They are the key planning method by which individuals can make provision for retirement. There is a variety of pension schemes available, ranging from those provided by employers to those that are run by the individual, known as self-directed schemes.

Pension funds are often large, long-term investors in shares, bonds and cash. Some also invest in physical assets, like property. To meet their aim of providing a pension on retirement, the sums of money invested in pensions are substantial.

5.5 Insurance Companies

One of the key functions of the financial services industry is to ensure risks are effectively managed. This includes the obvious insurance services such as car insurance, household contents insurance and life assurance. Car insurance will pay out in the event of a car accident, household contents will enable the replacement of possessions in the event of a burglary or flood and life assurance will pay out in the event that the insured person dies. However, the insurance industry provides solutions for much more than these standard areas of life and general insurance cover.

Protection planning is a key area of financial advice, and the insurance industry offers a wide range of products to meet many potential scenarios. These products range from payment protection policies designed to pay out in the event that an individual is unable to meet repayments on loans and mortgages, to fleet insurance against the risk of an airline's planes crashing.

Insurance companies also market a wide range of investment products, and have become large players in what is known as the 'structured products' market by offering guaranteed stock market related bonds.

Generally, insurance companies collect **premiums** in exchange for the cover provided, and this premium income is used to buy investments, such as shares and bonds. As a result, the insurance industry is a major player in the London stock market.

Insurance companies will subsequently realise these investments to pay any claims that may arise on the various policies.

The UK insurance industry is the largest in Europe and the fourth largest in the world after the US, Japan and China.

5.6 Fund Management

In essence, fund management is selecting the investments that make up the portfolios for pension funds, insurance companies and collective investment schemes and is also known as **asset management** or **investment management**.

Other areas of fund management include private wealth management and the provision of investment management services to institutional entities, such as companies, charities and local government authorities.

Individual fund managers, also known as investment or asset managers, run these portfolios of investments for others. They invest money held by institutions, such as pension funds and insurance companies, as well as for collective investment schemes (CISs), such as unit trusts and open-ended investment companies (OEICs), and for wealthier individuals. Some fund management organisations focus solely on this activity; others are divisions of larger entities, such as insurance companies or banks.

Investment managers who buy and sell shares, bonds and other assets in order to increase the value of their clients' portfolios can conveniently be subdivided into **institutional** and **private client** fund managers. Institutional fund managers work on behalf of institutions, for example, investing money for a company's pension fund or an insurance company's fund, or managing the investments in a unit trust. Private client fund managers invest the money of relatively wealthy individuals. Generally, institutional portfolios are larger than those of private clients.

Investment management firms charge their clients for managing their money, with their charges often based on a small percentage of the value of the fund being managed.

5.7 Stockbrokers and Wealth Managers

Stockbrokers traditionally arranged trades in financial instruments on behalf of their clients, which included investment institutions, fund managers and private clients. Today, most of these are institutional brokers who make their money by using their discretion and skill to execute large trades in the market. Others are execution-only brokers that offer trading services to retail clients. These firms earn their profits by charging commissions on transactions.

Stockbrokers also advised investors about which shares, bonds or funds they should buy and the services offered expanded to include investment management services and wealth management. As a result, many stockbrokers now offer wealth management services to their clients and so are referred to as wealth managers. These wealth management firms can be independent companies, but some are divisions of larger entities, such as investment banks. They earn their profits by charging fees for their advice and commissions on transactions. Also, like fund managers, they may look after client assets and charge custody and portfolio management fees.

5.8 Custodian Banks

Custodians are banks that specialise in keeping assets safe for others. These safe custody services typically involve looking after portfolios of shares and bonds on behalf of others, such as fund managers, pension funds and insurance companies.

The core activities they undertake include:

- holding assets in safekeeping, such as equities and bonds
- arranging settlement – making the appropriate payment for any purchases and collecting the proceeds of any sales of securities
- processing corporate actions, including collecting income from assets, namely dividends in the case of equities and interest in the case of bonds
- providing information on the underlying companies in which shares are held, such as their annual general meetings
- generally managing the cash held within the portfolios
- performing foreign exchange transactions when required
- providing regular reporting on all of their activities to their clients.

Competition has driven down the charges that a custodian can make for its traditional custody services and has resulted in consolidation within the industry. The custody business is now dominated by a small number of global custodians which are often divisions of large banks.

5.9 Platforms

Platforms are online services used by intermediaries, such as independent financial advisers (IFAs), to view and administer their clients' investment portfolios.

They offer a range of tools which allow advisers to see and analyse a client's overall portfolio and to choose products for them.

As well as providing facilities for investments to be bought and sold, platforms generally arrange custody for clients' assets. Examples of platforms include those offered by Cofunds and Hargreaves Lansdown.

The term 'platform' refers to both wraps and fund supermarkets. These are similar, but while fund supermarkets tend to offer wide ranges of unit trusts and OEICs, wraps often offer greater access to other products too, such as Individual Savings Accounts (ISAs), pension plans and insurance bonds.

Wrap accounts enable advisers to take a holistic view of the various assets that a client has in a variety of accounts. Advisers also benefit from using wrap accounts to simplify and bring some level of automation to their back office using internet technology.

Platform providers also make their services available direct to investors, and platforms earn their income by charging for their services.

The advantage of platforms for fund management groups is the ability of the platform to distribute their products to financial advisers.

5.10 Trade and Professional Bodies

The investment industry is a dynamic, rapidly changing business, and one that requires cooperation between firms to ensure that the views of various industry sections are represented, especially to government and regulators. The industry also facilitates and enables cross-firm developments to take place to create an efficient market in which the firms can operate.

This is essentially the role of the numerous professional and trade bodies that exist across the world's financial markets. Examples of such bodies include:

- In the **bonds** market – International Capital Market Association (ICMA).
- In the **derivatives** market – FIA Europe; International Swaps and Derivatives Association (ISDA).
- For **fund managers** – Investment Association (IA) (formerly the Investment Management Association (IMA)).
- For **insurance companies** – Association of British Insurers (ABI).
- For stockbrokers and investment managers providing **private client investment management** – Wealth Management Association (WMA).
- For **banks** – British Bankers' Association (BBA).
- For **investment funds** – the Tax Incentivised Savings Association (TISA) is an industry-funded body working to improve savings and investment schemes available to UK citizens.
- The Depositary and Trustee Association (DATA) represents the industry views of depositaries of open-ended investment companies (OEICs) and trustees of unit trusts within the UK.

5.11 Professional and Retail Business

As already seen in the first chapter of this manual, there are two distinct areas within the financial services industry, namely the wholesale or professional sector (also known as the institutional sector) and the retail sector.

The financial activities that make up the **wholesale/professional** sector include:

- **Equity markets** – the trading of quoted shares.
- **Bond markets** – the trading of government, supranational or corporate debt.

- **Foreign exchange** – the trading of currencies.
- **Derivatives** – the trading of options, futures and forwards.
- **Fund management** – managing the investment portfolios of collective investment schemes, pension funds and insurance funds.
- **Investment banking** – services tailored to organisations, such as undertaking mergers and acquisitions, raising finance by issuing equity or bonds and private equity.
- **Custodian banking** – provision of services to asset managers involving the safekeeping of assets; the administration of the underlying investments; settlement; corporate actions and other specialised activities.

By contrast, the **retail** sector focuses on services provided to personal customers including:

- **Retail banking** – the traditional range of current accounts, deposit accounts, lending and credit cards.
- **Insurance** – the provision of a range of life assurance and protection solutions for areas such as medical insurance, critical illness cover, motor insurance, property insurance, income protection and mortgage protection.
- **Pensions** – the provision of investment accounts specifically designed to capture savings during a person's working life and provide benefits on retirement.
- **Investment services** – a range of investment products and vehicles ranging from execution-only stockbroking to full wealth management services and private banking.
- **Financial planning and financial advice** – helping individuals to understand and plan for their financial future.

Exercise 5

All of the following financial institutions have been mentioned in the manual so far – who do they serve? Are their clients predominantly retail or professional, or a mix of both?

Please try to answer the exercise and then check your responses against the answer that can be found at the end of the chapter.

Financial Institution	Retail	Professional	Both
High street bank			
Pension fund			
Fund manager			
Building society			
Retail bank			
Insurance company			
Investment bank			
Stockbroker			
Institutional fund manager			
Custodian bank			
Private wealth manager			

6. Investment Distribution Channels

6.1 Financial Planning

Financial planning is a professional service available to individuals, their families and businesses, who need objective assistance in organising their financial affairs to achieve their financial and lifestyle objectives more easily.

Financial planning is clearly about financial matters, so it deals with money and assets that have monetary value. Invariably this will involve looking at the current value of clients' bank balances, any loans, investments and other assets. It is also about planning, ie, defining, quantifying and qualifying goals and objectives and then working out how those goals and objectives can be achieved. In order to do this, it is vital that a client's current financial status is known in detail.

Financial planning is ultimately about meeting a client's financial and lifestyle objectives, not the adviser's objectives. Any advice should be relevant to the goals and objectives agreed. Financial planning plays a significant role in helping individuals get the most out of their money. Careful planning can help individuals define their goals and objectives, and work out how these may be achieved in the future using available resources. Financial planning can look at all aspects of an individual's financial situation and may include tax planning, both during lifetime and on death, asset management, debt management, retirement planning and personal risk management – protecting income and capital in the event of illness and providing for dependants on death.

The Chartered Institute for Securities & Investment (CISI) offers qualifications and related products at all levels for those working in, or looking for a career in, financial planning. Further details can be found on the CISI's website (www.cisi.org).

6.2 Financial Advisers

Financial advisers are professionals who offer advice on financial matters to their clients. Some recommend suitable financial products provided by anyone – known as 'whole of market' advisors – while others can only recommend from a narrower range of products.

Typically, a financial adviser will conduct a detailed survey of a client's financial position, preferences and objectives; this is sometimes known as a 'fact-find'. The adviser will then suggest appropriate action to meet the client's objectives and, if necessary, recommend a suitable financial product to match the client's needs.

Investment firms must now clearly describe their services as either **independent advice** or **restricted advice**. Firms that describe their advice as independent will have to ensure that they genuinely do make their recommendations based on comprehensive and fair analysis of all products available in the market, and provide unbiased, unrestricted advice. If a firm chooses to only give advice on its own range of products – restricted advice – this will have to be made clear. Their activities are supervised by the Financial Conduct Authority (FCA).

6.3 Execution-only

As already mentioned, a firm carries out transactions on an execution-only basis if the customer asks it to buy or sell a specific named investment product without having been prompted or advised by the firm. In such instances, customers are responsible for their own decision about a product's suitability.

The practice of execution-only sales is long-established. To ensure that firms operate within regulatory guidelines they need to record and retain evidence in writing that the firm:

- gave no advice, and
- made it clear, at the time of the sale, that it was not responsible for the product's suitability.

6.4 Robo-Advice

Robo-advice is the application of technology to the process of providing financial advice, but without the involvement of a financial adviser. A prospective investor enters data and financial information about themselves, and the system then uses an algorithm to score the information and decide what investments should be chosen. The system then presents the investment strategy, which is usually passively focused around index funds or exchange-traded funds (ETFs), and allows easy implementation.

Robo-advice can be fully automated or provide guidance and tools to enable investors to choose their own solutions. The approach uses an asset and risk model, as well as the construction of risk-targeted portfolios or funds to achieve a client's objectives, and then the ongoing monitoring and rebalancing against those objectives.

Robo-advice is already established in the US, with some of the industry's largest players involved. More providers are expected to come online in the UK during 2017 to fill the gaps in the advice market and, particularly, for pensions planning, as a result of major changes to how pension benefits can be taken.

Answers to Chapter Exercises

Exercise 1

Jack Jones has just been left £250,000 by an elderly aunt. He is considering his options and has been told he could use the money to buy and then let a one-bedroom flat in a city centre location. Alternatively he could put the money on deposit with a bank.

a. What would make the one-bedroom flat the more attractive option?
b. How much interest could he earn, if instead of buying the flat Jack placed the £250,000 on deposit with a building society paying 1.75% each year, for three years?

a. For Jack to invest his £250,000 of capital in a buy-to-let flat, he is hoping for two things:
    *   For the value of that flat to rise, ie, for Jack's capital to grow.
    *   To earn a competitive rent from letting out the flat to tenants.

Obviously there is a risk of capital loss, if the value of the flat falls rather than increases and there is also a risk to the income, the rent. The rent may not be competitive due to oversupply, or the flat may be without a tenant for a time.

In contrast, if Jack put the money on deposit in the bank, his capital will not grow – when he withdraws his deposit, he will receive back his original sum. He will only earn interest income.

b. If Jack had placed the £250,000 of capital on deposit with a building society at 1.75% for three years:
    *   In the first year he would earn interest of £4,375 (£250,000 x 1.75%).
    *   Assuming he does not leave the interest in the account, he could earn the same in each of the other two years.
    *   In total the interest would be £13,125 (£4,375 x 3), but that would be before any income tax due on the interest earned.

Exercise 2

Mr Evans is a basic rate taxpayer. He has had £3,000 on deposit at XYZ Bank for a year, earning 4% gross interest. How much interest does Mr Evans receive, and how much would he be left with after tax assuming he pays tax at the basic rate of 20% and no other allowances are available?

Interest earned = £3,000 x 4% = £120

Income tax at 20% = £120 x 20% = £24

Earned by Mr Evans = £120 x 80% = £96

Exercise 3

This exercise returns to the earlier example of XYZ Hot Dog ltd utilising a £10,000 overdraft facility. XYZ Hot Dog ltd is worried that its bank might withdraw the overdraft facility without any warning. It is considering taking out a loan at 13% for £10,000 for a fixed, three-year period. What are the advantages and disadvantages of using a loan instead of an overdraft?

Advantages of the loan over an overdraft	Disadvantages of the loan over an overdraft
As long as XYZ Hot Dog ltd complies with the conditions of the loan agreement, the bank cannot demand repayment of the loan before the term expires.	XYZ Hot Dog ltd has to borrow the full amount of the loan, despite it perhaps being more than it needs for most of the time.
The interest rate on the loan at 13.0% is likely to be substantially cheaper than the rate applied to the overdraft.	It pays interest on the full amount of the loan.
	It may have to offer security to prove it can repay the loan.

Exercise 4

Company A is offering:

- Minimum agreement period of two years.
- 0% introductory rate for 14 months on all balance transfers.
- 2.98% fee payable upon transfer of balance.
- 16.6% APR on the balance from month 15 onwards.

Company B is offering:

- Minimum agreement period of two years.
- 3.5% monthly introductory rate for first 12 months on all balance transfers.
- No fee payable upon transfer of balance.
- 12% on the balance from month 13 onwards.

You have a credit card balance of £1,800. You want to switch to a new credit card company. You are determined not to put any more spending on your new card at all. You just want the cheapest cost over the life of the two year deal. Which offer do you choose?

Company A – 24-month deal	
Balance transferred	£1,800.00
Fee of 2.98% on balance transferred	£53.64
New balance after the addition of the 2.98% transfer fee	£1,853.64
Introductory interest rate quoted on the new balance for the first 14 months	0.00%
16.6% APR interest charge on the new balance for the remaining 10 months	£256.42
Total cost of the Company A deal (53.64 + 256.42)	£310.06

Company B – 24-month deal	
Balance transferred	£1,800
Introductory rate (APR) charged for first 12 months (3.56% x 1,800)	£64.08
New balance after first 12 months	£1,864.08
Rate (APR) charged for the remaining 12 months (1,864.08 x 12.68%)	236.37
Total cost of Company B deal	£300.49

The Company B deal is the cheaper option.

Exercise 5

All of the following financial institutions have been mentioned in the manual so far – who do they serve? Are their clients predominantly retail or professional, or a mix of both?

Financial Institution	Retail	Professional	Both
High street bank			√
Pension fund	√		
Fund manager			√
Building society	√		
Retail bank	√		
Insurance company			√
Investment bank		√	
Stockbroker			√
Institutional fund manager		√	
Custodian bank		√	
Private wealth manager	√		

Learning Objectives

Chapter Two has covered the following Learning Objectives:

1.1.1   Know the role of the following within the financial services industry: retail banks; building societies; investment banks; pension funds; insurance companies; fund managers; platforms; stockbrokers; custodians; industry trade and professional bodies; peer-to-peer lending/crowdfunding

1.1.2   Know the function of and differences between retail and professional business and who the main customers are in each case: retail clients and professional clients

1.1.3   Know the role of the following investment distribution channels: independent financial adviser; restricted advice; execution-only; robo-advice

3.1.1   Know the characteristics of fixed term and instant access deposit accounts

3.1.2   Understand the distinction between gross and net interest payments

3.1.3   Know the characteristics of Bitcoin

10.1.1 Know the differences between bank loans, overdrafts; credit card borrowing and payday loans

10.1.2 Know the difference between the quoted interest rate on borrowing and the effective annual rate of borrowing

10.1.3 Be able to calculate the effective annual rate of borrowing, given the quoted interest rate and frequency of payment

10.1.4 Know the difference between secured and unsecured borrowing

Based on what you have learned in Chapter Two, try to answer the following end of chapter questions.

End of Chapter Questions

Think of an answer for each question and refer to the appropriate section for confirmation.

1. What are the two major types of saving institution in the UK?
    Answer Reference: Section 2

    ....

    ....

2. What makes a building society different?
    Answer Reference: Section 2

    ....

    ....

3. How do traditional banks make money?
    Answer Reference: Section 3

    ....

    ....

4. What two factors typically determine the amount of interest received from a savings institution?
    Answer Reference: Section 3.1

    ....

    ....

5. What is the FSCS?
    Answer Reference: Section 3.4

    ....

    ....

CISI
CHARTERED INSTITUTE FOR
SECURITIES & INVESTMENT

6. What are the three main ways that individuals use to borrow from financial institutions?

   Answer Reference: Section 4

   ....

   ....

7. What are the two forms of overdraft and which form is the most expensive?

   Answer Reference: Section 4.1

   ....

   ....

8. What are the two forms of loan?

   Answer Reference: Section 4.3

   ....

   ....

9. How does the flat rate differ from the effective annual rate?

   Answer Reference: Section 4.4

   ....

   ....

10. How does the annual percentage rate differ from the effective annual rate?

    Answer Reference: Section 4.4

    ....

    ....

11. What does an investment bank do?

    Answer Reference: Section 5.1

    ....

    ....

12. What are the two types of client that investment managers serve?

    Answer Reference: Section 5.6

    ....

    ....

13. Who do custodian banks serve?

    Answer Reference: Section 5.8

    ....

    ....

Chapter Three
Equities

3

1. Introduction

The workbook has already mentioned both equities and bonds as investment possibilities. This chapter looks in detail at the features of equities. The next chapter (Chapter 4) provides further detail about how equities are traded on stock markets. Bonds will be covered in detail in Chapter 5.

So, what is equity? Well, in the stock market, it refers to shares in a company. Shares and equities are alternative terms for the same thing, and it is the shareholders that own and control companies. Shareholders generally hope that the value of their shares will increase (they will make a 'capital gain') and that the company will pay regular and increasing amounts of income to them each year in the form of 'dividends'.

In contrast a bond is basically a certificate that represents a loan. It is the equivalent of an IOU

(I owe you) and could be issued by a company or another issuer, such as a government. Bondholders are rewarded for lending money to the bond issuer, by receiving regular income in the form of interest or **coupons**.

This chapter considers equities, which are shares in companies – initially outlining how a company is formed, before moving on to the requirements for the company to become listed on a stock exchange. It then considers the features of equities – the benefits and risks of owning them.

2. Company Formation and Administration

2.1 Forming a Company

Many businesses, large and small, are set up as companies. It is important to appreciate that, while shareholders provide the capital to form a company, they are run by directors. In many smaller companies the shareholders and the directors are the same people, but in larger companies the majority of the shareholders are not directors. Because of this potential separation between the running of the company (by the directors) and the ownership of the company (by shareholders), the law includes the requirement for the company to hold regular meetings at which the directors consult with their shareholders, and report on company progress. This concept can be illustrated by the following example.

Example _____

Local Veg ltd

Jake Onions is a recent school leaver and he and his friends Johnny and Jenny Plant have come up with an idea for a business – buying locally grown vegetables from within the community (either grown in allotments or gardens), and selling them from a market stall. As the business begins to generate income Jake and his friends may decide to formalise things by setting it up as a company 'Local Veg ltd'. At this stage it is Jake and his friends that both own the shares and are also directors running the company.

_____

To form a simple company (like Local Veg ltd) is inexpensive and requires the founders of the company to complete a series of documents and lodge these with the appropriate authority. In the UK these documents are required to be lodged with the Registrar of Companies at Companies House.

To form a company, two constitutional documents are required:

- Memorandum of Association
- Articles of Association.

The **Memorandum of Association** confirms the subscribers' intention to form a company under the Companies Act 2006 and that they have agreed to become a member of that company and to take at least one share each. A simplified example of a memorandum of association for Local Veg ltd can be seen on the following page.

In contrast to the memorandum, the **Articles of Association** detail the relationship between the company and its shareholders. The articles include details such as the rights of the shareholders to appoint and remove directors and the frequency of company meetings.

2.2 Private and Public Companies

Companies are established either as:

- **private companies**, such as Local Veg ltd, when ltd stands for Limited. Such companies can have just a single shareholder, or
- **public companies**, such as International Veg plc, where plc stands for public limited company. Plcs are required to have a minimum of two shareholders.

It is only plcs that are permitted to issue shares to the public. As a result, Local Veg ltd would need to become a plc before it could issue shares to the general public (termed an initial public offering (IPO)).

Example _____

Local Veg ltd becomes a plc

Local Veg ltd is doing so well that it is becoming difficult for Jake, Johnny and Jenny to keep control and grow the business further. They find a more experienced person (Vicky Mature) to join as a director, Vicky has got plans for the company including spreading the concept internationally and raising the money to do so

---

PRIVATE COMPANY LIMITED BY SHARES
MEMORANDUM OF ASSOCIATION
OF
LOCAL VEG LTD

1. The company's name is Local Veg Limited.

2. The Company's registered office is:

   Under the Arches, 6 High Street, Newtown, Newtownshire, NE61 5SW.

3. The Company's objects are to carry on the business of a general commercial company, principally this will involve buying vegetables from producers and selling those vegetables on to consumers.

4. The liability of the shareholders/members is limited.

5. The Company's authorised and issued share capital is £1,000 divided into 1,000 Ordinary £1 Shares of £1 each.

   We, the subscribers to this Memorandum of Association, wish to be formed into a Company pursuant to this Memorandum and to take the number of shares shown beneath our respective names.

   Jake Onions, 42A High Street, Newtown, Newtownshire, NE61 5SW.

   Number of shares taken: 400

   Johnny Plant, 36 High Street, Newtown, Newtownshire, NE61 5SW.

   Number of shares taken: 300

   Jenny Plant, 36 High Street, Newtown, Newtownshire, NE61 5SW.

   Number of shares taken: 300

---

by selling shares to the public in an IPO. Jake, Johnny and Jenny are all in agreement and the first step is for Local Veg has to become a plc, so Vicky organises the amendment of the constitutional documents to rename the business 'International Veg plc'.

It is a requirement for companies that are listed on stock exchanges to be plcs, because listed companies have all gone through an IPO stage selling shares to the public. However not all plcs are listed. It is perfectly possible for a company like International Veg to 'just be' a plc, and not be listed on a stock exchange.

Virgin Holdings, the business empire of Richard Branson, is a public limited company but is not listed on any stock exchanges. In contrast, the global bank HSBC Holdings is a public limited company and is listed on a number of stock exchanges including: the London Stock Exchange (LSE), the New York Stock Exchange (NYSE), the Tokyo Stock Exchange (TSE) and the Hong Kong Stock Exchange (HKSE).

'Limited', whether as in 'ltd' for a private company or within 'plc' for a public company, means that the liability of shareholders for the debts of the company is limited to the amount they agreed to pay to the company on initial subscription. This is explained in the following example.

Example

Slip Up ltd is a UK company that is created with a share capital of £100 which is made up of 100 ordinary £1 shares.

Assuming that each share is fully paid, an initial shareholder who subscribes for 20 shares will pay £20.

In the event that Slip Up ltd is unsuccessful and goes into liquidation, the liability of that shareholder for the company's debts is limited to the amount they subscribed, that is £20.

The position would be different if the shares were only partly paid. For example, the shares might be ordinary £1 shares but only require 80p per share to be paid at the outset, the remainder being payable at some future date. In the event of liquidation, the shareholder may be required to subscribe the balance of 20p per share to help meet the company's debts.

2.3 Company Meetings

As mentioned earlier, companies have meetings between the directors that are running the business and the shareholders. Public companies must hold **annual general meetings (AGMs)** at which the shareholders are given the opportunity to question the directors about the company's strategy and operations. Public companies must hold an AGM within six months of the financial year end.

The Companies Act provides shareholders with the right to attend, speak and vote at the AGM or to appoint a proxy to vote (but not speak) on their behalf at the meeting.

The shareholders are also given the opportunity to vote on matters such as the appointment and removal of directors and the payment of the dividend recommended by the directors. Most matters put to the shareholders are **ordinary resolutions**, requiring a simple majority of those shareholders voting to be passed. Matters of major importance, such as a proposed change to the company's constitution, require a **special resolution** and at least 75% to vote in favour.

Example

The appointment of Vicky Mature as a director at Local Veg ltd would have only required a majority of the shareholders to vote in favour. Given that Jake Onions held 40% of the votes (with 400 of the 1,000 shares) and Johnny and Jenny Plant each held 30% (with 300 shares each), a combination of Jake and either of the Plants would be sufficient (at 70%), or alternatively the two Plants voting in favour (at 60%).

In contrast, changing Local Veg ltd into International Veg plc would require a special resolution and at least 75% to vote in favour. Presuming Jake, Johnny and Jenny all voted, they would all have to vote in favour for the change in name to take effect.

The shareholders can either attend the meeting and vote in person, or if they prefer, they might not attend but they can still have their vote counted at the meeting by appointing someone else to vote on their behalf, known as **proxy voting**. This involves the completion of a proxy voting form, enabling someone else to register their vote on their behalf.

Companies may also hold other meetings during the year to deal with important issues, such as a takeover or capital raising. These are known simply as general meetings. Until 2009, they were referred to as extraordinary general meetings (EGMs), and you may come across that term as it is still often used to differentiate between the two types of meeting.

3. Listing

3.1 Primary and Secondary Markets

When a company like International Veg plc decides to seek a listing for its shares, the process is known by a number of terms:

*   making an 'Initial Public Offer' (IPO)
*   becoming 'listed' or 'quoted'
*   'floating' on the stock market, or
*   'going public'.

Typically, the company making the IPO will have been in existence for many years, and will have grown to a point where it wishes to expand further. The IPO will enable the company to raise money by selling shares to the public, which will help finance the expansion of the company.

Other relevant terminology is 'primary market' and 'secondary market'. The term **primary market** refers to the marketing of new shares in a company to investors for the first time. So clearly, an IPO is a primary market transaction. Once they have acquired shares, investors will at some point wish to dispose of some or all of their shares and will generally do this through the stock exchange trading system. This latter process is referred to as 'dealing on the **secondary market**'.

Primary markets exist to facilitate the raising of capital and enable surplus funds to be matched with investment opportunities. The secondary market is necessary because investors would not be willing to invest in shares unless there was some sort of mechanism to sell them. So the secondary market allows the primary market to function efficiently by providing trading in issued securities.

3.2 Requirements for Listing on the LSE

The London Stock Exchange (LSE) is one of the most well-known stock exchanges in the UK and lists some very large companies like the mobile telecommunications company Vodafone, banks like Barclays and HSBC and the oil giant BP. However, it is not necessary to be quite as large as these companies to be listed on the LSE.

The requirements to be met before a company is allowed to be listed on the LSE are laid down by a division of the UK regulator, the Financial Conduct Authority (FCA). The particular division is known as the United Kingdom Listing Authority (UKLA).

The UKLA's requirements for companies seeking a listing for their shares are mainly aimed at making sure the company is sizeable and well established, and that it discloses sufficient information to potential investors so that they can decide whether or not they want to invest. The main requirements are as follows:

*   The company must be a public limited company (plc).
*   The company's expected market capitalisation (the share price multiplied by the number of shares in issue) must be at least £700,000.
*   The company should have been trading for at least three years and at least 75% of its business must be supported by a historic revenue-earning record for that period.
*   At least 25% of the company's shares should be in public hands or available for purchase by the public. The term 'public' excludes directors of the company and their associates, and significant shareholders who hold 5% or more of the company's shares.
*   A trading company must demonstrate that it has sufficient working capital for the next 12 months.

Please try the following exercise in relation to the eligibility of companies seeking a listing.

Exercise 1

Based solely on the information provided below, which of the following three companies would NOT be eligible to list on the LSE?

1. Langley Property Rentals plc

    - Established five years ago.
    - First rental properties acquired two years ago.
    - 100% of revenues from property rentals.
    - Directors, associates and significant shareholders own 70% of the shares.
    - Expected market cap £2 million.

2. Kelsey Market Research ltd

    - Established ten years ago.
    - Company has been trading profitably since 2nd year of operation.
    - 85% of revenues from market research.
    - Has sufficient working capital for 14 months of operations.

3. Eden Park IT Services plc

    - Established four years ago.
    - 75% of revenues from IT services.
    - Been trading profitably from company's inception.
    - Directors, associates and significant shareholders own 25% of the shares.
    - Expected market cap £1 million.

The answer and explanation can be found at the end of this chapter.

Once listed, companies are expected to fulfil rules known as the **continuing obligations**. For example, they are obliged to issue a half-yearly report that includes financial information, such as trading performance, and listed companies are required to notify the market of any new 'price-sensitive' information. An example would be when the oil giant BP had a major oil spill in the Gulf of Mexico in 2010.

A listing on the LSE is often referred to as a 'full listing'. This distinguishes it from cases where a company's shares are admitted to the **Alternative Investment Market (AIM)**, a market also run by the LSE where the requirements are less demanding, as explained below.

3.3 The Alternative Investment Market (AIM)

The Alternative Investment Market (AIM) was established by the LSE as a 'junior' market targeted at younger, smaller companies than those eligible for a full listing. Such companies apply to the LSE to join AIM, whereas full listing requires application to the UKLA. The requirements for a listing on AIM, in comparison to the requirements for a full listing, are as shown in the table below.

Among the companies traded on the AIM are the wine retailer Majestic, the fashion label Mulberry, and the football club Celtic.

AIM	Full Listing
No trading history required; the company could be newly established.	Three years' trading history is needed.
No minimum market capitalisation required.	£700,000 is the minimum market cap.
No requirement for a minimum proportion of the shares to be held by the 'public'.	At least 25% of the shares must be held by outside investors.

A company wanting to gain admission to AIM is required to appoint a **nominated adviser (NOMAD)** and a **nominated broker**. The role of the NOMAD is to advise the directors of the company of their responsibilities in complying with AIM rules, including the information required to accompany the company's application for admission to AIM. The role of the nominated broker is to make a market and facilitate trading in the company's shares, as well as to provide ongoing information about the company to interested parties such as company presentations.

Certain rules are common to both AIM and fully listed companies. They must both release price-sensitive information promptly (such as legal cases lodged against them and the resignation of a director) and produce financial information at both the half-yearly (interim) stage and the full year (final) stage.

4. Types of Equities

Remember that the capital of a company is made up of a combination of borrowing and the money invested by its owners. The long-term borrowings, or debt, of a company are often a combination of bonds and long term bank loans, and the money invested by its owners are referred to as shares, stock or equity. Shares are the equity capital of a company, hence the reason they are referred to as equities; they may comprise ordinary shares and preference shares.

4.1 Ordinary Shares

Ordinary shares carry the full risk and reward of investing in a company. If a company does well, its ordinary shareholders should do well. As the shareholders of the company, it is the ordinary shareholders who vote 'yes' or 'no' to each resolution put forward by the company directors at company meetings. For example, an offer to take over a company may be made and the directors may propose that it is accepted but this will be subject to a vote by shareholders. If the shareholders vote 'no', then the directors will have to think again.

Ordinary shareholders share in the profits of the company by receiving dividends declared by the company, which tend to be paid half-yearly or even quarterly. For example, with the final dividend for the financial year, the company directors will propose a dividend which will need to be ratified by the ordinary shareholders before it is formally declared as payable. The amount of dividend paid will depend on how well the company is doing. However, some companies pay large dividends and others none as they plough all profits made back into the future growth.

Example

Company XYZ plc has been very profitable for many years but has never paid a dividend. Only now that its meteoric expansion is showing signs of slowing down will the company start to return cash to its shareholders.

If the company does badly, it is the ordinary shareholders that will suffer. If the company closes down, often described as the company being 'wound up', the ordinary shareholders are paid last, after everybody else. If there is nothing left, then the ordinary shareholders get nothing. If there is money left after all creditors and preference shareholders have been paid, it all belongs to the ordinary shareholders.

Some ordinary shares may be referred to as partly paid or contributing shares. This means that only part of their nominal value has been paid up. For example, if a new company was established with an initial capital of £100, this capital may be made up of 100 ordinary £1 shares.

If the shareholders to whom these shares are allocated have paid £1 per share in full, then the shares are termed **fully paid**.

Alternatively, the shareholders may contribute only half of the initial capital, say £50 in total, which would require a payment of 50p per share, ie, one-half of the amount due. The shares would then be termed **partly paid**, but the shareholder has an obligation to pay the remaining amount when called upon to do so by the company.

4.2 Preference Shares

Some companies have preference shares as well as ordinary shares. The company's internal rules (their Articles of Association) will set out precisely how the preference shares differ from the ordinary shares.

Preference shares have elements of both bonds and equities, so they are often referred to as 'hybrid' securities. Although they are technically a form of equity investment, they also have characteristics that are more like debt, particularly in that most preference shares pay a fixed income.

Preference shares have legal priority (known as seniority) over ordinary shareholders in respect of their dividends and, if the issuing company collapsed, they would get their money back ahead of the ordinary shareholders.

Normally, preference shares:

- are non-voting, so preference shareholders cannot vote at the General Meetings of the company. This may change in certain special circumstances, such as when their dividends have not been paid
- pay a fixed dividend each year, the amount being set when they are first issued and which has to be paid before dividends on ordinary shares can be paid
- rank ahead of ordinary shares in terms of being paid back if the company is wound up.

Preference shares may be non-cumulative, cumulative and/or participating.

If dividends cannot be paid in a particular year, perhaps because the company has insufficient profits, preference shares would get no dividend. However, if they were cumulative preference shareholders then the dividend entitlement accumulates. Assuming sufficient profits, the **cumulative** preference shareholders will have the arrears of dividend paid in the subsequent year. If the shares were **non-cumulative**, the dividend from the first year would be lost.

Participating preference shares entitle the holder to a basic dividend of, say, 3p a year, but the directors can award a bigger dividend in a year when the profits exceed a certain level. In other words, the preference shareholder can participate in bumper profits.

Preference shares may also be convertible or redeemable. **Convertible** preference shares carry an option to convert into the ordinary shares of the company at set intervals and on pre-set terms. **Redeemable** shares, as the name implies, have a date at which they may be redeemed; that is, the nominal value of the shares will be paid back to the preference shareholder and the shares cancelled.

5. Benefits of Owning Shares

Holding shares in a company is having an ownership stake in that company. Ownership carries certain benefits and rights, and ordinary shareholders expect to be the major beneficiaries of a company's success.

As we will see in Section 6 below, shares carry risks. As a reward for taking this risk, shareholders hope to benefit from the success of the company. This reward or return can take one of the following forms.

5.1 Dividends

A dividend is part of the return that an investor gets for providing the risk capital for a business. Dividends are typically an annual (or semi-annual) payment to equity investors. Dividends are paid out of the company's profits, which form part of their **distributable reserves**. Distributable reserves are the profits after tax, and after payment of dividends which have been accumulated over the life of the company. This is exhibited in the following example.

Example

XYZ plc was formed some years ago. Over the company's life it has made £20 million in profits and paid dividends of £13 million. Distributable reserves at the beginning of the year are, therefore, £7 million.

This year XYZ plc makes post-tax profits of £3 million and decides to pay a dividend of £1 million.

At the end of the year distributable reserves are:

Opening balance	£7m
Profits after tax for the year	£3m
	£10m
Less, dividend to be paid	(£1m)
Closing balance	£9m

Note, despite only making £3 million in the current year, it would be perfectly legal for XYZ plc to pay dividends of more than £3 million, because it can use the undistributed profits from previous years. This would be described as a **naked** or **uncovered** dividend, because the current year's profits were insufficient to fully cover the dividend. Companies occasionally do this, but it is obviously not possible to maintain this long term.

UK companies generally seek, when possible, to pay steadily growing dividends. A fall in dividend payments can lead to a negative reaction among shareholders and a general

XYZ plc share price compared to FTSE 100

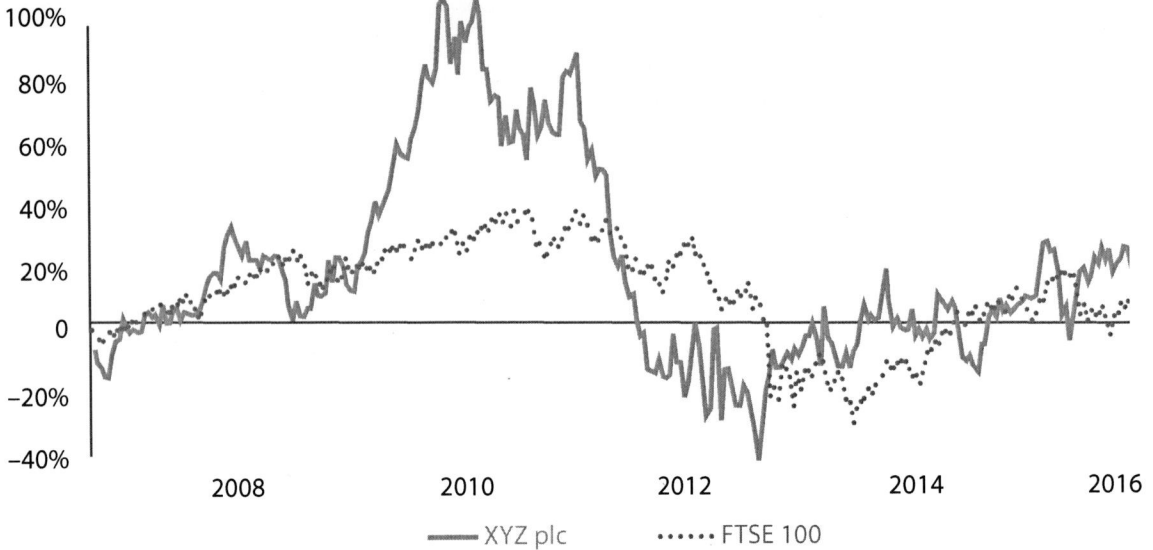

reduction in the willingness to hold the company's shares.

Potential shareholders will compare the dividend paid on a company's shares with alternative investments. These would include other shares, bonds and bank deposits. This involves calculating the **dividend yield**.

Example

ABC plc has 20 million ordinary shares, each trading at £2.50. It pays out a total of £1 million in dividends.

Its dividend yield is calculated by expressing the dividend as a percentage of the total value of the company's shares (the market capitalisation):

Dividend (£1m) ÷ Market capitalisation (20m x £2.50) x 100

So the dividend yield is:

[1m ÷ (20m x £2.50)] x 100 = 2%

Since ABC plc paid £1 million to shareholders of 20 million shares, the dividend yield can also be calculated on a per share basis by dividing the dividend per share by the share price.

The dividend per share is £1 million ÷ 20 million shares, ie, £0.05. So £0.05 ÷ £2.50 (the share price) is again 2%.

Some companies have a higher than average dividend yield, which may be for one of the following reasons:

* The company is mature and continues to generate healthy levels of cash, but has limited growth potential. For example, water and electricity supply companies ('utilities') have their prices regulated by the government and demand for water and electricity tends to grow at a steady but low rate.
* The company has a low share price for some other reason, perhaps because it is, or is expected to be, relatively unsuccessful; its comparatively high current dividend is, therefore, not expected to be sustained and its share price is not expected to rise.

In contrast, some companies might have dividend yields that are relatively low. This is generally because:

* the share price is high, because the company is viewed by investors as having strong growth prospects, or

- a large proportion of the profit being generated by the company is being ploughed back into the business, rather than being paid out as dividends (as shown with the Company XYZ example earlier).

5.2 Capital Gains

Capital gains can be made on shares if their prices increase over time.

If an investor purchases a share for £3.00, and two years later that share price has risen to £5.00, then the investor has made a £2.00 capital gain. However, the shares need to be sold to realise any capital gains. If he does not sell the share, then the gain is described as being 'unrealised'; and he runs the risk of the share price falling before he does realise the shares and 'bank' his profits. This is illustrated in the following example based on Company XYZ plc.

Example

Investors who bought the stock in 2005 had made a capital gain of 100% on their investment in 1½ years. Company XYZ plc was a 'growth' stock – expanding its operations across Europe and as its profits increased, investors bought the stock in anticipation of more capital gains and future dividends.

If a shareholder had bought XYZ plc in mid-2005 and sold the stock at the end of quarter 1 in 2007, a capital gain of 100% would have been realised. However, if the shareholder held onto the shares for another year until 2008, all that profit would have been wiped out. The lesson is that capital gains have to be 'banked' to be realised.

5.3 Shareholder Benefits

Some companies provide perks to shareholders, such as a telecoms company offering its shareholders a discounted price on their mobile phones or a shipping company offering cheap ferry tickets. Such trade benefits can be a pleasant bonus for small investors, but are not normally a major factor in investment decisions.

5.4 Shareholder Rights

5.4.1 Right to Subscribe for New Shares

If a company were able to issue new shares to anyone, then existing shareholders could lose control of the company, or at least see their share of ownership diluted. As a result, under UK legislation, existing shareholders in UK companies are given **pre-emptive** rights to subscribe for new shares. What this means is that, unless the shareholders agree to permit the company to issue shares to others, they must be given the option to subscribe for the new share offering, before it is offered to the wider public.

Pre-emptive rights are illustrated in the following example.

Example

An investor, Mr B, currently holds 20,000 ordinary shares of the 100,000 issued ordinary shares in ABC plc. He therefore owns 20% of ABC plc.

If ABC plc planned to increase the number of issued ordinary shares, by allowing investors to subscribe for another 100,000 new ordinary shares, Mr B would be offered 20% of the new shares, ie, 20,000 shares. This would enable Mr B to retain his 20% ownership of the enlarged company. In summary:

	Before the issue (000's)	%	New issue (000's)	After the issue (000's)	%
Mr B	20	20%	20	40	20%
Other share-holders	80	80%	80	160	80%
Total	100	100%	100	200	100%

If this were not the case, Mr B's stake in ABC plc could be diluted, as shown below:

	Before the issue (000's)	%	New issue (000's)	After the issue (000's)	%
Mr B	20	20%	nil	20	10%
Other share-holders	80	80%	100	180	90%
Total	100	100%	100	200	100%

A rights issue is one method by which a company can raise additional capital, complying with pre-emptive rights, with existing shareholders having the right to subscribe for new shares. The mechanics of a rights issue will be looked at in Section 7.2.

5.4.2 Right to Vote

As seen earlier in this chapter, ordinary shareholders have the right to vote on matters presented to them at company meetings. This would include the right to vote on proposed dividends and other matters, such as the appointment, or reappointment, of directors.

The votes are normally allocated on the basis of **one share = one vote**. The votes are cast in one of two ways:

- The individual shareholder can attend the company meeting and vote.
- The individual shareholder can appoint someone else to vote on his behalf – this is commonly referred to as **voting by proxy**.

However, some companies issue different share classes, for some of which voting rights are restricted or non-existent. This allows some shareholders to control the company while only holding a small proportion of the shares.

6. Risks of Owning Shares

Shares are generally considered to be relatively high risk, but have the potential for high returns when a company is successful.

The main risks associated with holding shares can be classified under the following three headings.

6.1 Market and Price Risk

Market risk is the risk that share prices in general might fall. Even though the company involved might maintain dividend payments, investors could face a loss of capital. Price risk can be illustrated by looking at the behaviour of the equity market over the past 25 years or so.

On 19 October 1987 worldwide equities once fell by nearly 20% in a single day, with some shares falling by even more than this. That is generally referred to as 'Black Monday' and the Dow Jones Industrial Average (DJIA) index of large US company shares fell by 22.3% on that day, wiping US$500 billion off share prices. Markets in every country around the world followed suit and collapsed in the similar fashion. Central banks intervened to prevent a depression and a banking crisis and, remarkably, the markets recovered much of their losses quite quickly from the worst-ever, one-day crash.

After the 1987 crash, global equity markets resumed an upward trend driven by computer technology. The arrival of the internet age sparked suggestions that a new economy was in development and led to a surge in internet stocks. Many of these stocks were quoted on the NASDAQ exchange, where share prices rapidly increased in the period leading up to the year 2000. This led the Chairman of the Federal Reserve to describe investor behaviour as 'irrational exuberance'.

In mid-2000, reality started to settle in and the 'dot.com' bubble was firmly popped, with

NASDAQ crashing to below the 2000 mark. Economies went into recession and heralded the decline in world stock markets, which continued in many until 2003.

The markets then had a period of growth, until the sub-prime crisis and credit crunch brought about another fall in stock markets. In 2008, the NASDAQ composite had its worst ever fall, declining by 40.54% over the year, the Dow Jones Industrial Average (DJIA) fell 33.84%, and the FTSE 100 tumbled 31% in the largest annual drop seen since its launch in 1984 (see following graph).

As well as general collapses in prices, any single company can experience dramatic falls in its share price when it discloses bad news, such as the loss of a major contract.

However, price risk does vary between companies: certain so-called 'defensive' shares, such as utility companies and general retailers tend to exhibit less price risk than many other companies. It takes something pretty major to stop households using gas and electricity or doing their weekly shop at the supermarket, so the shares in such companies do not tend to move in price as much as others.

6.2 Liquidity Risk

Liquidity risk is the risk that shares may be difficult to sell at a reasonable price or traded quickly enough in the market to prevent a loss. It essentially occurs when it is difficult to find a buyer willing to purchase the shares.

This typically occurs in respect of shares in 'thinly traded' companies – private companies that are not often bought and sold, or those public companies that may be listed, but in which there is not much trading activity.

Liquidity risk can also feature, to a lesser degree, when share prices in general are falling. In such circumstances the spread between the bid price (the price at which dealers will buy shares) and the offer price (the price at which dealers will sell shares) may become larger.

FTSE 100 Since 2000

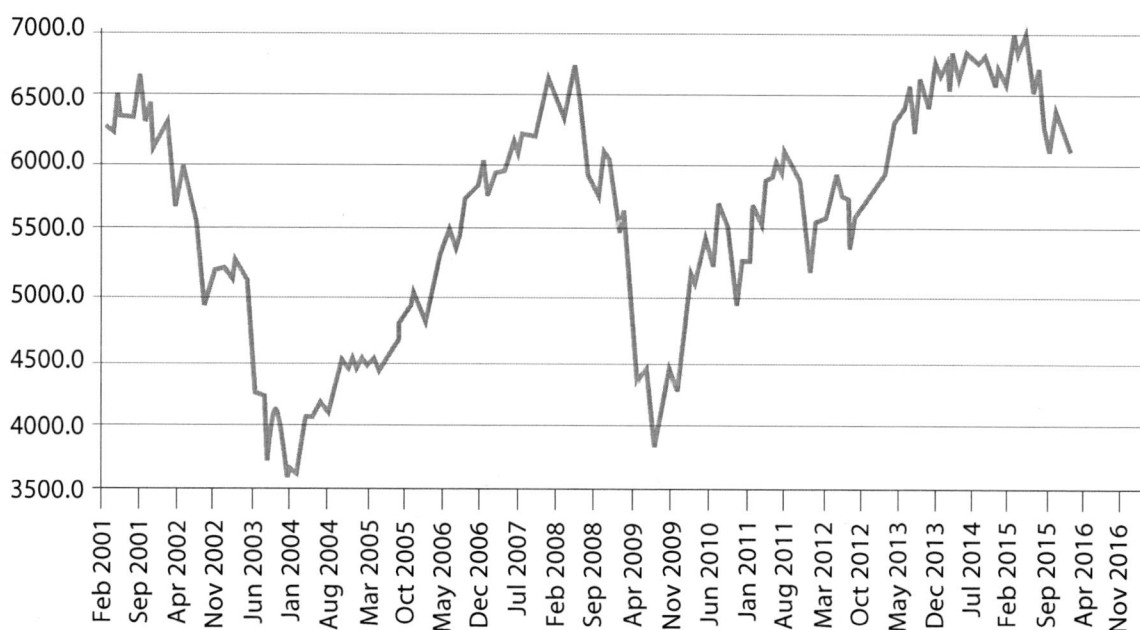

Example

Prices for ABC plc shares might be 720–722p on a normal day. This means investors can buy the shares for 722p each (at the dealer's offer price), and they can sell the shares to the dealer for 720p each (the dealer's bid price).

To begin to see a capital gain, an investor who buys shares (at 722p) needs the price to rise so that the bid (the price at which he could sell) has risen by more than 2p (eg, from 720 to 723p).

If there was a general market downturn, the dealer will reduce his prices and he might also widen the price spread to, say, 700–720p to deter sellers. An investor wanting to sell would be forced to accept the much lower price of 700p.

Unsurprisingly, shares in smaller companies tend to have a greater liquidity risk than shares in larger companies – with these smaller companies also tending to have a wider price spread between bid and offer prices than larger, more actively traded companies.

6.3 Issuer Risk

This is the risk that the issuing company collapses and the ordinary shares become worthless.

In general, it is very unlikely that larger, well-established companies will collapse, so the risk could be viewed as very small and insignificant. However, events such as the collapse of household names like Northern Rock, HBOS, Bradford & Bingley, Woolworths and Comet show that the risk is a real and present one and cannot be ignored.

Furthermore, shares in new companies, which have not yet managed to report profits, may have substantial issuer risk.

7. Corporate Actions

In simple terms, a corporate action is where a company (a corporate entity) does something that affects its investors, such as its shareholders. An obvious example is the payment of a dividend and many companies pay dividends to their shareholders twice a year.

Corporate actions can be classified into three types:

1. A **mandatory corporate action** gives the investors no choice. It is obligatory and mandated by the company, and does not require any intervention from the investors. The most obvious example of a mandatory corporate action is the payment of a dividend, since all qualifying shareholders automatically receive the dividend. Shareholders do not have to apply for the dividend.

2. A **mandatory corporate action with options** has an element of choice. It is an action that has some sort of default option that will occur if the shareholder does not intervene by selecting another option. Until the date at which the mandatory default option occurs, the individual shareholders are given the choice to select another option. Two examples of mandatory with options corporate actions are the rights issue (detailed below) and a dividend in the form of cash or additional shares. In the latter situation, the shareholder can choose whether he would prefer more shares or cash by a set deadline. If he does not express a preference by the deadline, he will typically receive his dividend in cash.

3. A **voluntary corporate action** gives the investor a choice. It is an action that requires the shareholder to make a decision. An example is where another company is bidding to take over the company (a takeover bid). To achieve the takeover the bidding company needs the shareholders of the company being bid for, to agree to sell their shares – each individual shareholder needs to choose whether to accept the offer or not.

This classification is the one that is used throughout Europe and by the international central securities depositories Euroclear and Clearstream. It should be noted that, in the US, corporate actions are simply divided into two classifications: voluntary and mandatory. The major difference between the two is therefore the existence of the category of mandatory events with options. In the US these types of events are split into two or more different events that have to be processed.

7.1 Securities Ratios

Before we look at various types of corporate action, it is necessary to know how the terms of a corporate action, such as a rights issue or bonus issue are expressed – a securities ratio. When a corporate action is announced, the terms of the event will specify what is to happen. This could be as simple as the amount of dividend that is to be paid per share. For other events, the terms will announce how many new shares the holder is entitled to receive for each existing share that they hold.

So, for example, a company might announce a bonus issue whereby it gives new shares to its investors in proportion to the shares it already holds. The terms of the bonus issue may be expressed as 1:4, which means that the investor will receive one new share for each existing four shares held. This is the standard approach used in European and Asian markets and can be simply remembered by always expressing the terms as the investor will receive 'X new shares for each Y existing shares'.

The approach differs in the US. The first number in the securities ratio indicates the final holding after the event; the second number is the original number of shares held. The above example expressed in US terms would be 5:4. so, for example, if a US company announced a 5:4 bonus issue and the investor held 10,000 shares, then the investor would end up with 12,500 shares.

7.2 Rights Issues

A company may wish to raise additional finance by issuing shares. This might be to provide funds to grow the company, Ryanair buying a new fleet of aircraft for example. In such circumstances, a company may approach its existing shareholders with an offer to buy some more shares. This is often termed a 'cash call' – they have already bought some shares in the company, so would they like to buy some more?

The announcement of a rights issue is not always greeted positively.

The initial response to the announcement of a planned rights issue will reflect the market's view of the scheme. If it is to finance expansion, and the strategy makes sense to the investors, the share price could well rise. If investors have a negative view of why a rights issue is being made (eg, to hastily find the cash to solve an issue that the directors perhaps should have anticipated), the share price could fall.

UK company law gives a series of protections to existing shareholders. As already stated, shareholders have pre-emptive rights – the right to buy shares so that their proportionate holding is not diluted. A rights issue is an offer of new shares to existing shareholders, in proportion to their initial holdings. It is an offer and each shareholder has a choice, but if they fail to make a choice the company can sell the right to buy the shares to someone else, paying the proceeds to the shareholder. So the rights issue is an example of a 'mandatory with options' type of corporate action.

As an example of a rights issue, the company might offer shareholders the right that for every four shares owned, they can buy one more at a specified price that is at a discount to the current market price, as shown below.

Example

ABC plc has 100 million shares in issue, currently trading at £4.00 each.

To raise finance for expansion, it decides to offer its existing shareholders the right to buy one new share for every four previously held. This would be described as a 1 for 4 rights issue.

The price of the rights would be set at a discount to the prevailing market price at, say, £2.00.

Each shareholder is given choices as to how to proceed following a rights issue. For an individual holding four shares in ABC plc, they could:

- Take up the rights, by paying the £2.00 and increasing their holding in ABC plc to five shares.
- Sell the rights on to another investor. The rights entitlement is transferable (often described as 'renounceable') and will have a value because it enables the purchase of a share at the discounted price of £2.00.
- Do nothing. If the investor chooses this option, the company's advisers will sell the rights at the best available price and pass on the proceeds (after charges) to the shareholder.

The share price of the investor's existing shares will also adjust to reflect the additional shares that are being issued. So, in the example above, the investor originally had four shares priced at £4 each, worth £16, and they can acquire one new share at £2.00. Assuming the rights are taken up by the investor, he will have five shares worth £18 or £3.60 each.

The share price will therefore change to reflect the effect of the rights issue once the shares go ex-rights. (This is the point at which the shares and the rights are traded as two separate instruments.)

This adjusted share price of £3.60 is known as the **theoretical ex-rights price** – it is theoretical as the actual price will depend upon the interaction of buyers and sellers in the market at the time and 'ex-rights' simply means after the rights issue has happened.

As mentioned above, the rights can be sold and the price is known as the **premium**. If the theoretical ex-rights price is £3.60 and a new share can be acquired for £2.00, then the right to acquire that share has a value. That value is the premium and should be approximately £1.60 (the difference between the £3.60 the shares will be worth and the £2.00 required to buy them).

The initial response to the announcement of a planned rights issue will reflect the market's view of the scheme. If it is to finance expansion, and the strategy makes sense to the investors, the share price could well rise. If investors have a very negative view of why a rights issue is being made (eg, to fund activities that investors view negatively) and what it says for the future of the company, the share price can fall substantially.

This situation was seen during the financial crisis with HBOS and RBS when the price of shares on the open market fell below the discounted rights issue price. The rights issues were flops and the underwriters ended up having to take up the new shares.

Underwriters of a share issue agree, for a fee, to buy any portion of the issue not taken up in the market at the issue price. The underwriters then sell the shares they have bought when market conditions seem opportune to them, and may make a gain or a loss on this sale. The underwriters agree to buy the shares if no one else will, and the company's investment bank will probably underwrite some of the issue itself.

The company and their investment banking advisers will have to consider the numbers carefully. If the price at which new shares are offered is too high, the cash call might flop. This would be embarrassing – and potentially costly for any institution that has underwritten the issue.

7.3 Bonus Issues

A bonus issue (also known as a **scrip** or **capitalisation** issue) is a corporate action when the company gives existing shareholders extra shares without their having to pay anything.

The company is simply increasing the number of shares held by each shareholder, and it is an example of a mandatory corporate action. Again, it is useful to look at an example.

Example

XYZ plc's shares currently trade at £12.00 each.

The company decided to make a 1 for 1 bonus issue, giving the shareholders an additional share for each share they currently hold.

The result is that a single shareholder who held one share worth £12.00 now has two shares worth the same amount in total. As the number of shares has doubled, the share price halves to £6.00.

Why do companies have bonus issues? The reason generally cited is that the bonus issue will increase the liquidity of the company's shares in the market because it brings about a lower share price. The logic is that, if a company's share price becomes too high, it may be unattractive to investors. Traditionally, most large UK companies tried to keep their share prices below £10, but that is less common today. For example, several years ago HSBC shares were trading at about £21 and were subject to a 2:1 scrip issue (two new shares for every one previously held), so that the share price fell to £7.

7.4 Dividends

The payment of a dividend is an example of a mandatory corporate action. The dividend represents the part of a company's profit that is passed to its shareholders.

Dividends for many large UK companies are paid twice a year, with the first dividend being declared by the directors and paid approximately halfway through the year (commonly referred to as the 'interim dividend'). The second dividend is paid after approval by shareholders at the company's AGM, held after the end of the company's financial year and is referred to as the 'final dividend' for the year. The amount paid per share may vary, as it depends on factors such as the overall profitability of the company and any plans it might have for future expansion.

The individual shareholders will receive the dividends by cheque, or by the money being transferred straight into their bank accounts or be paid through CREST (stock settlement system in the UK).

A practical difficulty, especially in a large company where shares change hands frequently, is determining the correct person to receive dividends. So, procedures have been established to minimise the extent that people receive dividends they are not entitled to, or fail to receive the dividend to which they are entitled.

Shares are bought and sold with the right to receive the next declared dividend up to the date shortly before the dividend payment is made. Up to that point the shares are described as **cum-dividend** ('cum' is the Latin word for 'with'). If the shares are purchased cum-dividend, the purchaser will receive the declared dividend. At a certain point between the declaration date and the dividend payment date, the shares go **ex-dividend** ('ex' is the Latin word for 'without'). Buyers of shares when they are ex-dividend are not entitled to the declared dividend.

In October 2014, the standard settlement period across Europe for equity trades changed to T+2 (up until October 2014 it was T+3); this means that a trade is settled two business days after it is executed so, for example, a trade executed on Monday would settle on Wednesday. As a result, the dividend timetable is also changed as the following example illustrates.

Example

The sequence of events might be as follows:

Holding plc calculates its interim profits (for the six months to 30 June) and decides to pay a dividend of 8p per share. It announces ('declares') the dividend on 1 September and states that it will be due to those shareholders who are entered on the shareholders' register on Friday 6 October.

This latter date (always on a Friday) is variously known as the:

- record date
- register date, or
- books closed date.

Given the record date of Friday 6 October, the LSE sets the ex-dividend date as Thursday 5 October.

On this day the shares will go ex-dividend and should fall in price by 8p. This is because new buyers of ABC plc's shares will not be entitled to the dividend.

Mistakes can happen. If an investor bought shares in ABC plc on 4 October, and for some reason the trade did not settle on Friday 6 October, they would not receive the dividend. A dividend claim would be made, and the buyer's broker would then recover the money via the seller's broker.

Why is the ex-dividend date a Thursday? Well, the settlement timetable for equity trades in London is that the shares are transferred to the buyer, and the money is paid to the seller two business days after day of the trade (T+2). So, if an investor (Jack Jones) purchased shares in Holding plc on Wednesday 5 October, he would be purchasing cum-dividend and his name would be entered into the shareholders'

register two business days later on Friday 7 October. It is the register at the end of this date that is used as basis for payment of the dividend, so Jack will get the dividend he is entitled to.

In contrast, if another investor (Cassie Smith) purchased shares in Holding plc on Thursday 6 October, she would be purchasing ex-dividend and her name would be entered into the shareholders' register two business days later on Monday 10 October. This is after the record date, so Cassie will not get the dividend.

7.5 Takeovers and Mergers

Companies seeking to expand can grow organically or by buying other companies. In a takeover, one company (the predator) seeks to acquire another company (the target). When they acquire shares in the other company they are under an obligation to report their share purchases once they reach a certain percentage. A relatively recent example was the purchase of Cadbury plc by the US food giant Kraft Foods.

The two parties to a takeover are the company bidding to buy the other, usually referred to as the 'predator' company, and the company that is being bid for, usually described as the 'target' company. In the above example Kraft Foods is the predator and Cadbury is the target.

Takeovers can be friendly or hostile. A friendly takeover is where the directors of the target company consider the terms of the takeover bid to be acceptable, and recommend acceptance to their shareholders.

The Kraft Cadbury bid was a friendly takeover as the directors recommended that Cadbury's shareholders accepted, and ultimately the bid was successful. Success is generally where the predator company manages to buy more than 50% of the shares of the target company – where the predator holds more than half of the shares of the target company, the predator is described as having 'gained control' of the target company. However, the predator company will usually look to buy all of the shares in the target company, perhaps for cash, perhaps in exchange for some of its own shares, or a mixture of cash and shares (as in the Kraft bid for Cadbury).

In contrast, a hostile takeover is one where the directors of the target company consider the terms of the offer are not attractive, perhaps undervaluing the target. As a result, the directors will recommend that their shareholders reject the offer. However, given that the shareholders can choose whether to accept or reject the bid (it is a voluntary corporate action), a hostile takeover bid can still be successful.

A **merger** is a similar transaction to a takeover. However the term 'merger' is reserved for situations when two companies of similar size come together to form a single, larger entity. The two companies agree to merge their interests. In a merger it is usual for one company to exchange new shares for the shares of the other entity. A recent example is the merger between British Airways and the Spanish airline Iberia to create the International Airline Group.

Answers to Chapter Exercises

Exercise 1

Which of the following three companies would NOT be eligible to list on the LSE?

1. Langley Property Rentals plc – ineligible for listing because it has only been revenue generating for two years. Companies need a revenue earning period of at least three years.

    *   Established five years ago.
    *   First rental properties acquired two years ago.
    *   100% of revenues from property rentals.
    *   Directors, associates and significant shareholders own 70% of the shares.
    *   Expected market cap £2 million.

2. Kelsey Market Research ltd – ineligible because it is a private (ltd) company rather than a public (plc) company.

    *   Established ten years ago.
    *   Company has been trading profitably since second year of operation.
    *   85% of revenues from market research.
    *   Has sufficient working capital for 14 months of operations.

3. Eden Park IT Services plc – eligible for listing.

    *   Established four years ago.
    *   75% of revenues from IT services.
    *   Been trading profitably from company's inception.
    *   Directors, associates and significant share-holders own 25% of the shares.
    *   Expected market cap £1 million.

Learning Objectives

Chapter Three has covered the following Learning Objectives:

4.1.1   Know how a company is formed and the differences between private and public companies

4.1.2   Know the features and benefits of ordinary and preference shares: dividend; capital gain, share benefits; right to subscribe for new shares; right to vote

4.1.3   Be able to calculate the share dividend yield

4.1.4   Understand the advantages, disadvantages and risks associated with owning shares: price risk; liquidity risk; issuer risk

4.1.5   Know the definition of a corporate action and the difference between mandatory, voluntary and mandatory with options

4.1.6   Understand the following terms: bonus/scrip/capitalisation issues; rights issues; dividend payments; takeover/merger

4.1.7   Know the purpose and format of annual general meetings

4.1.8   Know the function of a stock exchange: primary/secondary market; listing

Based on what you have learned in Chapter Three, try to answer the following end of chapter questions.

End of Chapter Questions

Think of an answer for each question and refer to the appropriate section for confirmation.

1. What are the two constitutional documents required in order to set up a UK company and with whom must they be lodged?

   Answer Reference: Section 2.1

   ....

   ....

2. What are the two types of company?

   Answer Reference: Section 2.2

   ....

   ....

3. What is the name of the meeting called by a public company?

   Answer Reference: Section 2.3

   ....

   ....

4. How does the primary market differ from the secondary market?

   Answer Reference: Section 3.1

   ....

   ....

5. How long does a company need to have been established to qualify for a listing in the UK?

   Answer Reference: Section 3.2

   ....

   ....

6. What is AIM and what two appointments are required of AIM companies?

    Answer Reference: Section 3.3

    ....

    ....

7. What are the two possible types of shares?

    Answer Reference: Section 4

    ....

    ....

8. What are the key benefits of owning shares?

    Answer Reference: Section 5

    ....

    ....

9. What is a 'naked' dividend?

    Answer Reference: Section 5.1

    ....

    ....

10. What is a pre-emptive right?

    Answer Reference: Section 5.4.1

    ....

    ....

11. What are the three main types of risk faced by equity investors?

    Answer Reference: Section 6

    ....

    ....

12. What are the three types of corporate action?

Answer Reference: Section 7

....

....

13. What is a rights issue?

Answer Reference: Section 7.2

....

....

14. What is a bonus issue?

Answer Reference: Section 7.3

....

....

15. What is most likely to happen to the price when a share goes ex-dividend?

Answer Reference: Section 7.4

....

....

16. How does a merger differ from a takeover?

Answer Reference: Section 7.5

....

....

Chapter Four
Equities Trading and Settlement

4

1. Introduction

This chapter follows on from Chapter 3 by considering how equities are bought and sold. This is done primarily through stock exchanges, and this chapter looks at how shares are traded on the London Stock Exchange, as well as the use of share indices worldwide.

2. Stock Markets

Stock exchanges, alternatively referred to as stock markets, have been around for hundreds of years. They began simply as meeting places where investors gathered to discuss companies and their shares, and to trade shares. As they became more formal, these meeting places became the trading floors of exchanges, where traders made deals face to face. At certain times, these floors became very noisy and busy and the trading was therefore described as **open outcry**. Today, many of these exchange floors have been replaced by sophisticated electronic dealing systems run on computer systems that now operate in major cities throughout the world.

As already seen, companies with shares traded on an exchange are said to be **listed**. Before they are admitted as listed companies, they must meet specific criteria. The requirements for the London Stock Exchange have already been encountered, and similar criteria exist across the various exchanges of the world.

2.1 London Stock Exchange (LSE)

The LSE is the most important exchange in Europe and one of the largest in the world. It has over 3,000 companies listed on it and is the most international of all exchanges, with 350 of the companies coming from 50 different countries.

Its main trading system is **SETS** (the Stock Exchange Electronic Trading Service), an automated trading system that operates on an **order-driven basis**. This means that when a buy and sell price match, an order is automatically executed.

For securities that trade less regularly, the LSE uses the **SETSqx** (the Stock Exchange Electronic Trading Service – quotes and crosses) and **SEAQ** (the Stock Exchange Automated Quotation) systems, where **market makers** keep the shares liquid.

The LSE is also the majority shareholder in MTS, the electronic exchange that dominates trading in the European government bond market. The MTS market model uses a common trading platform, while corporate governance and market supervision are based on the respective national regulatory regimes.

Each of these systems will be covered in more detail later in this chapter.

The London Stock Exchange also now has a new electronic order book for retail bonds (ORB) which offers continuous two-way pricing for trading in UK gilts and retail-size corporate bonds on-exchange.

3.   Stock Market Indices

The media constantly provides details of stock indices like the FTSE 100 (the 'Footsie' 100) and the Dow Jones Industrial Average. These stock indices provide a snapshot of how share prices are performing in a particular stock market, or across several markets. They can measure price movements across the following:

- A selection of shares from several different stock markets around the world.
- All shares listed on a single stock market.
- A selection of shares from a single stock market, perhaps:
  - shares classified according to the size of the company (its market capitalisation).
    - Large cap.
    - Mid cap.
    - Small cap:
  - shares classified according to business type.
- Industrials.
- Utilities.

- Pharmaceuticals:
  - shares classified according to business philosophy.
- 'Green' stocks (following sustainable, environmental friendly policies).
- 'Sin free' stocks (avoiding earnings from alcohol, tobacco, gambling and weapons).

A stock index calculates the aggregate price movement of its targeted stocks on a daily basis, providing a single figure for ease of comparison.

These stock indices are useful because it is very difficult for investors to gauge the overall performance of the market by looking at individual share price movements. On a given day some shares may have moved up sharply, others may have moved down sharply and some sector specific news may have had a strong influence on particular shares that are active in that sector. A stock index will smooth out these anomalies and provide a consistent picture of the mood across the market.

This is illustrated in the example charts on the following page.

In addition to providing a snapshot of how share prices are progressing across the whole group of constituent companies, stock indices also provide a benchmark for investors, allowing them to assess whether their portfolios of shares are doing better (outperforming) or worse (underperforming) than the market in general.

3.1 UK Indices

In the UK, the indices are provided by FTSE Russell, which is part of the London Stock Exchange Group. The relevant indices in the UK are:

- **FTSE 100** – this is an index of the largest 100 UK companies, commonly referred to as the 'Footsie'. The Footsie covers about 70% of the UK market by value.

Vodafone

Nov 12 20xx +2.05 (1.19%)

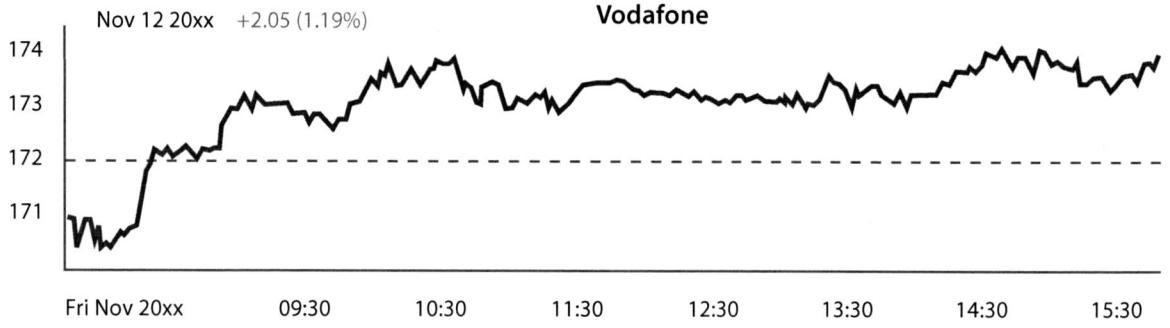

BP

Nov 12 20xx −3.85 (−0.86%)

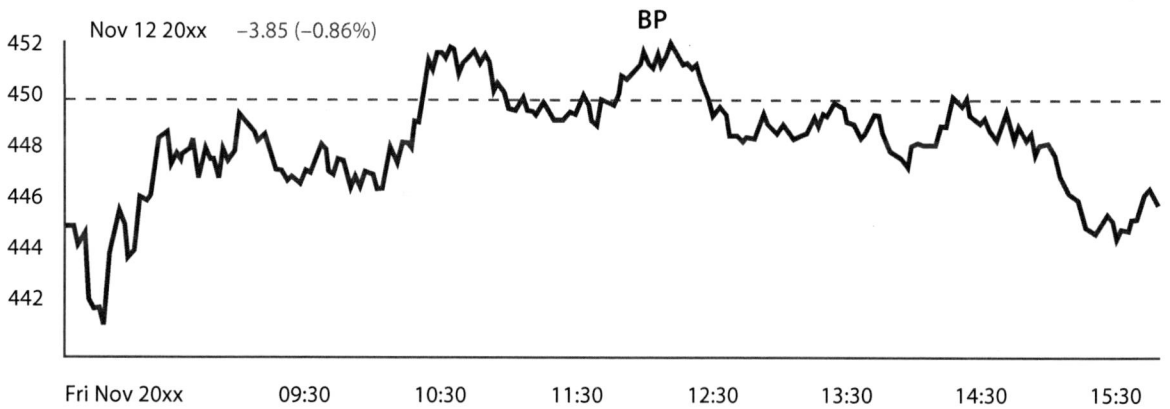

Barclays

Nov 12 20xx −4.4 (−1.54%)

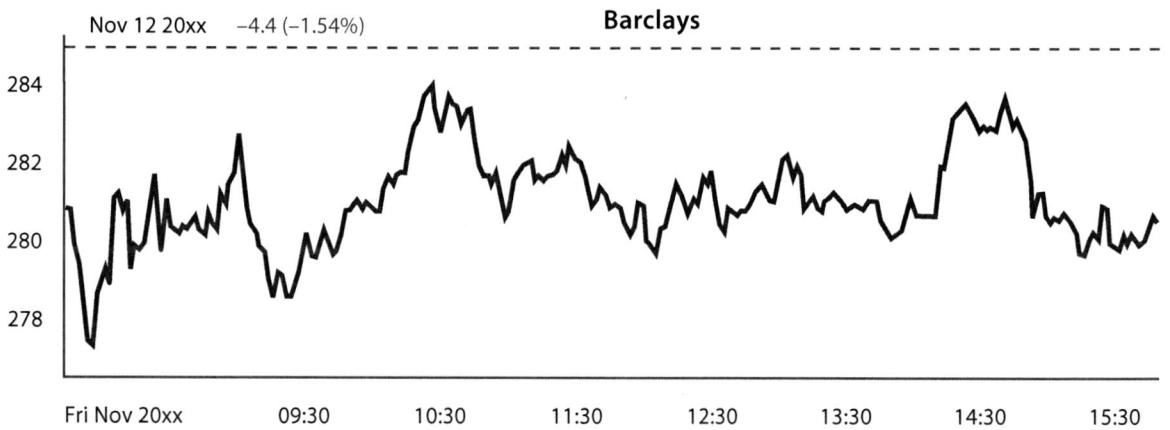

FTSE 100

Nov 12 20xx −18.36 (−0.32%)

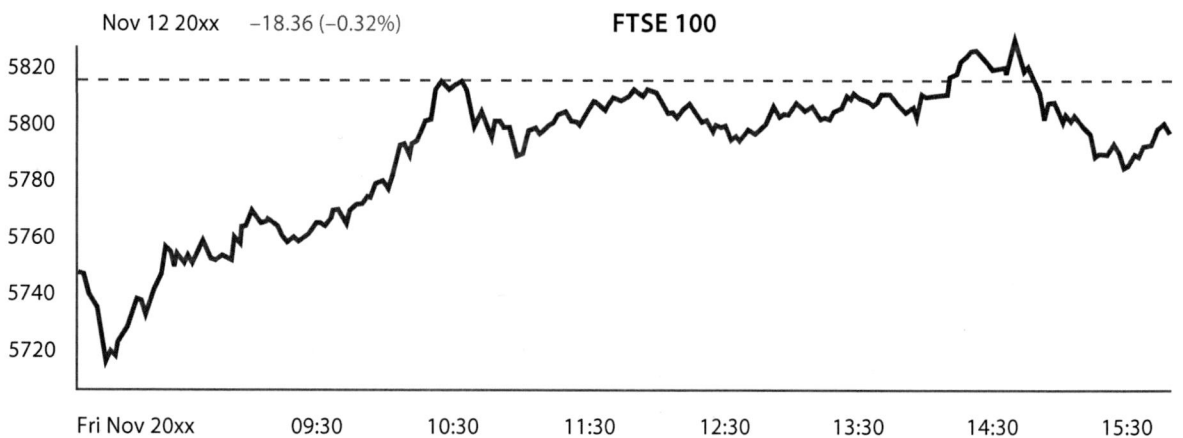

- **FTSE 250** – an index of the next 250 medium- or middle-sized (mid cap) companies below the 100.
- **FTSE 350** – a combination of the 100 and the 250 indices. The 350 is broken down into industry sectors, for example, retailing and transport.
- **FTSE All Share** – this index covers over 800 companies (including the FTSE 350) and accounts for about 98% of the UK market by value. It is often used as the benchmark against which diversified share portfolios are assessed.

Reviews of the 100, 250 and, therefore, 350 and the All Share index, are carried out every three months. Companies whose share price has grown strongly, and whose market capitalisation has increased significantly, will replace those whose price and, hence, market capitalisation is static or falling.

3.2 World Indices

Some of the other main indices that are regularly quoted in the financial press are shown in the table below.

4. Trading

Stock market trading is largely conducted on an exchange, through trading systems broadly categorised as either:

- quote-driven, or
- order-driven.

4.1 Quote-Driven Systems

Quote-driven trading systems employ market makers to provide continuous two-way, or bid and offer, prices during the trading day in particular securities, regardless of market conditions. Market makers make a profit, or turn, through this price spread. Compared to electronic order-driven systems, many practitioners argue that quote-driven systems provide liquidity to the market when trading would otherwise dry up. The NASDAQ and the LSE's Stock Exchange Automated Quotation (SEAQ) trading systems are two examples of quote-driven equity trading systems.

Country	Name	Main Stock Exchange
US	• Dow Jones Industrial Average (DJIA): providing a narrow view of the US stock market • S&P 500 (Standard & Poor's): providing a wider view of the US stock market • NASDAQ Composite: focusing on the shares traded on NASDAQ, including many technology companies	• New York Stock Exchange (NYSE) • NASDAQ
Japan	Nikkei 225	Tokyo Stock Exchange
France	CAC 40	Euronext
Germany	Xetra DAX	Deutsche Borse
Hong Kong/ China	Hang Seng	Hong Kong Stock Exchange (HKEX)

Example of the LSE's SEAQ Trading Screen

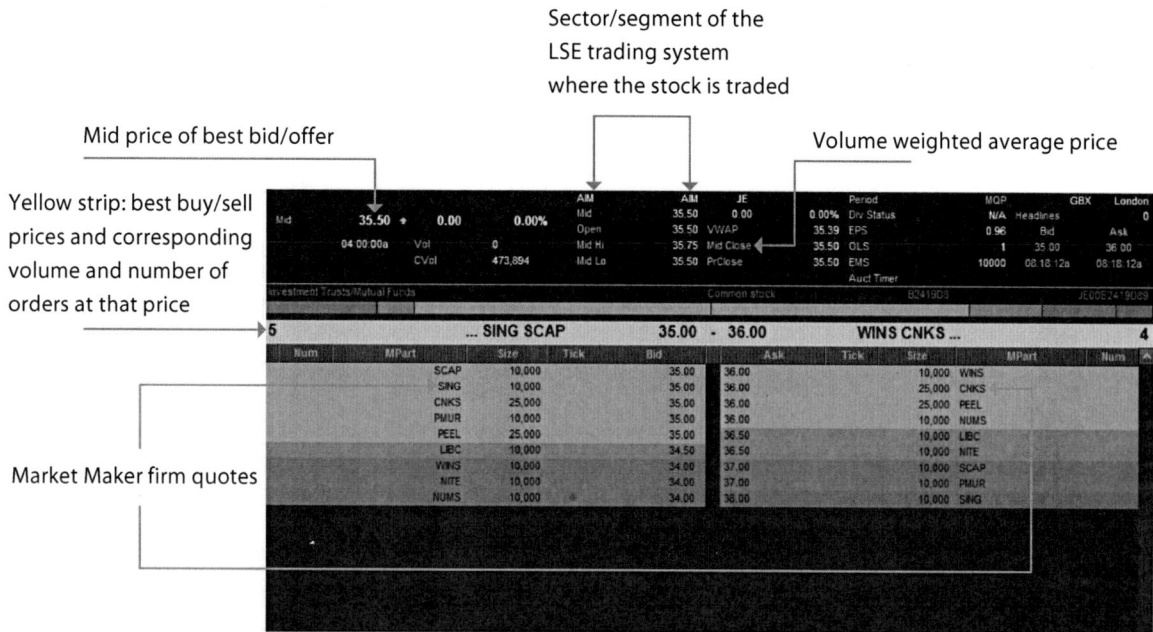

Source: London Stock Exchange

An example of the LSE's SEAQ trading screen is shown above.

4.2 Order-Driven Systems

An **order-driven** market is one that employs either an electronic order book, such as the LSE's SETS, or an auction process, such as that on the NYSE floor, to match buyers with sellers. In both cases, buyers and sellers are matched in strict chronological order by price and the quantity of shares being traded and do not require market makers.

Most stock exchanges operate order-driven systems; how they operate can be seen by looking at the LSE's SETS system as an example.

Example – SETS

The London Stock Exchange's main trading platform is SETS, which is used to trade shares that are contained within the FTSE All Share Index. It combines **electronic order-driven** trading with integrated **market maker**

liquidity provision, delivering guaranteed two-way prices for the most liquid securities.

In this system, LSE member firms (investment banks and brokers) input orders via computer terminals. These orders may be for the member firms themselves, or for their clients.

Very simply, the way the system operates is that these orders will be added to the 'buy queue' or the 'sell queue', or executed immediately. Investors who add their order to the relevant queue are prepared to hold out for the price they want.

Those seeking immediate execution will trade against the queue of buyers (if they are selling) or against the sellers' queue (if they are buying).

For a liquid stock, like Vodafone, there will be a 'deep' order book – the term 'deep' implies that there are lots of orders waiting to be dealt on either side.

CISI
CHARTERED INSTITUTE FOR
SECURITIES & INVESTMENT

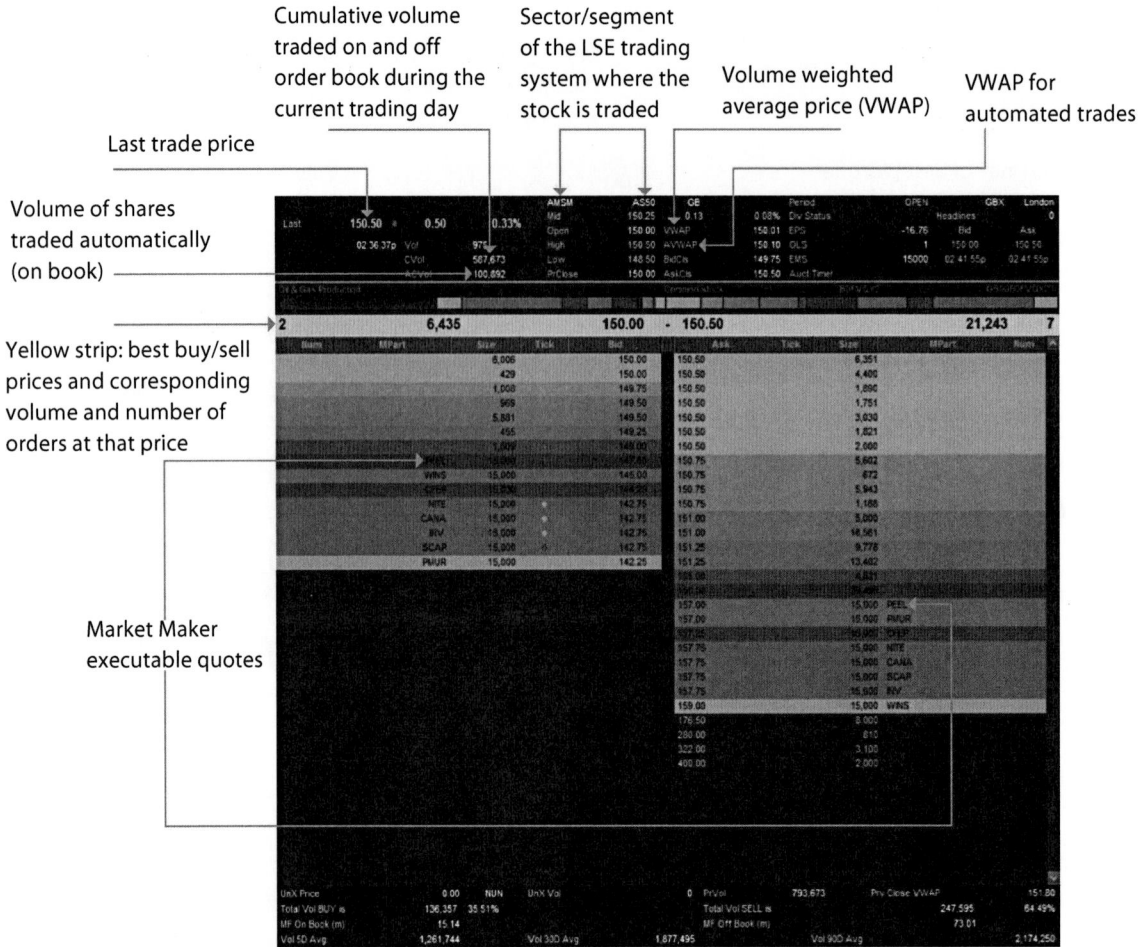

Cumulative volume traded on and off order book during the current trading day

Sector/segment of the LSE trading system where the stock is traded

Volume weighted average price (VWAP)

VWAP for automated trades

Last trade price

Volume of shares traded automatically (on book)

Yellow strip: best buy/sell prices and corresponding volume and number of orders at that price

Market Maker executable quotes

Source: London Stock Exchange

The top of the queues might look like this:

Buy Queue		Sell Queue	
We will buy for at most		We will sell for at least	
7,000 shares	£1.24	3,500 shares	£1.25
5,150 shares	£1.23	1,984 shares [2]	£1.26
19,250 shares [1]	£1.22	75,397 shares [2]	£1.26
44,000 shares [1]	£1.22	17,300 shares	£1.27

Queue priority is given on the basis of price and then time. So, for the equally priced orders noted [1], the order to buy 19,250 shares must have been placed before the 44,000 order – hence its position higher up the queue. Similarly, for the orders noted [2], the order to sell 1,984 shares must have been input before the order to sell 75,397 shares.

5. Settlement

Settlement is the process through which legal title (ie, ownership) of a security is transferred from seller to buyer in exchange for the equivalent value in cash. Ideally, these two transfers should occur simultaneously.

5.1 Methods of Holding Title

Before exploring how purchases and sales of shares are settled – ie, how the seller gets his money and the buyer gets her shares, it is important to consider how ownership of a share is evidenced. Shares can be issued in either registered or bearer form, with the former (registered) being a lot more common than the latter (bearer).

Holding shares in registered form involves the investor's name being recorded on the share register and, often, the investor being issued with a share certificate to reflect their ownership. However, many companies have today 'dematerialised' their shares. In other words, they do not use physical share certificates and instead use electronic records of ownership. This is often described as issuing shares on a **non-certificated basis**.

The alternative to holding shares in registered form is to hold **bearer** shares. As the name suggests, the person who holds, or is the 'bearer' of, the shares is the owner. Ownership passes by transfer of the share certificate to the new owner. This adds a degree of risk to holding shares – loss of the certificate might equal loss of the person's investment. As a result, holding bearer shares is relatively rare, especially in the UK.

As well as being a security risk, bearer securities are regarded unfavourably by the regulatory authorities due to the opportunities they offer for money laundering, and evading tax. As will be developed later in this workbook, money laundering is an attempt to make criminally derived money appear legitimate.

5.2 Share Settlement

With very few exceptions, UK companies are required to maintain a **share register**. As seen, this is simply a record of all current shareholders in that company, and how many shares they each hold. The share register is kept and maintained by the company registrar, who might be an employee of the company itself or a specialist firm of registrars. An electronic register is also kept by CREST so that trades can be settled electronically.

In contrast, bearer shares which have no register are usually kept safe in authorised depositories. These can be international organisations like Euroclear, or country based depositories like Singapore's central depository.

Bearer shares kept in this way are said to be 'immobilised' in depositories.

Returning to the more common situation of shares being registered, when a shareholder sells some, or all, of his shareholding, there must be a mechanism for updating the register to reflect the new buyer and for transferring the money to the seller. This is required in order to settle the transaction – accordingly, it is described as **settlement**.

Historically, when each shareholder held a **share certificate** as evidence of the shares they owned, the seller sent their share certificate and a stock transfer form, providing details of the new owner, to the company registrar. Acting on these documents, the registrar would delete the seller's name and insert the name of the buyer into the register. The registrar then issued a new certificate to the buyer. This was commonly referred to as 'certificated settlement' because the completion of a transaction required the issue of a new share certificate.

Certificated settlement is cumbersome and inefficient, and most markets have moved to having a single central securities depository which holds records of ownership, with transfer of ownership taking place electronically. In the UK, settlement has moved to a paperless, dematerialised (or uncertificated) form of settlement through a system called CREST.

Further developments in settlement took place in October 2014 when rules came in requiring European markets to move to a standardised T+2 settlement period. This reduction in the settlement period is intended to harmonise practices across Europe and help to reduce risk.

Some investors still hold physical share certificates and they have been unable to benefit from shorter settlement periods. Settlement of these trades usually takes place at T+10 or a shorter period to allow all of the paperwork to be completed. As part of the changes to settlement periods, there are separate proposals to phase out the use of paper share certificates.

Learning Objectives

Chapter Four has covered the following Learning Objectives:

4.1.9   Know the types and uses of a stock exchange index

4.1.10   Know to which markets and exchanges the following indices relate: FTSE, Dow Jones Industrial Average, S&P 500, Nikkei 225 CAC 40, Xetra DAX, NASDAQ Composite, Hang Seng

4.1.11   Know how shares are traded: order-driven/quote-driven

4.1.12   Know the method of holding title – registered/bearer/immobilised/dematerialised

4.1.13 Understand how settlement takes place and the key participants within the settlement process

Based on what you have learned in Chapter Four, try to answer the following end of chapter questions.

End of Chapter Questions

Think of an answer for each question and refer to the appropriate section for confirmation.

1. How does an open outcry method of trading work?

   Answer Reference: Section 2

   ....

   ....

2. What is the key use of a stock market index?

   Answer Reference: Section 3

   ....

   ....

3. What are the four main indices of the UK market and how often are the constituents reviewed?

   Answer Reference: Section 3.1

   ....

   ....

4. What are the three major indices in the US market?

   Answer Reference: Section 3.2

   ....

   ....

5. What is SETS and is it order-driven or quote-driven?

   Answer Reference: Section 4.2

   ....

   ....

6. What are the two methods of holding title to shares?
Answer Reference: Section 5.1

....

....

7. What is 'immobilisation'?
Answer Reference: Section 5.2

....

....

Chapter Five
Bonds

5

1. Introduction

Almost every newspaper and news bulletin mentions the shares market by giving the latest level of the FTSE 100 or the Dow Jones Industrial Average. In contrast, bonds generate little media attention despite the global investment value of bonds actually being greater than shares.

Bonds are roughly equally split between 'government' and 'corporate' bonds. Unsurprisingly, government bonds are issued by national governments such as the UK and the US, while corporate bonds are issued by companies. Most of the corporate bonds are issued by listed companies, such as the large banks and other large corporate like McDonald's.

In this chapter, we will first look at the common characteristics of bonds and then consider the key features of both government and corporate bonds.

2. Characteristics of Bonds

A bond is, very simply, a loan that is represented by an IOU (I owe you). So, if a company wants to borrow some money to enable it to expand, it could borrow it from a bank, or alternatively the company could issue bonds instead. With bonds, investors typically lend money to the company in return for the promise to have the loan repaid on a fixed future date and to receive a series of interest payments.

For example, Company A could decide to issue bonds in units of £10,000, promising to repay the £10,000 in 2022 and agreeing to pay 7% interest each year (or £700 per annum) to the holder of the bond until it is repaid. In the jargon of the bond market, Company A is the 'issuer' of the bond, the £10,000 is known as the 'face' value, the 'nominal' value, the 'par' value or the 'principal'. The date at which the £10,000 is scheduled to be repaid is the 'maturity' or 'redemption' date and the 7% interest paid each year is referred to as the 'coupon' on the bond.

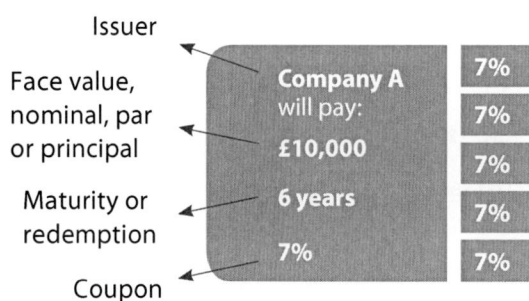

Bonds are also known by other names, such as loan stock, debt instruments and, because they tend to pay a fixed amount of interest each year, fixed interest securities. The key feature that distinguishes a bond from most loans is that a bond is tradeable – the investor in a bond could sell that bond onto another investor without the need to refer to the original borrower (Company A in the above example).

It is vital to appreciate that a bond will not always trade at its nominal value. For example, the above bond might have been issued for £10,000 to the original investor, but the original investor may choose to sell the bond after, say, two years. If the interest rate in the wider market has risen over those two years, the 7% available on the bond may not be competitive anymore, so the new buyer will only be willing to pay perhaps £9,950 for the bond. If he holds the bond until its maturity date, the new buyer will get £10,000 back. The difference between the two (£10,000 – £9,950) of £50 will be the new buyer's compensation for accepting the uncompetitive 7% coupon.

Although there is a wide variety of bonds in issue, they all share similar characteristics and some more of these characteristics will be described by looking at an example of a bond issued by the UK government.

Let us assume that an investor has purchased a holding of £10,000 nominal of 5% Treasury stock 2025. This is ultimately a loan to the UK Treasury that will pay 5% each year until it reaches its maturity date in 2025.

Nominal[1]	=	£10,000.00
Stock[2]	=	5%[3] Treasury stock 2025[4]
Price[5]	=	£133.20
Value[6]	=	£13,320.00

Each of the terms annotated above is explained below:

1. **Nominal** – as seen, this is the amount of stock purchased and is not necessarily the same as the amount invested or the cost of purchase. This is the amount on which interest will be paid and the amount that will eventually be repaid. It is also known as the 'par' or 'face' value of the bond.
2. **Stock** – 5% Treasury stock 2025 is the name given to identify the stock.
3. **5%** – this is the nominal interest rate payable on the stock, also known as the coupon. The rate is quoted gross (before the deduction of any tax that might be payable) and for UK government bonds it is normally paid in two separate and equal half-yearly interest payments. The annual amount of interest paid is calculated by multiplying the nominal amount of stock held by the coupon; that is, in this case, £10,000 times 5% (ie, £500).
4. **2025** – this is the year in which the stock will be repaid, known as the redemption date or maturity date. Repayment will take place at the same time as the final interest payment is made. The amount repaid will be the nominal amount of stock held; that is, £10,000.
5. **Price** – the convention in the bond markets is to quote prices per £100 nominal of stock. So, in this example, the price is £133.20 for each £100 nominal of stock.
6. **Value** – the value of the stock is calculated by multiplying the nominal amount of stock by the current price and the holding has a market value of £13,320.00 – that is, the nominal value of £10,000 multiplied by the price of £133.20..

Example

Government bonds are named by their coupon rate and their redemption date, for example, 6% Treasury stock 2028. These particular bonds pay coupons on 7 June and 7 December each year until the redemption date of 7 December 2028.

The coupon indicates the percentage of the nominal value that the holder will receive each year (assuming no tax is deducted at source). This interest payment is usually made in two equal semi-annual payments on fixed dates, six months apart.

An investor holding £1,000 nominal of 6% Treasury stock 2028 will receive two coupon payments of £30 each, on 7 June and 7 December each year, until the repayment of £1,000 on 7 December 2028.

3. Government Bonds

Governments issue bonds to finance their spending and investment and to bridge the gap between their actual spending and the tax and other forms of income that they receive. Clearly, issuance of government bonds will be high when tax revenues are significantly less than government spending.

Western governments like the UK, the US, Germany and France are major borrowers of money, so the volume of government bonds in issue is very large and forms a major part of the investment portfolio of many institutional investors (such as pension funds and insurance companies).

UK government bonds are known as gilts. This dates back to the days when the physical certificates were issued with a real gold or 'gilt' edge to them, so they became known as 'gilts' or 'gilt-edged stock'. The bonds are issued on behalf of the government by the Debt Management Office (DMO). The chart on the following page gives some detail of the UK government's sales of new gilts and redemptions of old gilts. The total amount of new gilts issued is called the 'gross' amount and the total amount less redemptions is the 'net' amount. The chart also shows the percentage of GDP represented by the total of gilts in issue.

3.1 Types of Government Bonds

There are two main types of UK government bond in issue – conventional bonds and index-linked bonds.

Conventional government bonds are instruments that carry a fixed coupon and a single repayment date, such as in the examples used above of 5% Treasury stock 2025 and 6% Treasury stock 2028. Conventional bonds typically represent around 75% of bonds in issue.

The coupon and redemption amount for index-linked bonds are increased by the amount of inflation over its lifetime. An example is 2½% Treasury index-linked stock 2020. When this stock was issued, it carried a coupon of 2½%, but this is uplifted by the amount of inflation at each interest payment. Similarly, the amount that will be repaid in 2020 is adjusted.

Index-linked bonds are attractive in periods when a government's control of inflation is uncertain because they provide extra protection to the investor. They are also attractive as long-term investments, eg, pension funds. Long-term investors need to invest their funds and know that the returns will maintain their real value after inflation so that they can meet their obligations to pay pensions.

Conventional bonds can be stripped into their individual cash flows – that is, the coupon payments and the bond repayment. 'Stripping' a gilt refers to breaking it down into its individual cash flows which can be traded separately as zero coupon gilts. A three-year gilt will have seven individual cash flows: six (semi-annual) coupon payments and the final maturity repayment. These are known as gilt STRIPS.

In the past, there have also been other types of government bonds, dual-dated and undated. Dual-dated bonds carried a fixed coupon but showed two dates between which they can be repaid. The decision as to when to repay is made by the government and depends on the prevailing rates of interest at that time. The final gilt of this type, 12% Exchequer stock 2013–17, was redeemed on 12 December 2013. Undated bonds have no fixed date for when they will be repaid.

4. Corporate Bonds

As the name suggests, a corporate bond is a bond that is issued by a corporate entity.

The term **corporate bond** is usually restricted to longer-term debt instruments, with a redemption date that is more than one year

Gross and Net Gilt Issuance

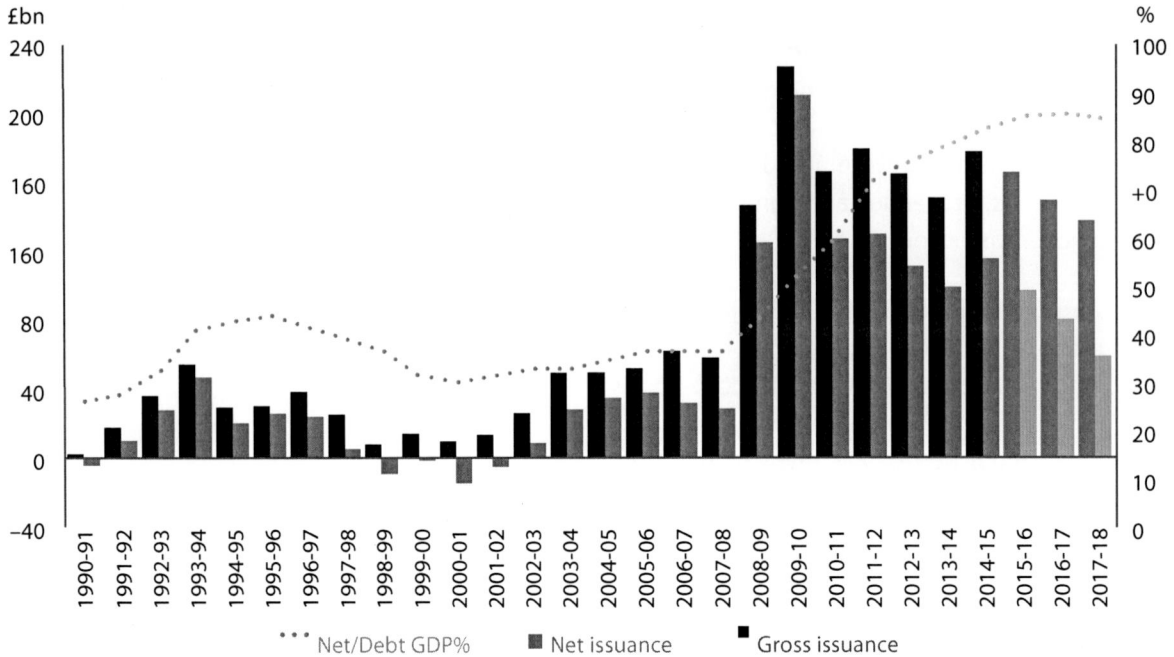

Source: Debt Management Office (DMO)

away at the point of issue. The term **commercial paper** is used for instruments with a shorter maturity. Furthermore, it only tends to be well established and relatively stable companies that can issue bonds with a maturity greater than ten years at an acceptable cost.

Most corporate bonds are listed on stock exchanges, however the majority of trading does not take place on the stock exchange systems. Instead, most bonds dealing is done in the 'over-the-counter' (OTC) market, between professionals – that is, directly between market counterparties.

4.1 Features of Corporate Bonds

There is a wide variety of corporate bonds and they can be differentiated by looking at some of their key features, such as security; and redemption provisions.

4.1.1 Bond Security

When an individual borrows money in the form of a mortgage, the lending bank or building

society makes sure that it has the ability to repossess the property if the scheduled mortgage payments are not made. In a similar way, when a company is seeking to raise new funds by way of a bond issue, it will often offer 'security' to provide the investor with some guarantee for the repayment of the bond.

In this context, security usually means a legal charge over some or all of the bond issuer's assets. These might include properties, like offices and factories, and other items such as the company's unsold goods or uncollected debts. If the issuer fails to pay the required coupons or the principal on the bonds, the bondholders can claim those assets in order to recoup the money that is owed to them. This enables the bondholders to regard their borrowings as safer than if there were no security. Logically, the greater the value of the security offered relative to the amount borrowed, the lower the cost of borrowing should be.

The security offered may be fixed or floating. Fixed security is where a specific asset, such as the head office of the company, or a particular factory, provides the security for the loan. Because there is a fixed legal charge over a particular asset, or a number of particular assets, this is commonly referred to as a 'fixed charge'. In contrast, a floating charge is where the general assets of the company are offered as security for the loan, which might include the company's cash at the bank, trade debtors and unsold stock.

In some cases, rather than being provided by something the company owns, the security takes the form of a third party guarantee – for example, a guarantee by a bank that, if the issuer defaults, the bank will repay the bondholders.

4.2 Types of Corporate Bonds

Over and above the considerations of security and redemption, there is a wide variety of corporate bonds that are traded around the world. The variety is largely due to innovative structures devised by banks to assist their client companies in raising finance – this is referred to as 'financial engineering'. Some of the main types are described below.

4.2.1 Fixed-Rate Bonds

The key features of fixed-rate bonds have already been described in Section 2. Essentially, they have fixed coupons which are paid either half-yearly or annually and predetermined redemption dates.

4.2.2 Floating Rate Notes (FRNs)

Floating rate notes are often referred to as FRNs – they are bonds that have variable rates, rather than a fixed rate of coupon.

The coupon rate will be linked to a published rate of interest, such as, the London InterBank Offered Rates (LIBOR) that are published daily by ICE (Intercontinental Exchange is a leading operator of global exchanges and clearing houses and a provider of data and listings services). LIBOR is the rate of interest at which

banks will lend to one another in London in a particular currency (eg, pounds sterling) for a particular period (eg, six months), and LIBOR rates are often used as a basis for cash flows on financial instruments.

An FRN will usually pay interest at LIBOR plus a quoted margin or spread.

4.3 Domestic and Foreign Bonds

Bonds can be categorised geographically. A **domestic bond** is issued by a domestic issuer into the domestic market, for example, a UK company issuing bonds, denominated in sterling, to UK investors.

In contrast, a **foreign bond** is issued by an overseas entity into a domestic market and is denominated in the domestic currency. Examples of foreign bonds include a German company issuing a sterling bond to UK investors, or a US dollar bond issued in the US by a non-US company.

4.4 Eurobonds

Despite what the name suggests, eurobonds are not necessarily denominated in the euro currency and may have little to do with Europe. Eurobonds are basically large international bond issues that are often made by governments and multinational companies.

Despite the first eurobond being issued on behalf of the Italian motorway operator, Autostrade, in 1963, the eurobond market really developed in the early 1970s when oil sales from the Middle East were generating substantial quantities of US dollars (because oil is priced in US dollars) and US financial institutions were subject to ceiling on the rate of interest that could be paid on dollar deposits. Bonds were issued from financial centres like London, denominated in US dollars to attract these international investors with dollars to invest. Since then, the eurobond market has grown rapidly to become the world's largest market for longer-term capital, and most eurobond activity is concentrated in London.

The defining characteristic of eurobonds is that they are denominated in a currency different from that of the financial centre or centres in which they are issued. So, a dollar denominated bond issued out of London is a eurobond, as is a Yen denominated bond issued out of Hong Kong. In fact, eurobond issues are often issued in a number of financial centres simultaneously.

Eurobonds issued by companies generally do not provide any underlying fixed or floating security to the bondholders, but instead tend to be assessed by one of the credit ratings agencies (see Section 5.3 below). To provide some measure of safety to the bondholders, the issuing company typically includes a 'negative pledge' clause in the bond's documentation. This prevents the company from subsequently making any secured bond issues, or bond issues that would confer a greater seniority or entitlement to the company's assets in the event of its liquidation, unless an equivalent level of security is provided to existing eurobond investors.

The eurobond market offers a number of advantages over a domestic bond market, making it attractive for companies as a way to raise capital, including:

- a choice of innovative products to more precisely meet issuers' needs
- the ability to reach potential lenders internationally rather than just domestically
- anonymity to investors as issues are made in bearer form (there is no register of bondholders maintained by the issuer)
- gross interest payments made to investors
- lower funding costs due to the competitive nature and greater liquidity of the market
- the ability to make bond issues at short notice, and
- less regulation and disclosure.

Most eurobonds are issued as conventional bonds (or 'straights'), with a fixed nominal value, fixed coupon and known redemption date.

5. Investing in Bonds

5.1 Advantages, Disadvantages and Risks

As one of the main asset classes, bonds clearly have a role to play in most portfolios.

The main **advantages** of bonds are:

- for fixed-coupon bonds, a regular and certain flow of income
- for most bonds, a fixed maturity date (however, there are bonds which have no redemption date, and others which may be repaid on either of two dates or between two dates – sometimes at the investor's option and sometimes at the issuer's option)
- a range of income yields to suit different investment and tax situations
- relative security of capital for more highly rated bonds.

The main **disadvantages** of bonds are:

- the 'real' value of the income flow is eroded by the effects of inflation (except in the case of index-linked bonds)
- default risk, namely the risk that the issuer will not be able to make the coupon payments as they fall due or repay the capital at the maturity date.

As has been seen, there are a number of **risks** attached to holding bonds.

Firstly, bonds generally have **default risk**, the possibility of the issuer defaulting on the payment of coupons and/or capital, for example a corporate issuer of a bond could go bust. Bonds also have **price risk or market risk**, which is the effect of **movements** in interest rates, which can have a significant impact on the value of bonds.

Highly rated government bonds are said to have only price risk, as there is little or no risk that the government will fail to pay the coupons or repay the capital on the bonds. However, recent turmoil in government bond markets has resulted from fears that certain European governments (such as Greece, Ireland and Portugal) may be unable to meet their obligations on these loans, and the prices of their bonds fell significantly as a result.

Price or market risk is best explained by two simple examples.

Example

Price Risk (Example 1)

Interest rates are approximately 5%, and the government issues a bond with a coupon rate of 5%. Three months later, interest rates have doubled to 10%. What will happen to the value of the bond?

The value of the bond will fall substantially. Its 5% coupon is no longer attractive, so its resale price will fall to compensate and make the return the bond offers more competitive.

Example

Price Risk (Example 2)

Interest rates are approximately 5%, and the government issues a bond with a coupon rate of 5%. Subsequently interest rates generally fall to 2.5%. What will happen to the value of the bond?

The value of the bond will rise substantially. Its 5% coupon is very attractive, so its resale price will rise to compensate and make the return it offers fall to more realistic levels.

With both of the above examples, remember that it is the current value of the bond that is changing. Changes in interest rates do not affect the coupon or the amount payable at maturity, which will remain as the nominal amount of the stock.

As the above examples illustrate, there is an inverse relationship between interest rates and bond prices:

- If interest rates increase, bond prices will decrease.
- If interest rates decrease, bond prices will increase.

interest rates   interest rates

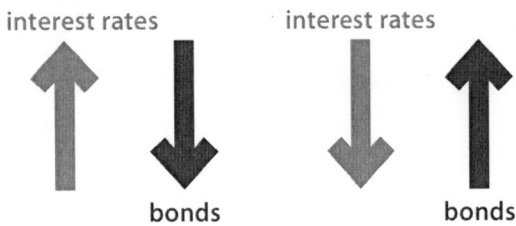

bonds   bonds

Some of the other main risks associated with holding bonds are:

- **Seniority risk** – the seniority with which corporate debt is ranked in the event of the issuer's liquidation. The issuer might issue new, additional bonds, which rank higher in seniority. These bonds will then be repaid first in the event of liquidation; so debt with the highest seniority has a greater chance of being repaid than debt with lower seniority. If the company raises more borrowing and it is entitled to be repaid before the existing bonds, then the bonds have suffered from seniority risk.
- **Inflation risk** – the risk of inflation rising unexpectedly and eroding the real value of the bond's coupon and redemption payment.
- **Liquidity risk** – liquidity is the ease with which a security can be converted into cash. Some bonds are more easily sold at a fair market price than others.
- **Exchange rate risk** – bonds denominated in a currency different from that of the investor's home currency are potentially subject to adverse exchange rate movements. The value of the issuer's currency might have declined relative to the investor's currency.

5.2 Flat Yields

Yields are measures of the return that can be earned on bonds.

However, remember that the coupon reflects the interest rate payable on the nominal or principal amount. An investor may have paid a different amount to purchase the bond, so a method of calculating the true return to him or her is needed. The return, as a percentage of the cost price, which a bond offers is often referred to as the bond's yield. The most straightforward yield is to look at the coupon paid on a bond as a percentage of its market price – this is referred to as the flat or **running yield**.

The flat yield is calculated by taking the annual coupon and dividing by the bond's price and then multiplying by 100 to obtain a percentage. The bond's price is typically stated as the price payable to purchase £100 nominal value. This is best illustrated by looking at the following examples.

Example _____

Flat Yields

1. A bond with a coupon of 5%, issued by XYZ plc, redeemable in 2020, is currently trading at £100 per £100 nominal.

   The flat yield is the coupon divided by the price expressed as a percentage, ie:

   £5 ÷ £100 x 100 = 5%.

2. A bond with a coupon of 4%, issued by ABC plc, redeemable in 2025, is currently trading at £78 per £100 nominal. So an investor could buy £100 nominal value for £78.

   The flat yield is the coupon divided by the price expressed as a percentage, ie:

   £4 ÷ £78 x 100 = 5.13%.

3. 5% Treasury stock 2028 is currently priced at £104. So an investor could buy £100 nominal value for £104.

   The flat yield on this gilt is the coupon divided by the price, ie:

   £5 ÷ £104 x 100 = 4.81%.

_____

The interest earned on a bond is only one part of its total return, however, as the investor may also either make a capital gain or a loss on the bond if it is held until redemption. The redemption yield is a measure that incorporates both the income and capital return – assuming the investor holds the bond until its maturity – into one figure.

5.3 Rating Agencies

Credit risk – the probability of an issuer defaulting on their payment obligations and the extent of the resulting loss – can be assessed by looking at the independent credit ratings given to most bond issues.

There are more than 70 agencies throughout the world, and preferred agencies vary from country to country. The three most prominent credit rating agencies that provide these ratings are Standard & Poor's; Moody's; and Fitch Ratings.

The following table shows the credit ratings available from the three companies.

Standard & Poor's and Fitch Ratings refine their ratings by adding a plus or minus sign to show relative standing within a category, while Moody's do the same by the addition of a 1, 2 or 3.

As can be seen, bond issues that have been subject to credit ratings can be divided into two distinct categories: those given an 'investment grade' rating, and those categorised as non-investment grade, or speculative. The latter are also known as 'high yield' or – for the worst-rated – 'junk bonds'. Investment grade issues offer the greatest liquidity and certainty of repayment.

Bonds will be assessed and given a credit rating when they are first issued and then re-assessed if circumstances change, so that their rating can be upgraded or downgraded with a consequent effect on their price.

Bond Credit Ratings				
Credit Risk		Moody's	Standard & Poor's	Fitch Ratings
Investment Grade				
Highest quality		Aaa	AAA	AAA
High quality	Very strong	Aa	AA	AA
Upper medium grade	Strong	A	A	A
Medium grade		Baa	BBB	BBB
Non-Investment Grade				
Lower medium grade	Somewhat speculative	Ba	BB	BB
Low grade	Speculative	B	B	B
Poor quality	May default	Caa	CCC	CCC
Most speculative		C	CC	CC
No interest being paid or bankruptcy petition filed		C	D	C
In default		C	D	D

Learning Objectives

Chapter Five has covered the following Learning Objectives:

5.1.1 Understand the characteristics and terminology of bonds: coupon; redemption; nominal value

5.2.1 Know the definition and features of government bonds: types; yields

5.3.1 Know the definitions and features of the following types of bond: domestic; foreign; eurobond

5.4.1 Know the advantages and disadvantages of investing in different types of bonds

5.4.2 Be able to calculate the flat yield of a bond

5.4.3 Understand the role of credit rating agencies and the differences between investment and non-investment grades

Based on what you have learned in Chapter Five, try to answer the following end of chapter questions.

End of Chapter Questions

Think of an answer for each question and refer to the appropriate section for confirmation.

1. What are the alternative terms for the face value of a bond?

    Answer Reference: Section 2

    ....

    ....

2. What is the market convention for quoting bond prices?

    Answer Reference: Section 2

    ....

    ....

3. What is a gilt?

    Answer Reference: Section 3

    ....

    ....

4. What are the two main types of government bond?

    Answer Reference: Section 3.1

    ....

    ....

5. What is a secured corporate bond?

    Answer Reference: Section 4.1.1

    ....

    ....

6. What is an FRN and what type of rates do they have?

   Answer Reference: Section 4.2.2

   ....

   ....

7. What distinguishes a domestic bond from a foreign bond?

   Answer Reference: Section 4.3

   ....

   ....

8. What is a eurobond?

   Answer Reference: Section 4.4

   ....

   ....

9. What are the main advantages of investing in bonds?

   Answer Reference: Section 5.1

   ....

   ....

10. What are the main risks involved in investing in bonds?

    Answer Reference: Section 5.1

    ....

    ....

11. How is the flat yield calculated?

    Answer Reference: Section 5.2

    ....

    ....

12. What does the flat yield ignore that is reflected in the redemption yield?

    Answer Reference: Section 5.2

    ....

    ....

13. What is the best credit rating that a bond can have?

    Answer Reference: Section 5.3

    ....

    ....

14. What is the lowest investment grade rating that a bond can have and how does the Moody's rating differ from the rating given by Standard & Poor's or Fitch Ratings?

    Answer Reference: Section 5.3

    ....

    ....

15. What is a 'junk bond'?

    Answer Reference: Section 5.3

    ....

    ....

Chapter Six
Other Financial Products

6

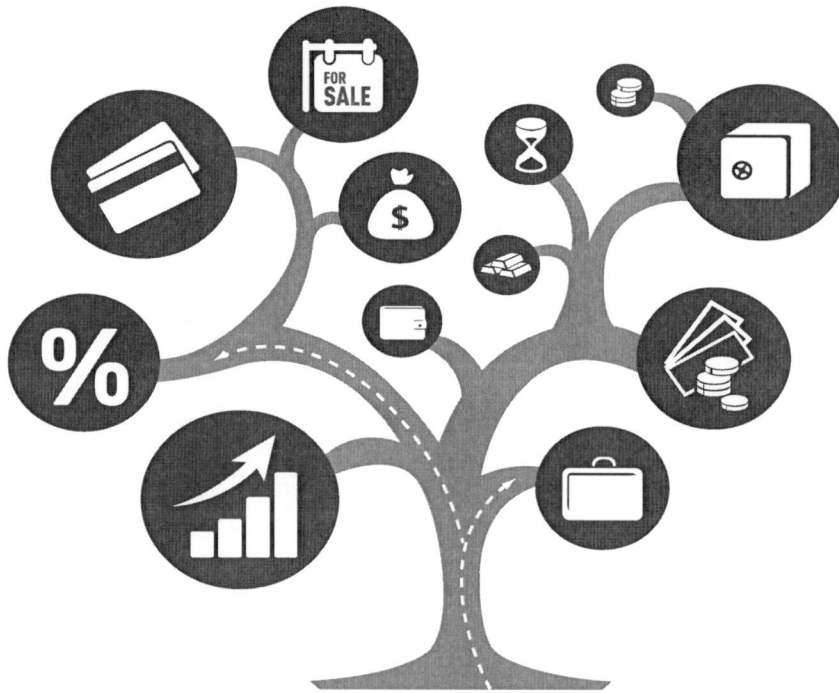

1. Introduction

Having already encountered equities and bonds, this chapter looks at a number of other financial instruments and products that are available – in particular, instruments and activities in the so-called 'money market', the foreign exchange market (or 'forex') plus a detailed look at the property market and the way property purchases can be financed through mortgage loans.

2. Money Markets

The term 'money market' is a little confusing – it can be thought of as the market for shorter term bonds. Remember that bonds are IOU (I owe you) instruments that generally pay a regular coupon and then repay the amount borrowed at the end of a particular period. The period between the issue and the maturity of a bond is typically years. In contrast, money market instruments are IOUs where the period between issue and maturity is much shorter, often just three months or less and certainly not exceeding a year.

Bonds and equities are used to raise relatively long term capital for the issuer – they are capital market instruments. Instruments issued to raise cash for shorter term periods of up to a year are referred to as money market instruments.

Direct investment in money market instruments is often subject to a relatively high minimum subscription and therefore tends to be more suitable for institutional investors like pension funds and insurance companies. Because of this, it is often described as a 'wholesale' or institutional market.

The short-term nature of the money markets means that issuers seek to avoid any excessive administrative costs. For most money market instruments, this is achieved by:

1. issuing the instruments in 'bearer' form and therefore removing the need to maintain a register of the holders of the instruments.
2. not paying a coupon and instead issuing the instruments at a discount to their face value.

It is now more usual to issue instruments in electronic form to enable electronic book transfer and custody of the securities.

The main types of UK money market instruments are:

- **Treasury bills** – like gilts, these are issued by the **Debt Management Office (DMO)** on behalf of the UK Treasury. However, Treasury bills are issued much more frequently than gilts, generally every week and the money is used to meet the government's short-term borrowing needs. Treasury bills are non-interest-bearing instruments. Instead of interest being paid out on them, they are issued at a **discount to par** – ie, a price of less than £100 per £100 nominal – and commonly redeem after one, three or six months. For example, a Treasury bill might be issued for £999 and mature at £1,000 three months later. The investor's return is the difference between the £999 they paid, and the £1,000 received on the Treasury bill's maturity.
- **Certificates of deposit (CDs)** – these are issued by banks in return for deposited money and are tradeable on the money markets. Until the late 1960s, a rigidity in the interbank market meant that deposits, once taken, could not be traded during their lifetime. To overcome this, CDs were introduced which could be traded on a secondary market. By market convention, it is a short-term marketable instrument with a maturity of up to five years, although the vast majority are issued for periods of less than six months. Interest can be at a fixed or variable rate, although they may also be issued at a discount and without a coupon. Most sterling CDs are held by banks, building societies and other money market participants.
- **Commercial paper (CP)** – this is the equivalent of a Treasury bill issued by a corporate entity (a company) rather than the government. Commercial paper tends to be issued by large companies to meet their short-term borrowing needs.

A company's ability to issue commercial paper is typically agreed with banks in advance. For example, a company might agree with its bank to a programme of £10 million-worth of commercial paper. This would enable the company to issue various forms of commercial paper with different maturities (eg, one month, three months and six months) and possibly different currencies, to the bank. As with Treasury bills, commercial paper is zero coupon and issued at a discount to its par value.

Settlement of money market instruments is typically achieved through CREST and is commonly settled on the day of the trade or the following business day.

Money market instruments provide a relatively low-risk way to generate an income or capital return, as appropriate, while preserving the nominal value of the amount invested. As a result, they tend to be particularly popular at times of market uncertainty. However, they are unsuitable for anything other than the short term since, historically, they have underperformed most other asset types over the medium to long term. Indeed, in the long term, returns from money market instruments have barely been positive once tax and inflation have been taken into account.

The money market is a highly professional market that is used by banks and companies to manage their liquidity needs. It is not accessible by private investors, who instead need to utilise either money market accounts offered by banks, or money market funds.

There is a range of money market funds available and they can offer some advantages over pure money market accounts. There is the obvious advantage that the pooling of funds with other investors gives the investor access to assets they would not otherwise be able to invest in. The returns on money market funds should also be greater than a simple money market account offered by a bank.

Placing funds in a money market account means that the investor is exposed to the risk of that bank. By contrast, a money market fund will invest in a range of instruments from many providers, and as long as they are AAA-rated they can offer high security levels. A rating of AAA is the highest rating assigned by a credit rating agency.

Under UK regulatory rules, money market funds may only invest in approved money market instruments and deposits with credit institutions and meet other conditions on the structure of the underlying portfolio.

The Investment Association (IA) introduced two money market sectors which came into effect on 1 January 2012. These are based on the European definitions of money market funds that have been adopted by the FCA – short-term money market funds and money market funds.

- **Short-term money market funds** can have a constant net asset value (NAV) or a fluctuating NAV. A constant NAV face value means they should have an unchanging net asset value when income in the fund is accrued daily and can either be paid out to the unitholder or used to purchase more units in the scheme.
- **Money market funds** by contrast must have a fluctuating net asset value.

It should be noted that money market funds may invest in instruments in which the capital is at risk and so may not be suitable for many investors. In addition, money market funds may invest in assets denominated in other currencies and so introduce exchange rate risk.

3. Foreign Exchange (FX)

The foreign exchange (FX) market refers to the trading of one currency for another. It is by far the busiest and most active of the financial markets, with turnover comfortably exceeding that of bonds and equities.

Most currencies are allowed by their central banks to 'float', so that the exchange rate between one currency and another can vary. This clearly creates risks for companies operating internationally, as can be seen in the following example.

Example

A British company, Union Jack plc manufactures and sells goods internationally. Union Jack is negotiating a sale with a large US customer, Stars & Stripes Inc. Because Stars & Stripes is potentially a very valuable client to Union Jack, the sale will be made in US dollars and Stars & Stripes will not be required to pay until a month after the sale is invoiced.

As far as Union Jack is concerned, there is a risk that the number of pounds the dollars will buy in a month's time may be less than when the sale is first made. This risk could be removed by using a FX forward contract, where Union Jack agrees to sell the US dollars it is anticipating to receive from Stars & Stripes in one month's time at a rate established now.

With currencies allowed to float freely against one another, trading in currencies has become 24-hour, and it can take place in the various time zones of Asia, Europe and America. London, being placed between the Asian and American time zones, is well placed to take advantage of this, and has grown to become the world's largest forex market. Other large centres include the US, Singapore, Hong Kong and Japan.

Trading of international currencies clearly involves selling one currency and buying another, the two currencies involved are described as 'pairs'. The price at which a pair is bought and sold provides the **exchange rate**. When the exchange rate is being quoted, the name of the each currency is abbreviated to a three letter reference; so, for example, sterling is abbreviated to GBP which is an abbreviation of Great British pounds.

The most commonly quoted currency pairs are:

- US dollar and Japanese yen (USD/JPY)
- Euro and US dollar (EUR/USD)
- US dollar and Swiss franc (USD/CHF)
- British pound and US dollar (GBP/USD)
- Euro and British pound (EUR/GBP).

When currencies are quoted, the first currency is the base currency and the second is the counter or quote currency. The base currency is always equal to one unit of that currency, in other words, one pound, one dollar or one euro. For example, if the EUR:USD exchange rate is 1:1.1165, this means that €1 is worth $1,1165. When the exchange rate is described as going up, it means that the value of the base currency is rising relative to the other currency and is referred to as the currency strengthening; where the opposite is the case, the currency is said to be weakening.

The graph below shows the British pound against the US dollar over the last ten years, showing a general weakening of the pound from being worth more than $2. In 2016, the Brexit vote saw sterling drop from around $1.45 in June 2016 to around $1.30 by the following month.

When currency pairs are quoted, a market maker or FX trader will quote a bid and ask price. Staying with the example of the EUR:USD the quote might be 1.1164/66 – notice that the euro is not mentioned, as standard convention is that the base currency is always one unit. So if a client wanted to buy €100,000 then he will need to pay the higher of the two prices and deliver $111,660; if a client wanted to sell €100,000 then he will get the lower of the two prices and receive $111,640.

The international currency market is primarily an over-the-counter (OTC) market, ie, one where brokers and dealers negotiate directly

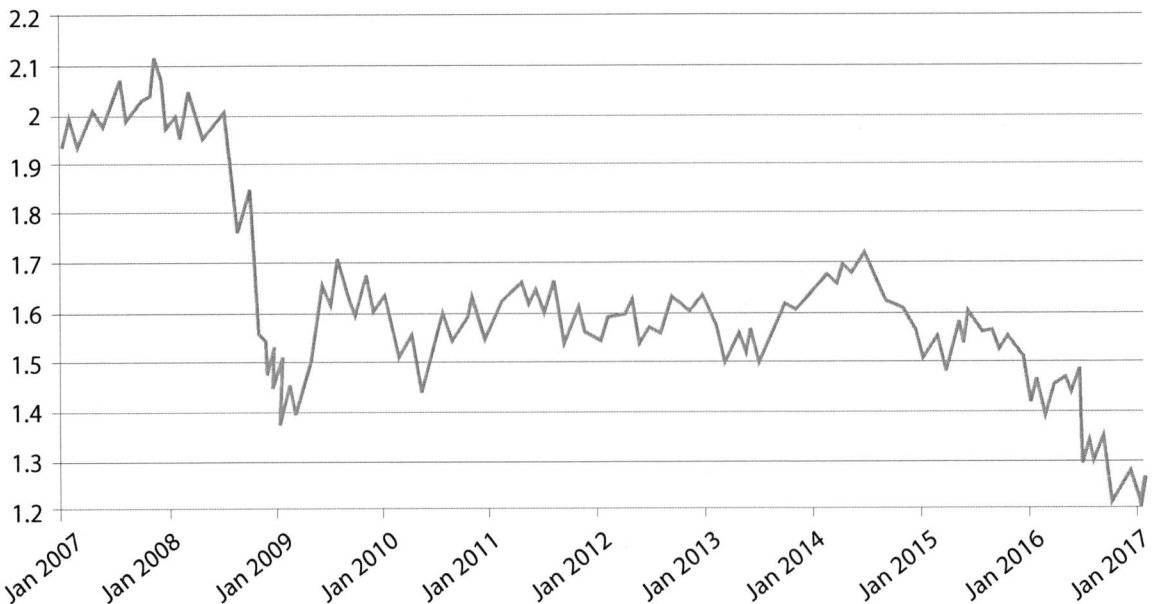

GBP:USD Exchange Rate

with one another. The main participants are large international banks, which continually provide the market with both bid (buy) and ask (sell) prices. Central banks are also major participants in FX markets, which they use to try to control money supply, inflation and interest rates.

There are several types of transactions and financial instruments commonly used:

- **Spot transaction** – the 'spot rate' is the rate quoted by a bank for the exchange of one currency for another with immediate effect. However in many cases spot trades are 'settled' – that is, the currencies actually change hands and arrive in recipients' bank accounts – two business days after the transaction date (T+2).
- **Forward transaction** – as seen in the earlier example, in a forward transaction money does not actually change hands until some agreed future date. A buyer and seller agree on an exchange rate for any date in the future, for a fixed sum of money, and the transaction occurs on that date, regardless of what the market rates are then. The duration of the trade can be a few days, months or years.

4. Property

Property is often considered as a separate type of asset in which to invest that is distinct from other asset classes such as shares and bonds. Property that is purchased for rental income and/or to make a profit on sale is generally referred to as commercial property. It includes retail and office developments, industrial property, agricultural land and residential property such as apartment blocks. As an asset class, property has a number of distinguishing features:

- Each individual property is unique in terms of location, structure and design.
- Individuals tend to find different characteristics attractive, so valuation is subjective.

- The transfer of property is subject to complex legal considerations and high transaction costs.
- It can take a considerable amount of time to buy or sell a property making property highly illiquid.
- Property is also illiquid in another sense: the investor generally has to sell all of the property or nothing at all. For example, a residential property owner cannot sell his spare bedroom to raise a little cash!
- Property can only be purchased in discrete and generally sizeable and relatively expensive units, making diversification difficult. In fact, only the largest investors, which generally means institutional investors, can purchase sufficient properties to build a diversified portfolio.

- The supply of land is finite and its availability can be further restricted by legislation and local planning regulations. Therefore, price is heavily driven by changes in demand and not supply.

As an asset class, direct investment in property has at times provided positive real long-term returns with a reliable stream of income and little volatility. An exposure to property can provide diversification benefits within a portfolio of investments due to its low correlation with other asset classes like equities and bonds. Many private investors have chosen to become involved in the property market by purchasing residential properties they intend to rent, known as the buy-to-let market.

Others with less money to invest wanting to include property within a diversified portfolio generally seek indirect exposure via a collective investment scheme (CIS), or shares in publicly quoted property companies.

Despite its unique features, investing in property does confer a number of advantages. As an asset class, it has provided positive real long-term returns, combined a reliable stream of income. However, property can also be subject to prolonged downturns, and its lack of liquidity, significant maintenance costs, high transaction costs on transfer and the risk of having commercial property with no tenant (and, therefore, no rental income) makes direct investment in commercial property only suitable for long-term investing institutions such as pension funds.

5. Mortgages

A mortgage is simply a secured loan, with the security taking the form of a property. The mortgage is typically provided to finance the purchase of that property, and for most people their main form of borrowing is the mortgage on their house or flat. Mortgages tend to be taken out over a long term, with most mortgages running for 20 or 25 years.

Whether a mortgage is to buy a house or flat in which the mortgagee will live, or to 'buy-to-let', the factors considered by the lender are much the same. The mortgage lender, such as the building society or bank, will consider each application for a loan in terms of the credit risk – the risk of not being repaid the principal sum loaned and the interest due.

Applicants are assessed in terms of:

- income and security of employment
- existing outgoings, eg, utility bills, other household expenses and school fees
- the size of the loan in relation to the value of the property being purchased. This is referred to as the loan-to-value ratio.

If the borrower fails to make the agreed repayments and/or the interest payments on the mortgage, the borrower is described as 'in default'. The lender can then re-possess the property, sell the property (often at auction) and then reimburse itself with the proceeds. Any money left over after repayment of the outstanding loan is returned to the former property owner.

A second mortgage is sometimes taken out on a single property. If the borrower defaults on his borrowings, the first mortgage ranks ahead of the second one in terms of being repaid out of the proceeds of the property sale.

5.1 Interest Rates

There are four main methods by which the interest may be charged. These are:

- variable rate
- fixed rate
- capped rate, and
- tracker rate.

In a typical **variable rate mortgage** the borrower pays interest at a rate that varies with prevailing interest rates. The rate is typically the lending bank or building society's 'standard variable rate'. This standard variable rate will reflect increases or decreases in the rates set by the Bank of England. So a borrower on a variable rate mortgage will benefit from rates falling and remaining low, but will suffer the additional costs when rates increase.

In a **fixed rate mortgage** the borrower's interest rate is set for an initial period, usually the first three or five years. If interest rates rise, the borrower is protected from the higher rates throughout this period, continuing to pay the lower, fixed rate of interest. However, if rates fall, and perhaps stay low, the fixed rate loan can only be cancelled if a redemption penalty is paid. The penalty is calculated to recoup the loss suffered by the lender as a result of the cancellation of the fixed rate loan.

It is common for fixed rate borrowers to be required to remain with the lender and pay interest at the lender's standard variable rate for a couple of years after the fixed rate deal ends – commonly referred to as a 'lock in' period.

Capped mortgages protect borrowers from rates rising above a particular rate – the 'capped rate'. For example, a mortgage might be taken out at 6%, with the interest rate based on the lender's standard variable rate, but with a cap at 7%. If prevailing rates fall to 5% the borrower pays at that rate, but if rates rise to 8% the rate paid cannot rise above the cap, and is only 7%.

A **tracker mortgage** is one that is linked to another rate such as the Bank of England base rate. The tracker rate will be set at a percentage above the Bank of England base rate, say 1% above, and will then increase or decrease as base rate changes, hence why it is called a tracker.

Lending institutions often attract borrowers by offering **discounted rate mortgages**. A 6% loan might be discounted to 5% for the first three years. Such deals might attract 'switchers' – borrowers who shop around and remortgage at a better rate; they may also be useful for first-time buyers as they make the transition to home ownership easier for those with a relatively low but growing level of income.

5.2 Types of Mortgage

5.2.1 Repayment Mortgages

The most straightforward form of mortgage is a repayment mortgage. This is simply a mortgage in which the borrower will make monthly payments to the lender, with each monthly payment comprising both interest and capital.

Example

Mr Mullergee borrows £100,000 from XYZ Bank to finance the purchase of a flat on a repayment basis over 25 years. Each month he is required to pay £600 to XYZ Bank.

In the above example, Mr Mullergee will pay in total £180,000 to XYZ Bank (£600 x 12 months x 25 years), a total of £80,000 interest over and above the capital borrowed of £100,000.

Each payment he makes will be partly allocated to interest and partly allocated to capital. In the early years the payments are predominantly interest. Towards the middle of the term the capital begins to reduce significantly, and at the end of the mortgage term the payments are predominantly capital.

The key advantage of a repayment mortgage over other forms of mortgage is that, as long as the borrower meets the repayments each month, he is guaranteed to pay off the loan over the term of the mortgage.

The main risks attached to a repayment mortgage from the borrower's perspective are:

- The cost of servicing the loan could increase, when interest is charged at the lender's standard variable rate of interest. This rate of interest will increase if interest rates go up. Mortgage repayments can rise significantly at the end of a fixed rate deal when they revert to the standard variable rate.

Illustration of Mortgage Repayments on a 25-year, £150,000 Mortgage with a 5% Interest Rate

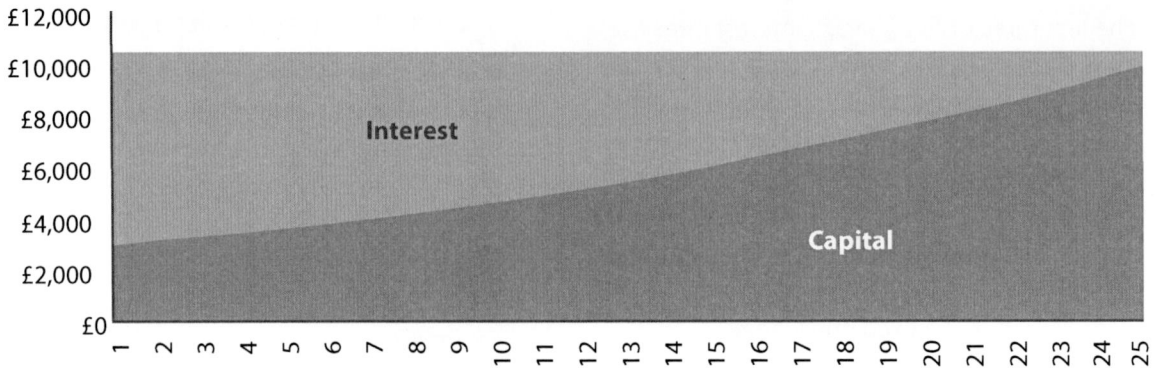

Source: CML calculations

- The borrower runs the risk of having the property repossessed if he fails to meet the repayments – remember the mortgage loan is secured on the underlying property.

These risks also apply to other forms of mortgage.

5.2.2 Interest-Only Mortgages

As the name suggests, an interest-only mortgage requires the borrower to make interest payments to the lender throughout the period of the loan. At the same time, the borrower generally puts money aside each month, into some form of investment.

The borrower's aim is for the investment to grow through regular contributions and investment returns (such as dividends, interest and capital growth) so that at the end of the mortgage the accumulated investment is sufficient to pay back the capital borrowed and perhaps offer some additional cash.

Example

Ms Ward borrows £100,000 from XYZ Bank to finance the purchase of a flat on an interest-only basis over 25 years. Each month she is required to pay £420 interest to XYZ Bank. At the same time, Ms Ward pays £180 each month into an investment fund run by an insurance company.

At the end of the 25-year period, Ms Ward hopes that the investment in the fund will have grown sufficiently to repay the £100,000 loan from XYZ Bank and offer an additional lump sum.

___

The main risks attached to an interest-only mortgage from the borrower's perspective are:

- Borrowers with interest-only mortgages still face the risks that repayment mortgage borrowers face – namely that interest rates may increase and their property is at risk if they fail to keep up the payments to the lender.
- There is also an additional risk that the investment might not grow sufficiently to pay the amount owing on the mortgage. In the example above, there is nothing guaranteeing that, at the end of the 25-year term, the investment in the fund will be worth £100,000 – indeed, it might be worth considerably less.

New rules from 2014 require lenders to ensure that borrowers have robust investment plans in place to repay their mortgage.

5.2.3 Offset Mortgages

An offset mortgage is a simple concept which works on the basis that, for the calculation and charging of interest, any mortgage is offset against, for example, any savings you may hold.

Example

Let's assume you have a mortgage of a £100,000 and have a savings account with £8,000 and £2,000 in a current account. For the purpose of calculating interest, the £100,000 is offset by the £10,000 worth of savings, so in effect you only pay interest on £90,000 of your mortgage borrowing. Obviously you would not receive any interest on your savings.

There are two main benefits to this approach:

- A higher-rate tax payer will not incur tax on any savings interest earned because it has been offset against the mortgage borrowing.
- As interest is being paid on a slightly lower mortgage, it provides some flexibility to manage finances, pay off the mortgage a little quicker and have more control.

5.3 Fees and Charges

There are a number of fees and charges you might need to pay when taking out a mortgage. These include:

- **Arrangement fees** – a fee for the mortgage itself and sometimes known as the product fee or completion fee.
- **Booking fee** – this is sometimes charged when you simply apply for a mortgage deal and is not usually refundable even if your mortgage falls through.
- **Valuation fee** – a charge made by the mortgage provider to value your property and make sure it is worth the amount you wish to borrow.
- **Broker fee** – this fee is for a mortgage broker, if you use one, for arranging the mortgage or giving you advice.
- **Early repayment charge** – this is a charge a mortgage provider might impose if you want to repay your mortgage early.

- **Exit fee** – a fee to your lender when you repay your mortgage, even if you are not repaying it early.

6. Life and Protection Insurance

Life assurance and protection policies are designed and sold by the insurance industry to provide individuals with some financial protection in case certain events occur. Although product details may vary from country to country, the general principles of what the individual (and their adviser) should be looking for in the products and their main features tend to be consistent. The big insurance companies are global operations, so the range of products they offer have common features and are similar whether offered in North America, Europe or the Asia/Pacific regions.

The following table gives some indication of the range of needs and products available.

Areas in need of protection	Protection products
Life and family	Life cover. Critical illness cover. Life or earlier critical illness cover. Medical cover. Long-term care.
Lifestyle and income	Income protection. Accident and sickness cover. Unemployment cover.
Home and contents	Household cover. Mortgage income protection.
Business	Key person protection. Shareholder protection. Partnership protection.

Key Terms	
Proposer	The person who proposes to enter into a contract of insurance with a life insurance company to insure themselves or another person on whose life they have insurable interest.
Life Assured	The person on whose life the contract depends is called the 'life assured'. Although the person who owns the policy and the life assured are frequently the same person, this is not necessarily the case. A policy on the life of one person, but effected and owned by someone else, is called a 'life of another' policy. A policy effected by the life assured is called an 'own life policy'.
Single Life	A single life policy pays out on one individual's death.
Joint Life	When cover is required for two people, this can typically be arranged in one of two ways, through a joint life policy or two single life policies.
	A joint life policy can be arranged so that the benefits would be paid out following the death of either the first, or, if required for a specific reason, the second life assured. The majority of policies are arranged ultimately to protect financial dependants, with the sum assured or benefits being paid on the first death.
	With two separate single life policies, each person is covered separately. If both lives assured were to die at the same time, as the result of a car accident for example, the full benefits would be payable on each of the policies. If one of the lives assured died, benefits would be paid for that policy, with the surviving partner having continuing cover on their life.
Insurable Interest	To buy a life insurance policy on someone else's life, the proposer must have an interest in that person remaining alive, or expect financial loss from that person's death. This is called an insurable interest.

6.1 Life Cover

Life assurance is a form of insurance policy where the event insured is a death. Such policies involve the payment of premiums in exchange for life cover – a lump sum that is payable upon death. These life policies are commonly taken out to provide for dependants after death (typically the spouse and children), or, when associated with a mortgage payment, to pay off the loan on the death of the borrower.

There are two types of life cover we need to consider, namely whole-of-life assurance and term assurance. A **whole-of-life policy** provides permanent cover, meaning that the sum assured will be paid whenever death occurs, as opposed to if death occurs within the term of a **term assurance policy**.

Before looking at these, it is important to know some key terms which are shown in the table above.

6.1.1 Term Assurance

A **term assurance** policy is for a set period, say 25 years. If the policy holder dies during the term, then his/her beneficiaries receive the insured sum. Term assurance has a variety of uses, such as ensuring there are funds available to repay a mortgage in case someone dies or providing a lump sum that can be used to generate income for a surviving partner or to provide funds to pay any tax that might become payable on death.

When taking out life cover, the individual selects the amount that they wish to be paid out if the event happens and the period that they want the cover to run for. If, during the period when the cover is in place, they die, then a lump sum will be paid out that equals the amount of life cover selected. With some policies, if an individual is diagnosed as suffering from a terminal illness which is expected to cause death within 12 months of the diagnosis, then the lump sum is payable at that point.

The amount of the premiums paid for term assurance will depend on:

- the amount insured
- age and family history
- other risk factors, including state of health (for example, whether the individual is a smoker or non-smoker), their occupation and whether they participate in dangerous sports such as hang-gliding, and
- the term over which cover is required.

When selecting the amount of cover, an individual is able to choose three types of cover, namely level, increasing or decreasing cover.

Level cover, as the name suggests, means that the amount to be paid out if the event happens remains the same throughout the period in which the policy is in force, eg, £500,000 cover over the whole 25 years. As a result, the premiums are fixed at the outset and do not change during the period of the policy.

With **increasing cover**, the amount of cover and the premium rise, for example with inflation or by a set percentage each year, on each anniversary of the taking out of the policy.

As you would expect, with **decreasing cover** the amount that is originally chosen as the sum to be paid out decreases each year. The amount by which it decreases is agreed at the outset and, if it is used to repay a mortgage, it will be based on the expected reduction in the outstanding mortgage that would occur if the client had a repayment mortgage. Although the amount of cover will diminish year by year, the premiums payable will remain the same throughout the policy.

Note: 'Insurance' refers to something that *might* happen – for example, an individual might die at some stage in the next 25 years. 'Assurance' relates to something that *will* happen – every individual is going to die at some stage. Technically therefore, life assurance should be used to refer to a whole-of-life policy that will pay out on death, while life insurance should be used in the context of term policies that pay out only if death occurs within a particular period.

6.1.2 Whole-of-Life Assurance

Whole-of-life plans are generally investment-based policies (usually 'with-profits' schemes – see below). Essentially, they combine insurance (a pre-determined payout if the insured dies during a particular period) with savings. The savings part of these policies involves the money being invested in a fund that is often run by the insurance company, and invests in a combination of shares and bonds. A slightly simplistic policy might guarantee to pay out £100,000 if the insured dies during a 25 year period, or alternatively pay the accumulated value of the savings part of the policy at the end of 25 years if the insured survives.

The total paid out, therefore, depends on the guaranteed sum, the date of death and the investment performance of the fund.

There are three main types of whole of life policy:

- non-profit
- with-profits, and
- unit-linked.

A **non-profit policy** guarantees to pay a set amount of life cover on the death of the person, regardless of when that might occur. It can be thought of as the equivalent of a term policy where the term will only end when the insured dies. There is no 'savings' portion for this type of policy, and the guaranteed amount paid out means that the policy does not depend on investment growth. As a result, the premiums are often very high. The insured sum is chosen at the outset and is fixed, eg, £500,000 whenever death occurs.

With-profits policies usually have a minimum amount of life cover. However, if the insured dies during the policy period, the minimum is increased each year by the addition of annual bonuses. These bonuses are based on the performance of the underlying investment portfolio run by the insurance company, often termed the 'with-profits fund'. However, these annual bonuses are usually spread out over a number of years to smooth the effect of fluctuating stock market returns. In other words, in a good year not all of the positive return will be added to the allocated bonus which should enable the insurance company to add a bonus even in a bad year.

One advantage of with-profits schemes is that profits are locked in each year, ie, the bonuses permanently increase the basic guaranteed sum. So, if the with-profits policy is being used to pay off a loan such as an interest-only mortgage, there is no risk that a general decline in the stock market just before the repayment date will suddenly remove the ability to repay the loan. If the investor had bought shares or bonds directly, or within a collective fund, the value of the investments could fall just before the repayment date.

A typical scheme might pay out:

- the **sum assured** or **guaranteed sum**, which is usually an amount a little less than the premiums paid over the term
- **annual bonuses**, as seen these are declared each year by the insurance company, and can vary. If the underlying performance of the investments in the fund is better than expected part of the surplus will be held back to enable the insurance company to award an annual bonus when returns are worse than expected. In this way, the returns 'smooth' the peaks and troughs that may be occurring in the underlying stock market
- a **terminal bonus** at the end of the period. The terminal bonus can be substantial, for example 20% of the sum insured, but is not declared until the end of the policy term. It is essentially topping-up the policy to give it the appropriate share of the with-profits fund.

With **unit-linked policies** or a **unitised scheme**, the savings portion of the premium is used to buy units in the insurance company's investment fund rather than just allocated to the with-profits fund. The other portion of the premium is used to pay for the life assurance cover. The eventual return will be dependent upon the performance of the funds selected.

The reason for such policies being taken out is not normally just for the insured sum itself. Usually they are bought as part of a protection planning exercise to provide a lump sum in the event of death to pay off the principal in a mortgage or to provide funds to assist with the payment of any tax that might become payable on death. They can serve two purposes, therefore, both protection and investment.

Purchasing a life assurance policy is the same as entering into any other contract. When a person completes a proposal form and submits it to an insurance company, that constitutes a part of the formal process of entering into a contract. The principle of utmost good faith applies to insurance contracts. This places an obligation on the person seeking insurance to disclose any material facts that may affect how the insurance company may judge the risk of the contract they are entering into. Failure to disclose a material fact gives the insurance company the right to avoid paying out in the event of a claim.

There is a wide range of variations on the basic life policy that are driven by mortality risk, investment and expenses and premium options – all of which impact on the structure of the policy itself.

6.2 Protection Planning

There are four main areas that might be in need of protection – family and personal, mortgage, long-term care and business protection.

Each area is briefly considered below:

Family and Personal

The main wage-earner or another family member might suffer a serious illness. In some cases the illness may be critical. Without protection, the family could lose its main source of income and may have insufficient funds to live on. Additionally, there may be medical bills and care costs arising.

Similarly, the main wage-earner could lose his or her job. The family will lose its main source of income and may have insufficient funds to live on.

Other family and personal issues include the possibility that the family home is burgled, or suffers damage from extreme weather such as flooding or wind. Again, without protection, major expenditure will be required to buy new contents and repair any damage.

Mortgage

Job loss or illness suffered by the main wage-earner could result in difficulty in meeting mortgage payments. Furthermore, the main wage-earner might die before the mortgage is repaid, saddling the family with ongoing mortgage repayments. Protection policies could be used to address these issues.

Long-Term Care

If an individual suffers mental and/or physical incapacity, the cost of care could drain and perhaps exhaust the individual's savings.

Business Protection

A key person within a business might die or suffer a serious illness. The business will no longer be able to generate sufficient profits without the key person's contribution.

Alternatively, a substantial shareholder or partner within the business may die. Their shareholding or partnership stake may need to be bought out by the remaining shareholders/partners.

6.3 Personal Protection Products

There is a wide range of protection products marketed by insurance companies and the characteristics of some of the more common types of products are considered below.

6.3.1 Critical Illness Insurance Cover

Critical illness cover is designed to pay a lump sum in the event that a person suffers from any one of a wide range of critical illnesses. Looking at how many people suffer from a major illness before they reach 65, its use and value can readily be seen. Illness may force an individual to give up work and so could cause financial hardship, to say nothing of how they will pay for specialist medical treatment or afford the additional costs that permanent disability may bring about.

The cover provided by these types of policies is constantly changing as insurance companies develop the product further and policies adapt to changing medical diagnoses and claims experience.

6.3.2 Income Protection Cover

Income protection insurance is designed to pay out an income benefit when a person is unable to work for a prolonged period due to sickness or incapacity. Since this may be paid for a significant period of time, the premiums are relatively expensive. Their use and value can be readily appreciated by considering how a family would continue to pay its bills if the main income-earner were to fall ill.

Income protection cover and critical illness insurance are complementary in the cover they offer. For most people, an element of each may be required so some insurance companies offer menu products that allow a combination of covers under one policy.

6.3.3 Mortgage Payment Protection Cover

Mortgage payment protection is designed to ensure that the payments that are due for a mortgage continue to be paid if the borrower is unable to work because of accident, sickness or unemployment.

They tend to be available from the lending institution, as well as insurance companies, although costs need to be carefully compared. They are designed to cover short-term problems, such as covering the costs if an individual loses their job and until they find alternative work, rather than long-term benefits.

6.3.4 Accident and Sickness Cover

Personal accident policies are generally taken out for annual periods and can provide for income or lump sum payments in the event of an accident. Although they are relatively inexpensive, care needs to be taken to look in detail at the exclusions and limits that apply.

6.3.5 Household Cover

House and contents insurance are well established products and are well understood by consumers, so these will only be covered briefly.

Key considerations include:

- Is the cover enough to pay for the complete rebuild of a home?
- To what extent are external features of a house covered, such as walls, gates, drives and pathways?
- What cover is there in case a neighbour sues you for your tree falling on their property or a similar accident?
- What is the extent of cover for personal possessions?
- Is legal cover included?

6.3.6 Medical Insurance

Private medical insurance is obviously intended to cover the cost of medical and hospital expenses. It may be taken out by individuals, or provided as part of an individual's employment.

6.3.7 Long-Term Care

The purpose of long-term care cover is to provide the funds that will be needed in later life to meet the cost of care. Simply considering the cost of nursing home care explains the need for such a policy, but its value to an individual will depend on the amount of state funding for care costs that will be available.

Premiums will be expensive, reflecting the cost of care, and the benefit will normally be paid as an income that can be used to cover the expenditure.

Learning Objectives

Chapter Six has covered the following Learning Objectives:

3.2.1 Know the difference between a capital market instrument and a money market instrument

3.2.2 Know the definition and features of the following: Treasury bill; commercial paper; certificate of deposit; money market funds

3.2.3 Know the advantages and disadvantages of investing in money market instruments

3.3.1 Know the characteristics of property investment: commercial/residential property; direct indirect investment

3.3.2 Know the advantages and disadvantages of investing in property

3.4.1 Know the basic structure of the foreign exchange market including: currency quotes; settlement; spot/forward

10.2.1 Understand the characteristics of the mortgage market: interest rates; loan to value

10.2.2 Know the definition of and types of mortgage: repayment; interest-only; offset

10.2.3 Know the fees applicable

10.3.1 Understand the basic principles of life assurance

10.3.2 Know the definition of the following types of life policy: term assurance; whole-of-life

10.4.1 Know the main areas in need of protection: family and personal; mortgage; long-term care; business protection

10.4.2 Know the definition of the following types of protection insurance: critical illness insurance; income protection; mortgage protection; accident and sickness cover; household cover; medical insurance; long-term care insurance

Based on what you have learned in Chapter Six, try to answer the following end of chapter questions.

End of Chapter Questions

Think of an answer for each question and refer to the appropriate section for confirmation.

1. How do money market instruments differ from capital market instruments?
   Answer Reference: Section 2

   ....

   ....

2. What are the three major types of money market instruments found in the UK and how do they pay their returns?
   Answer Reference: Section 2

   ....

   ....

3. Are exchange rates between most currencies fixed or floating?
   Answer Reference: Section 3

   ....

   ....

4. Where is the world's largest foreign exchange market centre?
   Answer Reference: Section 3

   ....

   ....

5. What are the most commonly quoted currency pairs?
   Answer Reference: Section 3

   ....

   ....

6. The number of US dollars that can be purchased with a British pound has increased over a period. Which currency is said to have 'strengthened'?

   Answer Reference: Section 3

   ....

   ....

7. Who are the major participants in the foreign exchange market?

   Answer Reference: Section 3

   ....

   ....

8. Why is property different to other asset classes such as shares and bonds?

   Answer Reference: Section 4

   ....

   ....

9. What is a mortgage loan's typical term and what is it secured on?

   Answer Reference: Section 5

   ....

   ....

10. What is a mortgage default, and what is the likely result?

    Answer Reference: Section 5

    ....

    ....

11. What are the four main methods of charging interest on a mortgage?

    Answer Reference: Section 5.1

    ....

    ....

12. What are the two forms by which a mortgage loan is repaid?

Answer Reference: Section 5.2

....

....

13. In a repayment mortgage, what proportion of the monthly payment is capital towards the beginning and end of the term?

Answer Reference: Section 5.2.1

....

....

14. How is an interest-only mortgage typically repaid?

Answer Reference: Section 5.2.2

....

....

15. What form of term assurance policy is typically used to cover a repayment mortgage loan?

Answer Reference: Section 6.1.1

....

....

16. How does a with-profits policy smooth investment returns?

Answer Reference: Section 6.1.2

....

....

Chapter Seven
The Economic Environment

7

1. Introduction

This chapter looks at economics. Economics is important as it is a key driver of the performance of both equities and bonds. For example, when the economy is generally doing well, most companies generate healthy profits and their shareholders benefit. When the economy suffers, interest rates tend to fall which boosts the value of bonds.

Initially, the chapter looks at how economic activity is determined in various economic and political systems, and then looks at the role of central banks, particularly the Bank of England (BoE), in the management of that economic activity.

The chapter concludes with an explanation of some of the key economic measures that provide an indication of the state of an economy.

2. Factors Determining Economic Activity

2.1 Factors of Production

Any economic activity, such as running a business, requires four different kinds of input – land, labour, capital and enterprise. In economics these are commonly referred to as the 'factors of production'.

1. The land represents the physical space that is required, such as the fields required for agriculture, the factory for manufacturing, the shop for a retail business and office space.
2. The labour is the workforce, which could be skilled workers, unskilled workers or a mix of both.
3. The capital is the plant and equipment required to run the business, like production machinery in a manufacturing business, or computer equipment and ATMs for a retail bank.

4. Finally enterprise is the 'know how' – the knowledge or ability to put the first three factors to productive use.

The extent to which these factors are in private hands, or government hands, differs from country to country.

2.2 State-Controlled Economies

A state-controlled economy is one where the state (ie, the government) decides what is produced and how it is distributed. These are also called 'planned', 'centrally planned', or 'command' economies, because all economic activity is supposed to be carried out according to a plan.

The Soviet Union (formed after the Russian Communist revolution in 1918) was the first modern, centrally planned economy. However, since the fall of Communism in the 1990s, Russia no longer plans its economy.

Similarly, China became a centrally planned economy after their revolution in 1949 and China has adopted market-based policies since the 1980s. North Korea is probably the last-surviving, true centrally-planned economy.

In a centrally planned (or 'command') economy, the factors of production are owned by the state and the motivation of the workforce is presumed to be the collective good of society, not individual gain. Every aspect of the economy is planned by the state in accordance with national priorities. This can result in excessive layers of bureaucracy, and state control inevitably removes a great deal of individual choice.

2.3 Market Economies

In a market economy, the factors of production – land, labour, capital and enterprise – are privately owned. Businesses produce goods and services to meet the demand from consumers. The interaction of demand from consumers and supply from businesses in the market will determine the **market-clearing price**. This is the price that reflects the balance between what consumers will willingly pay for goods and services and what suppliers will willingly accept for them.

If consumers demand more of a good, then shortages may occur. A shortage causes the price to rise, and the price rise provides the signal to the producing firms to produce more and attract new firms into the market.

In contrast, if the firms are producing too much of a particular good and the consumers are not buying all of the products, the price will be driven lower. The result will be that some producers will leave the market, as they will be unable to make a profit at the lower price.

In this way, the market directs resources and in a pure market system, the government merely operates as supervisor by issuing currency and providing a legal system.

Furthermore, there is a market not only for goods and services, but also for productive assets, such as capital goods (eg, machinery), labour and money. For the labour market, it is the wage level that is effectively the 'price', and for the money market it is the interest rate.

So, people compete for jobs and companies compete for customers in a market economy. Scarce resources, including skilled labour, such as a particularly skilful football player, or a financial asset, such as a share in a successful company, will have a high value. In a market economy, competition means that inferior football players and shares in unsuccessful companies will be much cheaper and ultimately competition could bring about the collapse of the unsuccessful company, and result in the inferior football player searching for an alternative career.

2.4 Mixed Economies

A mixed economy combines a market economy with some element of state control. The vast majority of economies are mixed to a greater or lesser extent.

While most would agree that unsuccessful companies should be allowed to fail, people also generally feel that the less able in society should be cushioned against the full force of the market economy. In a mixed economy, the government will provide a welfare system to support the unemployed, the infirm and the elderly, in tandem with the market-driven aspects of the economy. The government will also spend money running key areas such as defence, education, public transport, health and police services.

Governments raise finance for their public expenditure by:

- collecting taxes directly from wage-earners and companies

- collecting indirect taxes (eg, VAT and taxes on petrol, cigarettes and alcohol), and
- raising money through borrowing in the capital markets.

Civil servants, primarily working for the government to raise money and spend it, tend to be one of the largest groups in the labour market. In the UK it is the civil servants working for the Treasury who raise money and allocate it to the 'spending departments', such as the National Health Service.

Virtually every economy in the world contains a mix of market activity and government intervention and the extent of the mix can be measured by government spending as a percentage of gross domestic product (GDP). GDP is a key measure of economic output and will be explored in more detail later in this chapter. Clearly, the bigger the percentage, the more government control within the mixed economy.

UK Government Expenditure as % of GDP

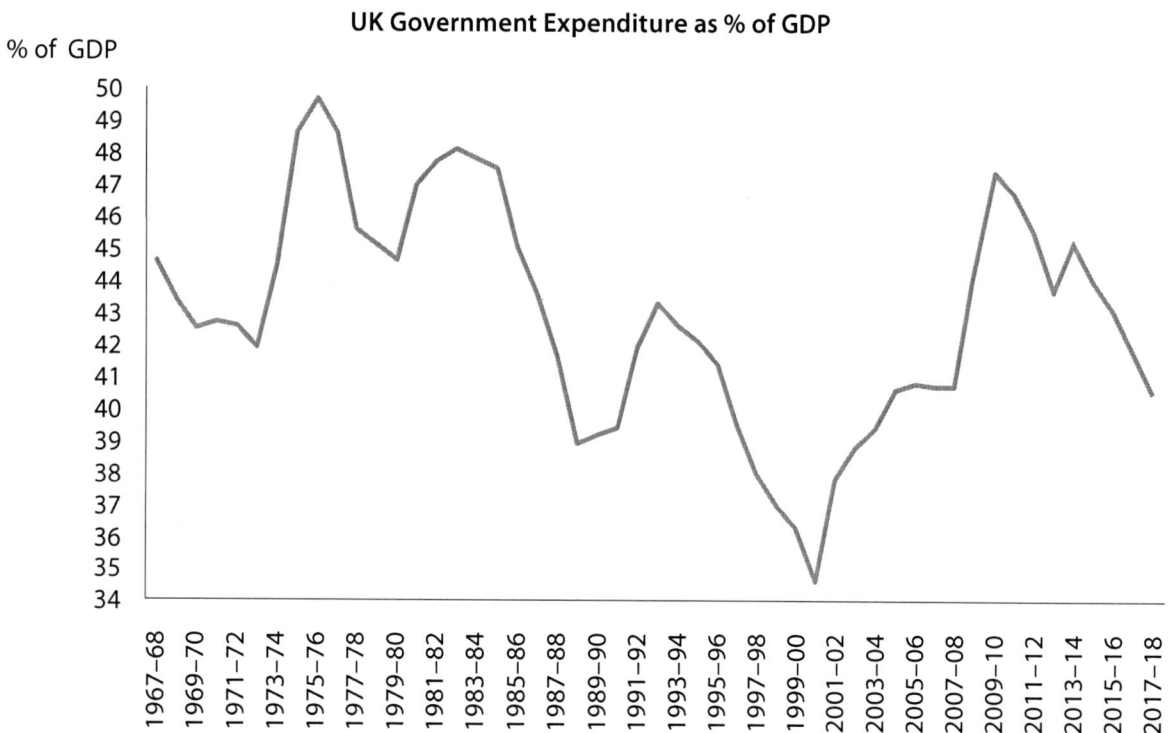

Source: HM Treasury (Public Finances Databank)

2.5 Open Economies

The term 'open economy' relates to a country's economic relationship with outside countries. In an open economy there are few barriers to trade or controls over foreign exchange. Most developed nations are relatively open economies. For example, although most western governments create barriers to protect their citizens against illegal drugs and other dangers, they generally have policies to allow or encourage free trade.

From time to time, issues will arise when one country believes another is taking unfair advantage of trade policies and takes some form of retaliatory action, possibly including the imposition of sanctions. These sanctions might take the form of special tariffs that are applied to imports. When a country prevents other countries from trading freely with it in order to preserve its domestic market, it is usually referred to as **protectionism**.

The **World Trade Organisation (WTO)** exists to promote the growth of free trade between economies. It is, therefore, sometimes called upon to arbitrate when disputes arise.

3. Central Banks

Traditionally, the role of government has been to manage the economy through taxation and through economic and monetary policy, and to ensure a fair society by the state provision of welfare and benefits to those who meet certain criteria, while leaving business relatively free to address the challenges and opportunities that arise.

Governments can use a variety of policies when attempting to reduce the impact of fluctuations in economic activity. Collectively these measures are known as stabilisation policies and are categorised under the broad headings of fiscal policy and monetary policy. Fiscal policy involves making adjustments using government spending and taxation, while monetary policy involves making adjustments to interest rates and the money supply. Rather than following one or another type of policy, most governments now adopt a pragmatic approach to controlling the level of economic activity through a combination of fiscal and monetary policy. In an increasingly integrated world, however, controlling the level of activity in an open economy in isolation is difficult, as financial markets, rather than individual governments and central banks, tend to dictate economic policy.

Governments implement their economic policies using their central bank, and a consideration of their role in this implementation is explained below.

3.1 The Role of Central Banks

Central banks operate at the very centre of a nation's financial system. They are usually public bodies but, increasingly, they operate independently of government control or political interference. They usually have some or all of the following responsibilities:

- Acting as banker to the banking system by accepting deposits from, and lending to, commercial banks.
- Acting as banker to the government.
- Managing the national debt.
- Regulating the domestic banking system.
- Acting as lender of last resort to the banking system in financial crises to prevent the systemic collapse of the banking system.
- Setting the official short-term rate of interest.
- Controlling the money supply.
- Issuing notes and coins.
- Holding the nation's gold and foreign currency reserves.
- Influencing the value of a nation's currency through activities such as intervention in the currency markets.
- Providing a depositors' protection scheme for bank deposits.

3.2 The Bank of England

The Bank of England is the central bank of the UK. It was founded in 1694 and is often referred to as the 'Old Lady of Threadneedle Street' because its headquarters building is situated in Threadneedle Street in the City of London.

The Bank's roles and functions have evolved and changed over its 300-year history. Since its foundation it has been the government's banker and, since the late 18th century, it has been banker to the banking system or, more generally, the bankers' bank. As well as providing banking services to these customers, the Bank of England also manages the UK's foreign exchange and gold reserves.

The Bank has two core purposes – monetary stability and financial stability.

- **Monetary stability** – monetary stability means stable prices and confidence in the currency. Stable prices are defined by the Government's inflation target, which the Bank seeks to meet through its decisions in relation to interest rates.
- **Financial stability** – a stable financial system is a key ingredient for a healthy and successful economy. People need to have confidence that the system is safe and stable, and functions properly. The Bank of England's role in relation to this involves detecting and reducing threats to the financial system as a whole. Such threats are detected through the Bank's surveillance and market intelligence functions. They are reduced by the Bank overseeing the payments systems, banking and market operations, including, in exceptional circumstances by acting as lender of last resort, and resolution work to deal with distressed banks.

The Bank of England's role in the management of the UK economy is reflected in its strategic priorities.

Core Purpose	Strategic Priorities
Monetary Stability	Keep inflation on track to meet the government's 2% target.
	Ensure the Bank has the policies, tools and infrastructure in place to implement monetary policy and issue banknotes.
	Sustain public support for the monetary policy framework and the benefits of low inflation.
Financial Stability	Deliver macroprudential policy, operating through the Financial Policy Committee (FPC).
	Complete the transition of microprudential supervision and infrastructure oversight.

In addition to these responsibilities, the Bank also assumes responsibility for all other traditional central bank activities listed in Section 3.1 – with the exception of managing the national debt and providing a depositors' protection scheme for bank deposits. Managing the national debt is undertaken by the Debt Management Office (DMO), and operating the depositor protection scheme by the Financial Services Compensation Scheme (FSCS).

The Bank's financial stability role has changed significantly from 2013.

Since the financial crisis of 2007–08, the Bank's role of protecting and enhancing the stability of the financial system has gained greater emphasis and importance. The purpose of preserving financial stability is to maintain the three vital functions which the financial system performs in the economy:

- providing the main mechanism for paying for goods, services and financial assets

- intermediating between savers and borrowers, and channelling savings into investment, via debt and equity instruments, and
- insuring against, and dispersing, risk.

In April 2013, the government brought in a major reform of the UK regulatory regime which has significantly increased and broadened the Bank's role and responsibilities for financial stability. These changes are a result of the weaknesses identified as a result of the financial crisis, of which perhaps the most significant failing was that no single institution had responsibility, authority or powers to oversee the financial system as a whole.

In June 2011, the government announced the details of its plans to establish a new committee at the Bank of England – the Financial Policy committee (FPC). The FPC is tasked with monitoring the stability and resilience of the UK financial system and using its powers to tackle those risks. It also gives direction and recommendations to the newly formed Prudential Regulation Authority (PRA) and Financial Conduct Authority (FCA). The PRA is part of the BoE and has assumed responsibility for the supervision of banks and key market infrastructure firms (such as the London Clearing House and Euroclear UK & Ireland).

The Bank is perhaps most visible to the general public through its banknotes and, since the late 1990s, its interest rate decisions. The Bank has had a monopoly on the issue of banknotes in England and Wales since the early 20th century. But it is only since 1997 that the Bank has had statutory responsibility for setting the UK's official interest rate.

Interest rate decisions are taken by the Bank's **Monetary Policy Committee (MPC)**. The MPC's primary focus is to ensure that inflation is kept within a government-set range. Inflation is prices persistently increasing, and the impact of this will be considered in greater detail in the next section.

The MPC can then set the 'base rate', an officially published short-term interest rate, to meet the inflation target. The inflation target is set each year by the Chancellor of the Exchequer.

At its monthly meetings, the MPC must gauge all of those factors that can influence inflation over both the short and medium term. These include the level of the exchange rate, the rate at which the economy is growing, how much consumers are borrowing and spending, wage inflation, and any changes to government spending and taxation plans. When setting the base rate, however, it must also be mindful of the impact any changes will have on the sustainability of economic growth and employment in the UK and the time lag between a change in rate and the effects it will have on the economy. If the Bank fails to keep inflation close to the government target, the Governor of the Bank of England is required to write a letter of explanation to the Chancellor of the Exchequer.

Controlling inflation using the interest rate is a delicate balancing act. Increasing interest rates to curb inflation puts people off borrowing to buy, but can also slow down the economy because reduced demand means less production of goods and services, and less production means less employment, and slower economic growth. In contrast, low interest rates stimulate the economy, but could lead to inflation.

The last economic cycle saw governments across the world, including the UK, follow a policy of reducing interest rates to counter the effect of a slowing global economy and the risks of depression.

When a central bank is concerned about the risks of very low inflation, it cuts the base rate to reduce the cost of money and provide a stimulus to the economy.

The key difference in the last recession was that interest rates were reduced massively by central banks in developed countries. When they are close to zero, central banks need an alternative policy instrument. This involves injecting money directly into the economy in a process that has become known as **quantitative easing**.

Quantitative easing involves the central bank creating money, which it then uses to buy assets such as government bonds and high quality debt from private companies, resulting in more money in the wider economy.

Creating more money does not involve printing more banknotes. Instead, the central bank buys assets from private sector institutions and credits the seller's bank account, so the seller has more money in their bank account, while the central bank holds assets as part of its reserves. The end result is more money out in the wider economy.

Injecting more money into the economy through the purchase of bonds can have a number of effects:

- The seller of the bonds ends up with more money and so may spend it, which will help boost growth.
- Alternatively, they may buy other assets instead and in doing so boost prices and provide liquidity to other sectors of the economy, resulting in people feeling better off and so spending more.
- Buying assets means higher asset prices and lower yields, which brings down the cost of borrowing for businesses and households, encouraging a further boost to spending.
- Banks find themselves holding more reserves, which might lead them to boost their lending to consumers and business; again, borrowing increases and so does spending.

The theory is that the extra money works its way through the economy, resulting in higher spending and therefore growth, or reducing the impact of recession and preventing the onset of a depression.

3.3 The Federal Reserve (the FED)

The Federal Reserve System in the US dates back to 1913. The Fed, as it is known, comprises 12 regional Federal Reserve Banks, each of which monitors the activities of, and provides liquidity to, the banks in its region. Although free from political interference, the Fed is governed by a seven-strong board appointed by the President of the United States. This governing board, together with the presidents of five of the 12 Federal Reserve banks, makes up the Federal Open Market Committee (FOMC). The chairman of the FOMC, also appointed by the US President, takes responsibility for the committee's decisions, which are directed towards its statutory duty of promoting price stability and sustainable economic growth.

The FOMC meets every six weeks or so to examine the latest economic data in order to gauge the health of the economy and determine whether the economically sensitive Fed funds rate should be altered. In late 2015, it made the decision to raise interest rates for the first time since the 2008 financial crisis. Very occasionally it meets in emergency session, if economic circumstances dictate. As lender of last resort to the US banking system, the Fed has rescued a number of US financial institutions and markets from collapse during the financial crisis. In doing so, it has prevented widespread panic, and stopped systemic risk from spreading throughout the financial system (known as 'contagion').

3.4 The European Central Bank (ECB)

Based in Frankfurt, the ECB assumed its central banking responsibilities upon the creation of the euro, on 1 January 1999. The ECB is principally responsible for setting monetary policy for the entire eurozone, with the objective of maintaining internal price stability. Its objective of keeping inflation, as defined by the harmonised index of consumer prices (HICP), *'close to but below 2% in the medium term'* is achieved by influencing those factors that may influence inflation, such as the external value of the euro and growth in the money supply.

The ECB sets its monetary policy through its president and council; the latter comprises the governors of each of the eurozone's national central banks. Although the ECB acts independently of European Union (EU) member governments when implementing monetary policy, it has on occasion succumbed to political persuasion. It used to be one of the few central banks that did not act as a lender of last resort to the banking system, but that changed when the eurozone crisis forced it to support banks and economies in struggling European countries.

In 2014, the ECB was given a supervisory role to monitor the financial stability of banks in eurozone states. The Single Supervisory Mechanism (SSM) is a new framework for banking supervision in Europe and comprises the ECB and national supervisory authorities of participating EU countries. Its main aims are to:

*   ensure the safety and soundness of the European banking system, and
*   increase financial integration and stability in Europe.

The SSM is an important milestone towards a banking union within the EU.

3.5 Brexit

In June 2016, the UK voted to exit the EU and the impact of the move will have a significant effect on the UK economy for years to come.

The decision to leave the EU was made in a referendum on 23 June 2016. The referendum result roiled global markets, including currencies, causing the pound to fall to its lowest level in decades although, in some cases, the effects were short-lived. Equities fell as a result of the vote, but reversed fairly quickly. London's FTSE 100 fell 8.7% and closed down 3.1% on June 24 at 6,138; however, it ended the year up at 7,142.

Article 50 was invoked at the end of March 2017, which officially informed the EU of the intention to withdraw. Unless both sides agree on an extension, the UK and the EU have two years to agree a deal before the bloc's treaties cease to apply to Britain. The approximate timeline of events is as follows:

*   March-April 2017 – the EU draws up guidelines to handle British withdrawal that need to be endorsed by a summit of the remaining 27 EU countries.
*   May-June 2017 – once the guidelines are decided the EU27 must formally nominate the European Commission as its lead negotiator and give it a detailed mandate.
*   May 2017 – Britain to introduce legislative measures (the Great Repeal Bill) which will repeal EU regulations to give legal continuity after Brexit and which will come into effect once the UK completes its exit.
*   December 2017 – the EU expects the principles on which the UK will leave the UK to be agreed before trade talks begin.
*   March 2018 – from a UK perspective, the terms of a transition deal need to be agreed, otherwise companies will need to take steps to protect their interests, eg, airlines have warned that the UK must have signed new open skies agreements by this point, because they sell tickets one year in advance. The EU27, however, sees the

Impact of Brexit Vote on GBP

Brexit – US$ to GBP

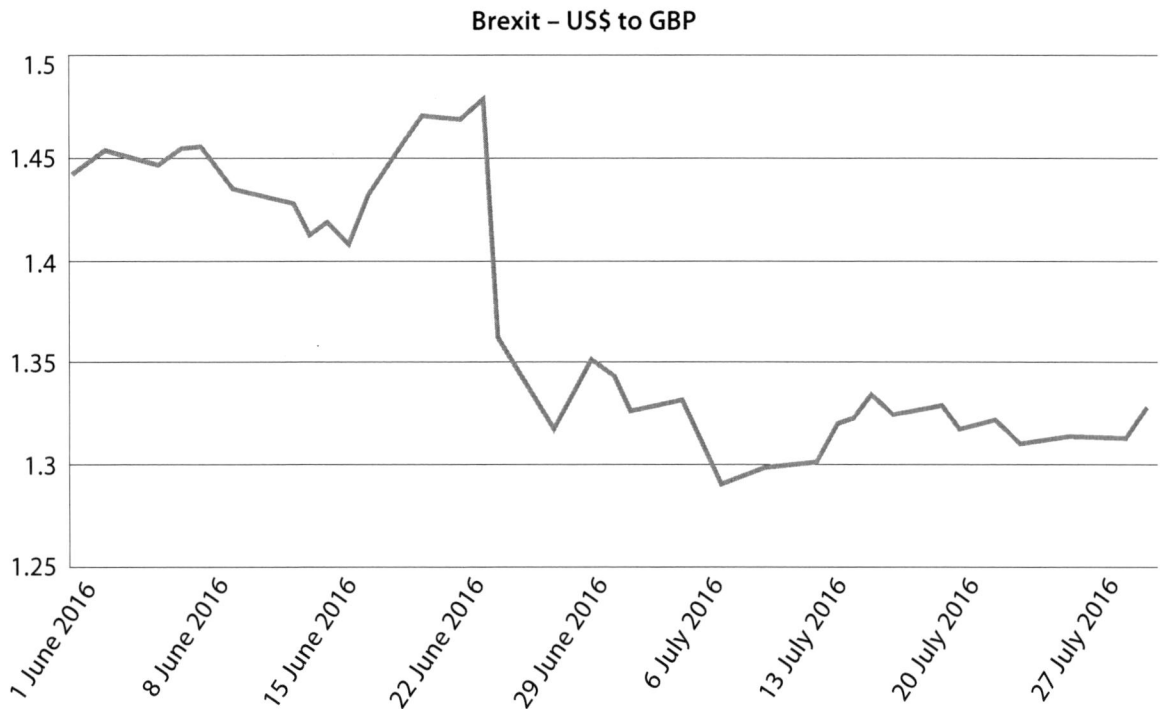

- transition as being the final piece of the negotiation.
- October 2018 – the EU expects talks to be completed to allow both sides to ratify the deal in time.
- March 2019 – ratification by the EU27 and a vote in the European parliament need to have taken place before the deal can take effect.
- April 2019 – UK departure from the EU.

A major area of the Brexit negotiations will be the trade deal that the UK can secure with the EU once it leaves. While the UK is a member of the EU, there are no tariffs on trade with other EU member states. Goods imported into the EU from non-EU countries pay the EU's common external tariff, unless there is a preferential trade agreement.

The UK has traditionally had strong trade links with the EU and, taken as a whole, the EU is the UK's largest trading partner. However, the share of UK exports going to the EU has declined gradually over recent years as trade with developing economies has grown. While exports to the EU are declining, it is still the UK's most important trading partner and so the terms of the trade deal are very important.

As the exit process will stretch over two years, it is important to remember that predictions about the future impact on the UK economy are mostly speculation; however, the Office for Budget Responsibility predicts slower economic growth for the next few years before the economy resumes its long-term rate of growth.

4. Inflation

This section will first consider the way goods and services are paid for, including the ability of banks to create credit, and then move on to look at how this interacts with inflation, and the impact inflation can have on an economy.

UK Inflation (CPI) 1976–2017

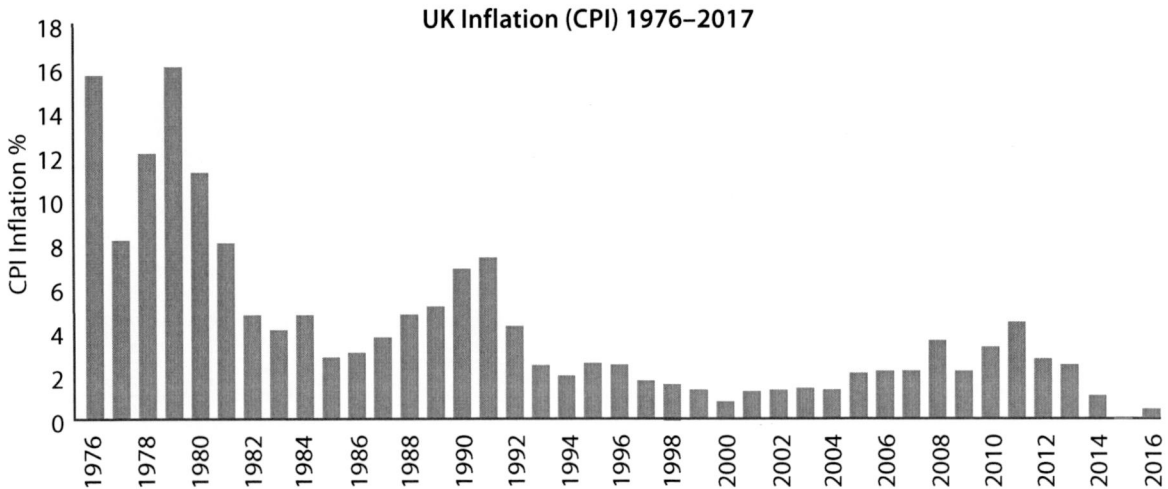

Source: Office for National Statistics (ONS)

4.1 Credit Creation

Most of what is purchased by consumers is not paid for using cash. It is generally more convenient to pay by card or cheque and it is fairly easy (subject to the borrower's credit status) to buy something now and pay later, for example, by going overdrawn, using a credit card or taking out a loan. Loans will often be for more substantial purchases such as a house or a car. Buying now and paying later is generally referred to as purchasing goods and services 'on credit'.

The banking system provides a mechanism in which credit can be created. This means that banks can increase the total amount of spending power in the economy, as shown in the following example.

Example

New Bank plc sets up business and is granted a banking licence. It is authorised to take deposits and make loans. Because New Bank knows that only a small proportion of the deposited funds are likely to be demanded at any one time, it will be able to lend most of the deposited money to others. New Bank will make profits by lending money out and charging a higher rate of interest than it pays depositors.

These loans provide an increase in the money supply in circulation – New Bank is creating credit.

By lending, banks create money and advance this to borrowers that may be businesses, consumers and governments. As soon as the borrowed money is spent on goods and services, the people to whom it is paid (the providers of those goods and services) will then deposit it in their own bank accounts, allowing the banks to use it to create fresh credit all over again.

It is estimated that this 'credit creation' process accounts for 96% of the money in circulation in most industrialised nations, with only 4% being in the form of notes and coins created by the government.

If this process were uncontrolled it could lead to a rapid increase in the money supply and, with too much money chasing too few goods, the result would be a rise in prices leading to an increase in inflation. Understandably, therefore, central banks aim to keep the amount of credit creation under control as part of their overall monetary policy. They aim to ensure that the amount of credit creation is below the level at which it would increase the money supply so much that inflation accelerates.

As seen earlier, the MPC of the Bank of England does this by influencing people's willingness to borrow by setting the interest rate.

UK Inflation (Dec 2006–Dec 2016)

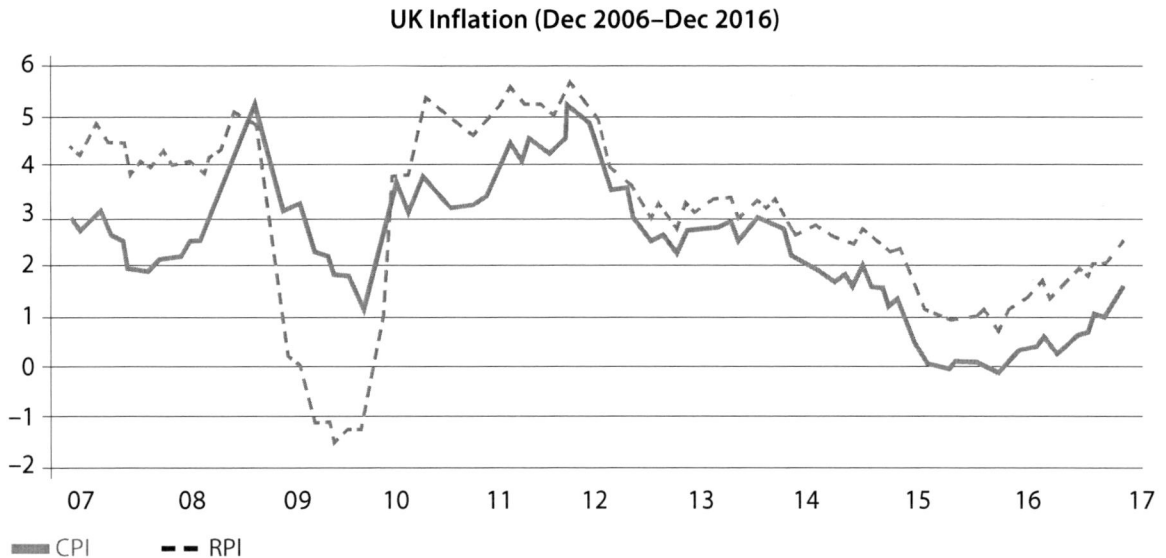

CPI ━━ RPI ― ―

Source: Office for National Statistics (ONS)

4.2 The Impact of Inflation

As already seen, inflation is a persistent increase in the general level of prices. There are a number of reasons why prices might increase, such as:

- Excess demand in the economy – too much money chasing too few goods.
- Scarcity of resources – when goods or services are in short supply, the prices paid for them tend to increase.
- Rapidly increasing government spending.

Most western governments seek to control inflation at a level of about 2-3% per annum without letting it get too high, or too low.

High levels of inflation can cause the following problems:

- Businesses have to continually update prices to keep pace with inflation.
- Employees find the real value of their salaries eroded.
- Those on fixed levels of income, such as pensioners, will suffer as the price increases are not matched by increases in income.
- Exports may become less competitive.
- The real value of future pensions and investment income becomes difficult to

assess, which might act as a disincentive to save.

There are, however, some positive aspects to high levels of inflation:

- Rising house prices contribute to a 'feel good' factor (although this might contribute to further inflation as house owners become more eager to borrow and spend).
- Borrowers benefit, because the value of their debt falls in 'real terms' – ie, after adjusting for the effect of inflation.
- Inflation also erodes the real value of a country's national debt and so can benefit an economy in difficult times.

Deflation is defined as a general fall in price levels. Although not experienced as a worldwide phenomenon since the 1930s, it has been seen more recently in many economies.

Deflation typically results from negative demand shocks, such as the recent falls in oil and commodity prices, and from excess capacity and production. It creates a vicious circle of reduced spending and a reluctance to borrow as the real burden of debt in an environment of falling prices increases.

Consumer Prices Index (2009–16)

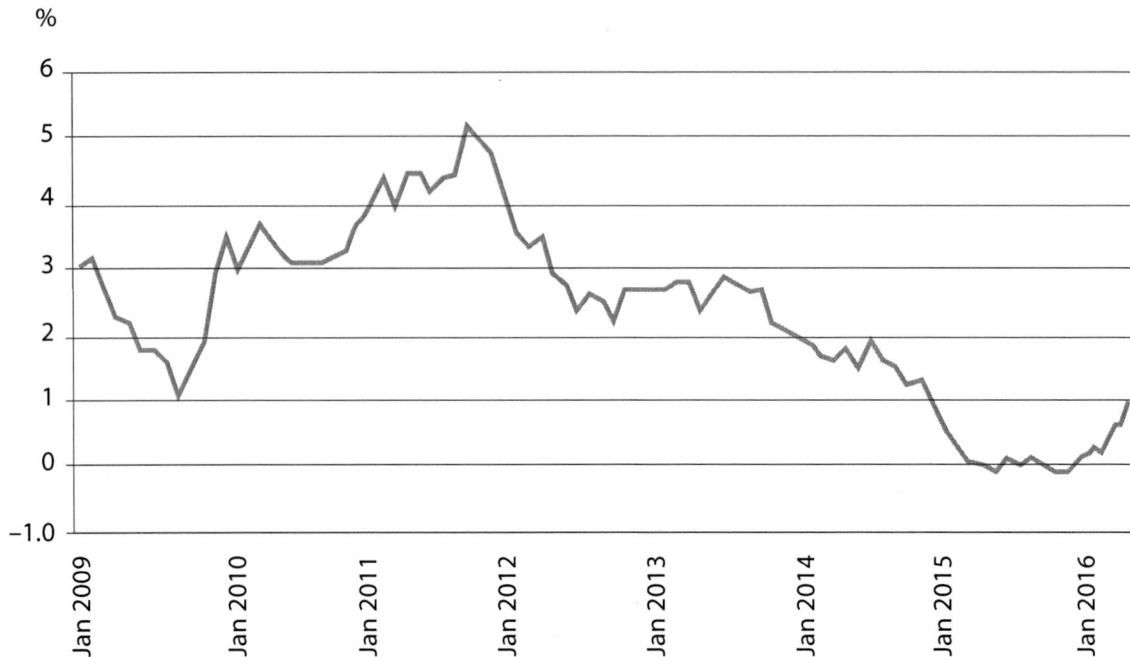

Source: Office for National Statistics

It should be noted that falling prices are not necessarily a destructive force per se and; indeed, they can be beneficial if they are as a result of positive supply shocks, such as rising productivity growth and greater price competition caused by the globalisation of the world economy and increased price transparency.

5. Key Economic Indicators

This section looks at a number of key economic statistics that can provide investors with a guide to the health of the economy and aid long-term investment decisions. These statistics are often called economic 'indicators', because they indicate how well the economy is performing. They are watched carefully by the government as well as by financial analysts.

5.1 Inflation Measures

Inflation is generally measured by selecting a 'basket' of goods and services that are typically purchased by consumers. The basket of goods

and services forms the basis for an index to measure inflation. The index simply takes this basket of goods and services and works out how much each price has changed and then weights the price changes according to their importance.

Some price changes have a much bigger impact on people than others. For example, an increase of 5% in the price of bread is likely to affect people much more than a 100% increase in the price of a box of matches. So bread therefore gets a much bigger weighting than matches, and changes in the price of bread will have a bigger effect on the index than changes in the price of matches.

There are various measures of inflation, including the following:

- **Retail Prices Index (RPI)** – the RPI (also known as the 'headline' rate) measures the increase in general household spending, including mortgage and rent payments, food, transport and entertainment.

- **RPIX** – this is the RPI, but excluding mortgage interest payments. This is often referred to as the 'underlying' rate of inflation. Excluding mortgage interest payments removes much of the impact of interest rate changes in general from the measure of inflation.
- **Consumer Prices Index (CPI)** – this is a measure of inflation that is prepared in a standard way throughout the EU. Like the RPIX, it excludes mortgage interest payments, largely because a substantial proportion of the population in continental Europe rent their homes, rather than buy them. Unlike the RPIX, however, it also excludes other housing costs aside from mortgage interest costs (for example, it excludes the 'depreciation component', an amount which the RPI uses to allow for the cost of maintaining a home in a constant condition). It was originally known as the **Harmonised Index of Consumer Prices (HICP)**.

Clearly, the different measures of inflation tend to show similar patterns but will not move perfectly in step as illustrated in the graph on the previous page.

In the UK, the government uses the CPI for a range of purposes, principally those where it needs to measure inflation on a like-for-like basis with other European countries.

5.2 Measures of Economic Data

In addition to inflation measures like the CPI, there are a number of other economic statistics carefully watched by the government and by other market participants as potentially significant indicators of how the economy is performing.

5.2.1 Gross Domestic Product (GDP)

At the very simplest level, an economy comprises two distinct groups: individuals and firms. Individuals supply firms with the productive resources (such as their labour) in exchange for an income. In turn, these individuals use this income to buy the entire output produced by firms employing these resources. This gives rise to what is known as the **circular flow** of income.

However, as can be seen by the diagram below, there is a little more to the 'circular flow' than just the individuals and firms. The government takes taxes from both firms and individuals and provides benefits to the unemployed and needy in the form of 'transfer payments' as well as spending on areas like defence and healthcare. There are exports from the firms to overseas economies and imports from overseas economies into the UK and there is money channelled through the financial markets in the form of savings and investment.

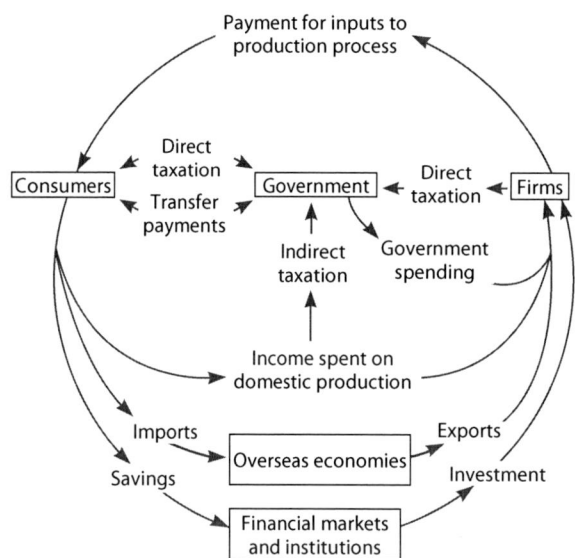

Using the circular flow, economic activity can be measured in one of three ways:

- by the total income paid by firms to individuals
- by individuals' total expenditure on firms' output, or
- by the value of total output generated by firms.

Gross domestic product is most commonly measured by looking at expenditure to calculate a country's output. This is known as the 'expenditure basis' and is typically calculated quarterly as follows:

Gross Domestic Product	
	consumer spending
+	government spending
+	investment
+	exports
–	imports
=	GDP

Clearly, an increasing level of GDP usually signifies an economy in a healthy state, with economies ideally looking for a consistent **trend of growth** over time.

If GDP falls, it is described as 'negative growth' and two consecutive quarters of negative growth is defined as a 'recession'. In a recession, consumers spend less, jobs are lost and output falls with the government usually trying to make up for the shortfall by spending more. However, this may be difficult if the government concerned has already built up too much debt and cannot borrow any more money.

The fact that actual growth fluctuates and deviates from trend growth in the short term is often termed the economic cycle, or business cycle. When an economy is growing in excess of its trend growth rate, actual output will exceed potential output, often leading to inflation. However, when a country's output contracts and the economy is in recession, there is likely to be spare capacity and unemployment.

5.2.2 Balance of Payments

The balance of payments is a summary of all the transactions between the UK and the rest of the world. If the UK imports more than it exports, there is a **balance of payments deficit**. If the UK exports more than it imports, there is a **balance of payments surplus**.

The main components of the balance of payments are the current account and the capital account.

The balance of trade comprises a visible trade balance – the difference between the value of imported and exported goods – and an invisible trade balance – the difference between the value of imported and exported services. The trade balance is detailed in the **current account**, which is used to calculate the total value of goods and services that flow into and out of a country. The results of the current account calculations provide details of the balance of trade a country has with the rest of the world. The UK typically runs a deficit on visible trade but an invisible trade surplus. Also, because it is an open economy, imports and exports combined total over 50% of UK GDP.

The **capital account** records international capital transactions related to investment in business, real estate, bonds and stocks. This includes transactions relating to the purchase and sale of domestic and foreign investment assets. These are usually divided into categories such as foreign direct investment when an overseas firm acquires a new plant or an existing business; portfolio investment which includes trading in stocks and bonds; and other investments which include transactions in currency and bank deposits.

For the balance of payments to balance, the current account must equal the capital account plus or minus a balancing item – used to rectify the many errors in compiling the balance of payments – plus or minus any change in central bank foreign currency reserves. In other words, a current account deficit resulting from a country being a net importer of overseas goods and services must be met by a net inflow of capital from overseas, taking account of any measurement errors and any central bank intervention in the foreign currency market.

Having a favourable **exchange rate** can be critical to the level of international trade undertaken, to a country's international competitiveness and therefore to its economic position. This can be understood by looking at what happens if a country's exchange rate alters.

- If the value of the domestic currency (eg, £ sterling) **rises** relative to other currencies, then exports will be less competitive unless producers reduce their prices and imports will be cheaper and therefore more competitive. The result will be either to reduce a trade surplus or worsen a trade deficit.
- If the value of the domestic currency **falls** against other currencies then the reverse happens: exports will be cheaper in foreign markets and thus more competitive, and imports will be more expensive and therefore, less attractive. A trade surplus or deficit is likely to see an improving position.

5.2.3 Budget Deficit and National Debt

A key function of government is to manage the public finances, and so a key economic indicator is the level of public sector debt, or the national debt as it is more frequently referred to.

In the past a state would incur budget deficits, usually as a result of wars, and finance these through taxation. In the UK, this changed in the late 1600s when the government's need to finance another war with France led to the creation of the Bank of England in 1694 and the first issue of state public debt in England.

Following on from this, the early 1700s saw the emergence of banking and financial markets and the ability to raise money by creating debt through the issue of bills and bonds and the beginning of the national debt. Some key statistics from the Office for National Statistics (ONS) show how the national debt has grown since then:

- The national debt rose from £12 million in 1700 to £850 million by the end of the Napoleonic Wars in 1815.
- The two world wars of the 20th century caused debt levels to rise, from £650 million in 1914 to £7.4 billion by 1919 and from £7.1 billion in 1939 to £24.7 billion in 1946.
- The period of relatively high inflation in the 1970s and 1980s saw debt rise from £33.1 billion in 1970 to £197.4 billion in 1988.
- The national debt has since ballooned to over £1,600 billion.

The national debt continues to rise as the effects of previous overspending and the recession are felt.

There are a wide number of measures used as key economic indicators which can be quite confusing. This is due to each measuring different sets of data but essentially they fall into two main types:

- **Government debt** – essentially this is what the government owes. The most widely quoted is the **public sector net debt**.
- **Budget deficit** – essentially the shortfall between what the government receives in tax receipts and what it spends. The most widely quoted is in the **Public Sector Net Cash Requirement (PSNCR)**.

Debt measures are also usually presented as a percentage of GDP since comparisons over time need to allow for effects such as inflation. Dividing by GDP is the conventional way of doing this.

The PSNCR is the difference each year between government expenditure and government income, the latter mainly from taxes. In a buoyant economy, government spending tends to be less than income, with substantial tax revenues generated from corporate profits and high levels of employment. This enables the government to reduce public sector (ie, government) borrowing.

UK Unemployment Rate

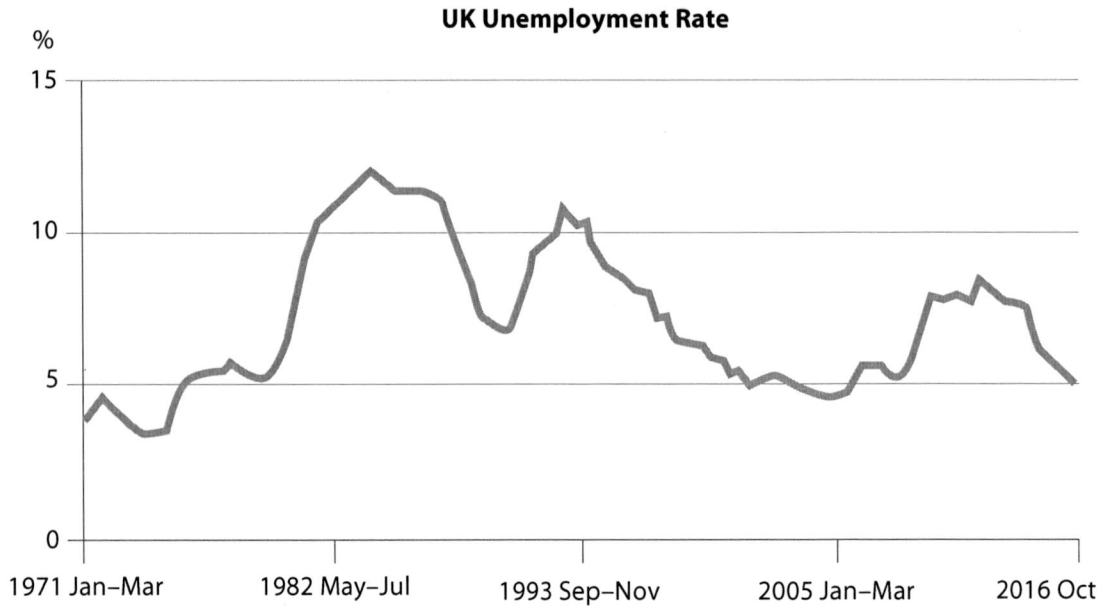

In a slowing economy, spending tends to exceed tax revenues and the government will need to raise borrowing by issuing government bonds. In the UK, the budget deficit exploded as the recession reduced tax receipts and pushed up spending on unemployment benefit before later reducing. If left unaddressed, high levels of public borrowing and debt risk undermining growth and economic stability.

5.2.4 Level of Unemployment

The extent to which those seeking employment cannot find work is an important indicator of the health of the economy. There is always likely to be some unemployment in an economy – some people might lack the right skills and/or live in employment black spots. Higher levels of unemployment indicate low demand in the economy for goods and services produced and sold to consumers and therefore low demand for people in the UK to provide them.

In addition, high unemployment levels will have a negative impact on the government's finances. The government will need to increase social security payments, and its income will decrease because of the lack of any tax revenues from the unemployed.

Learning Objectives

Chapter Seven has covered the following Learning Objectives:

2.1.1 Know the factors which determine the level of economic activity: state-controlled economies; market economies; mixed economies; open economies

2.1.2 Know the functions of central banks: the Bank of England; the Federal Reserve; the European Central Bank

2.1.3 Know the functions of the Monetary Policy Committee

2.1.4 Know how goods and services are paid for and how credit is created

2.1.5 Understand the impact of inflation/deflation on economic behaviour

2.1.6 Know the meaning of the following measures of inflation: retail prices index; RPIX; consumer prices index

2.1.7 Understand the impact of the following economic data: gross domestic product; balance of payments; budget deficit/surplus; level of unemployment; exchange rates

Based on what you have learned in Chapter Seven, try to answer the following end of chapter questions.

CISI
CHARTERED INSTITUTE FOR
SECURITIES & INVESTMENT

End of Chapter Questions

Think of an answer for each question and refer to the appropriate section for confirmation.

1. What are the four factors of production?
    Answer Reference: Section 2.1

    ....

    ....

2. What are two alternative terms for a state-controlled economy?
    Answer Reference: Section 2.2

    ....

    ....

3. Give an example of a state-controlled economy.
    Answer Reference: Section 2.2

    ....

    ....

4. In a market economy, how are prices determined?
    Answer Reference: Section 2.3

    ....

    ....

5. The vast majority of countries are neither state-controlled nor market economies. What are they?
    Answer Reference: Section 2.4

    ....

    ....

6. What is an open economy?

    Answer Reference: Section 2.5

    ....

    ....

7. Who arbitrates in disputes over international trade?

    Answer Reference: Section 2.5

    ....

    ....

8. What are the two core functions of the Bank of England?

    Answer Reference: Section 3.2

    ....

    ....

9. Who decides on the UK's official interest rate?

    Answer Reference: Section 3.2

    ....

    ....

10. Who decides on the UK's inflationary target?

    Answer Reference: Section 3.2

    ....

    ....

11. What happens if the Bank of England fails to keep inflation close to target?

    Answer Reference: Section 3.2

    ....

    ....

12. List the two typical central bank roles that are not undertaken by the Bank of England.

Answer Reference: Section 3.2

....

....

13. How are most goods and services paid for in the UK?

Answer Reference: Section 4.1

....

....

14. What is credit creation?

Answer Reference: Section 4.1

....

....

15. What is inflation?

Answer Reference: Section 4.2

....

....

16. List at least three problems caused by high levels of inflation.

Answer Reference: Section 4.2

....

....

17. What are the three major measures of inflation published in the UK and how do they differ?

Answer Reference: Section 5.1

....

....

18. How is GDP usually calculated?

Answer Reference: Section 5.2.1

....

....

19. What is a recession?

Answer Reference: Section 5.2.1

....

....

20. What is a balance of payments surplus?

Answer Reference: Section 5.2.2

....

....

21. What is the current account made up of?

Answer Reference: Section 5.2.2

....

....

22. What is the likely impact on the balance of trade if the domestic currency exchange rate weakens?

Answer Reference: Section 5.2.2

....

....

23. What is the PSNCR?

Answer Reference: Section 5.2.3

....

....

24. What impact is high unemployment likely to have on government finances?

Answer Reference: Section 5.2.4

....

....

Chapter Eight
Derivatives

8

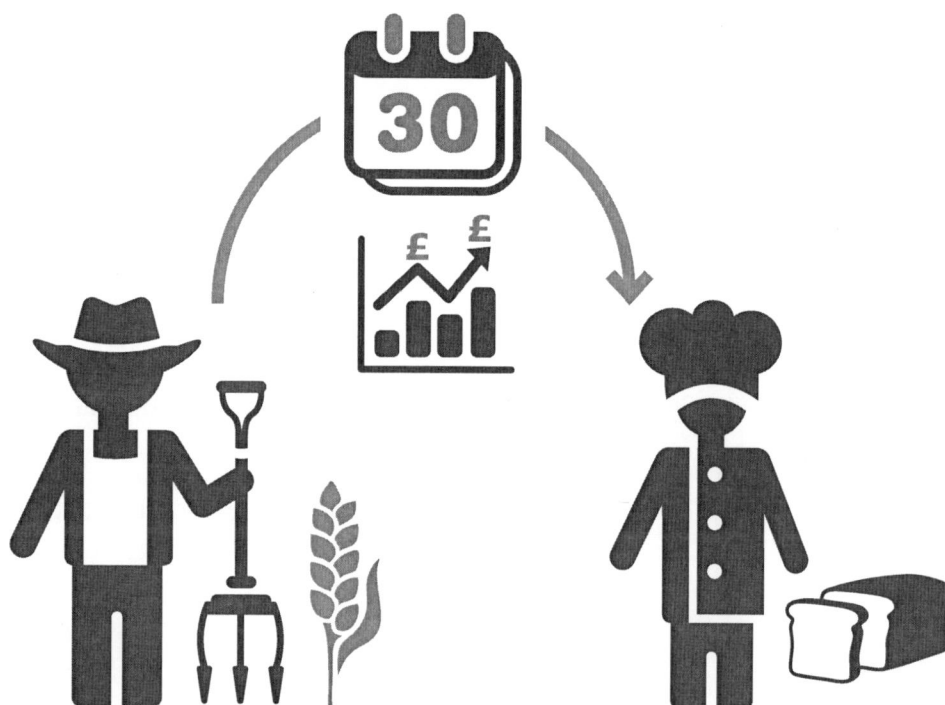

1. Uses of Derivatives

A derivative is a financial instrument where the value of the instrument is derived from the price of another underlying asset. This underlying asset could be a financial asset, such as those considered in the previous chapters, or a commodity. Examples of financial assets include bonds, shares, stock market indices and interest rates; for commodities they include oil, silver or wheat.

A simple example would be an airline committing to buy jet fuel from an oil company now, with the delivery not taking place until two months later. This is termed a 'forward' contract. The price the airline will have to pay will obviously be closely related to prevailing price of the underlying asset, jet fuel.

The trading of derivatives can take place directly between **counterparties** (such as the airline and the oil company seen above) or on an organised exchange. Where trading takes place directly between counterparties it is referred to as **over-the-counter (OTC)** trading.

When a derivative is traded on an exchange, it is no longer an OTC trade and is instead referred to as **exchange-traded**.

Derivatives tend to be used for two purposes – hedging and speculating.

Hedging is reducing the risk of adverse price movements. In the brief example outlined above, the airline is removing the risk that the cost of jet fuel may increase in the next two months and the oil company is guaranteeing that it will not suffer if the price of jet fuel falls in the next two months. So, both participants are hedging.

Speculation is where the motivation behind the derivative trade is to make money. Developing the earlier example of the airline hedging its risk in relation to the price of jet fuel, imagine that the deal is done between the airline and a bank, rather than the airline and an oil company. Clearly the airline's motivation is still to hedge, but why would a bank be willing to be involved? Well, if the bank thought that the price of jet fuel was likely to fall over the next two months, then the derivatives contract might make some money for the bank. The bank is speculating. As long as the bank is correct and the price of jet fuel falls over the next two months, the bank will make money because it has agreed to sell jet fuel at a higher price than it needs to pay for the fuel two months later.

As will be detailed in the remainder of this chapter, most derivatives take one of the following forms:

- Forwards.
- Futures.
- Options.

2. Futures

2.1 Development of Futures

Derivatives are not a new concept and, in fact, have been around for hundreds of years. Their origins can be traced back to agricultural markets where farmers needed a mechanism to guard against price fluctuations caused by gluts of produce or periods of drought. So, in order to fix the price of agricultural produce in advance of harvest time, farmers and merchants entered into forward contracts. Like the jet fuel example encountered above, these agricultural forward contracts set the price at which a stated amount of a commodity (for example, a bushel of wheat) would be delivered between a farmer and a merchant at a pre-specified future time.

Because these early derivative contracts removed risks they were very popular and led to the opening of the world's first derivatives exchange, the Chicago Board of Trade (CBOT), in 1848.

The exchange introduced a **futures contract**. The futures contract involved the purchase or sale of a standardised quantity and quality of grain (such as 100 bushels of wheat containing no more than 5% moisture) for a price agreed now and for delivery on a stated future delivery date, such as three months later. Unlike the forward contracts that preceded it, these futures contract are traded on the exchange, rather than over the counter. These futures contracts have subsequently been extended to a wide variety of commodities and are offered by an increasing number of derivatives exchanges.

It was not until 1975 that CBOT introduced the world's first **financial futures contract**. Rather than being based on a commodity like wheat, oil or metal, financial futures are based on financial assets like shares and bonds.

2.2 Definition and Function of a Future

A future is an agreement between a buyer and a seller. A futures contract is a legally binding obligation between two parties: the buyer agrees to pay a pre-specified amount for the delivery of a particular pre-specified quantity of an asset at a pre-specified future date. The seller agrees to deliver the asset at the future date, in exchange for the pre-specified amount of money.

Example ───────────────

A buyer might agree with a seller to pay US$50 per barrel for 1,000 barrels of crude oil in three months' time. The buyer might be an electricity-generating company wanting to fix the price it will have to pay for the oil to use in its oil-fired power stations and the seller might be an oil company wanting to fix the sales price of some of its future oil production. Both of the counterparties to the trade are using the futures contract to hedge.

───────────────

A futures contract has two distinct features:

- It is **exchange-traded** – for example, on the derivatives exchanges, such as ICE Europe in London or the Chicago Mercantile Exchange (CME) in the US.
- It is dealt on **standardised terms** – the exchange specifies the quality of the underlying asset, the quantity underlying each contract, the future date and the delivery location – only the price is open to negotiation. In the above example, the oil quality will be based on the oil field from which it originates (eg, Brent crude – from the Brent oil field in the North Sea), the quantity is 1,000 barrels, the date is three months ahead and the location might be the port of Rotterdam.

2.3 Futures Terminology

Derivatives markets have specialised terminology that is important to understand.

Staying with the example above, the buyer of the contract to purchase 1,000 barrels of crude oil at US$50 per barrel for delivery in three months is said to go **long** of the contract, while the seller is described as going **short**.

The definition of these key terms that the futures market uses are as follows:

- **Long** – the term used for the position taken by the buyer of the future. The person who is 'long' of the contract is committed to buying the underlying asset at the pre-agreed price on the specified future date.
- **Short** – the position taken by the seller of the future. The seller is committed to delivering the underlying asset in exchange for the pre-agreed price on the specified future date.

3. Options

3.1 Development of Options

Options are another form of derivative. They did not really start to flourish until two US academics produced an option pricing model in 1973 that allowed them to be readily priced. This paved the way for the creation of standardised options contracts and the opening of the Chicago Board Options Exchange (CBOE) in the same year. This in turn led to an explosion in product innovation and introduction of options onto other exchanges.

3.2 Definition and Function of an Option

An option gives a buyer the right, but not the obligation, to buy or sell a specified quantity of an underlying asset at a pre-agreed **exercise price**, on or before a pre-specified future date or between two specified dates. The seller, in exchange for the payment of a **premium**, grants the option to the buyer.

As further detailed below, an option could be sold by one party (such as a bank) to another (such as an investor). In exchange for a premium, the bank might agree to sell the investor 1,000 shares in a particular company (XYZ plc) in three months' time for £5 each, if the investor wishes. In other words, the investor (the buyer of the option) has a choice of either going ahead and buying the shares at the exercise price of £5 each (exercising the option), or deciding not to go ahead and letting the option lapse. Clearly, the choice the investor makes will be driven by whether or not the shares in XYZ plc are worth more or less than £5 in three months. If they are worth more than £5, the investor will go ahead. If they are trading at less than £5, the investor will let the option lapse.

When options are traded on an **exchange**, they will be in standardised sizes (such as for 1,000 shares) and terms (such as for a period of three months). From time to time, however, investors may wish to trade an option that is outside these standardised terms and they will do so in the **over-the-counter (OTC)** market. Options can therefore also be traded off-exchange, or OTC, where the contract specification determined by the parties is bespoke.

3.3 Options Terms

There are two main classes of options:

- A **call option** is when the buyer has the right to buy the asset at the exercise price, if he chooses to. The seller is obliged to deliver if the buyer exercises the option. The above example relating to XYZ plc shares was a call option.
- A **put option** is when the buyer has the right to sell the underlying asset at the exercise price. The seller of the put option is obliged to take delivery and pay the exercise price, if the buyer exercises the option.

The buyers of options are the owners of those options. They are also referred to as **holders**.

The sellers of options are referred to as the **writers** of those options. Their sale is also referred to as 'taking for the call' or 'taking for the put', depending on whether they receive a premium for selling a call option or a put option.

For exchange-traded contracts, both buyers and sellers settle the contract with a clearing house that is part of the exchange, rather than directly with each other. The **premium** is the money paid by the buyer to the exchange (and then by the exchange to the writer) at the beginning of the option contract; it is not refundable.

The following simplified example of an options contract is intended to assist in understanding the way in which option contracts might be used. The answer can be found at the end of this chapter.

Exercise 1

Suppose shares in Beckenham Venture plc are trading at 125p and an investor buys a 150p call for three months. The investor, Frank Smith, has the right to buy Beckenham Venture shares from the writer of the option (another investor – Steve Jones) at 150p if he chooses, at the end of the next three months.

If Beckenham Ventures shares are below 150p three months later, Frank will abandon the option and Steve will keep the premium. If they rise to, say, 200p, Frank will contact Steve and either:

- exercise the option (buy the shares at 150p and keep them, or sell them at 200p), or
- persuade Steve to give him 200 – 150p = 50p to settle the transaction.

1. What does Frank hope will happen to the shares in Beckenham Ventures plc in the next three months?
2. What does Steve hope will happen to the shares in Beckenham Ventures plc in the next three months?
3. If Frank paid a premium of 20p to Steve, what is Frank's maximum loss and what level does Beckenham Ventures plc have to reach for Frank to make a profit?

4. Derivatives and Commodity Markets

A derivative is a financial instrument whose price is derived from that of another asset, and the other asset is generally referred to as the 'underlying asset', or sometimes just 'the underlying'.

The physical trading of commodities tends to take place side by side with the trading of derivatives on those commodities. The physical market is simply the buying, selling and subsequent delivery of commodities like oil, wheat, barley and aluminium. This trading is dominated by major international trading houses, governments, and the major producers and consumers. The derivatives markets exist in parallel and enable the participants in the physical markets to hedge the risk of adverse price movements.

4.1 Physical Markets

There are a number of different commodity markets, which are differentiated by the commodity that is traded there. Some of the major commodities are:

- agricultural commodities (such as wheat, potatoes and livestock)
- base metals (such as aluminium and copper)
- precious metals (such as gold and silver)
- energy commodities (such as crude oil and natural gas).

The features of the base and precious metals markets and energy markets are considered in more detail below.

4.1.1 Base and Precious Metals

There are numerous metals produced worldwide and subsequently refined for use in a large variety of products and processes.

As with all other commodity prices, metal prices are influenced by supply and demand. The factors influencing supply include the availability of raw materials and the costs of extraction and production. Demand comes from underlying users of the commodity, for example, the demand for metals in rapidly industrialising economies, including China and India.

Demand also originates from investors that might buy metal futures in anticipation of excess demand, or incorporate commodities into specific funds. Producers use the market for hedging their production. Traditionally, the price of precious metals, such as gold, will rise in times of crisis – gold is seen as a safe haven.

4.1.2 Energy Markets

The energy market includes the market for oil (and other oil-based products like petroleum), natural gas and coal.

Oil includes both crude oil and various 'fractions' produced as a result of the refining process, such as naptha, butanes, kerosene, petrol and heating/gas oil. Crude oil is defined by three primary factors:

- Field of origin, for example, Brent, West Texas Intermediate, Oman.
- Density, ie, low density or 'light', high density or 'heavy'.
- Sulphur content, ie, low sulphur (known as 'sweet') or high sulphur (known as 'sour').

Demand for oil and gas is ultimately driven by levels of consumption, which in turn is driven by energy needs, eg, from manufacturing industry and transport. Supply of these commodities is finite, and countries with surplus oil and gas reserves are able to export to those countries with insufficient oil and gas to meet their requirements. In the past, oil producing countries that are members of the Organisation of Petroleum Exporting Countries (OPEC) would regularly restrict the supply of oil in order to keep prices high or to drive them up. More recently, prices of oil have dropped significantly due to a combination of oversupply and competition between oil-producing states.

8

4.2 Derivatives Markets

As seen, there are two distinct groups of derivatives, which are differentiated by how they are traded. These are OTC derivatives and exchange-traded derivatives (ETD).

OTC derivatives are negotiated and traded privately between parties without the use of an exchange. Products such as interest rate swaps and foreign exchange forwards are traded in this way.

The OTC market is the larger of the two in terms of value of contracts traded daily. Trading takes place predominantly in Europe and, particularly, in the UK. (Note: there is considerable activity taking place at the moment to move OTC trading on-exchange in response to regulatory concerns about the risks posed by OTC derivative trading.)

Exchange-traded derivatives are ones that have standardised features and can therefore be traded on an organised exchange. The main types are futures and options. The role of the exchange is to provide a marketplace for trading to take place as well as to provide some sort of guarantee that the trade will eventually be settled. The exchanges do this by using an intermediary (known as the 'central counterparty') for their trades.

4.2.1 Derivatives Exchanges

Details of some of the main derivatives exchanges in Europe are shown below.

ICE Futures Europe

In 2001, Euronext purchased a derivatives exchange in London called LIFFE (pronounced 'life') and renamed it Euronext.liffe. LIFFE was originally an acronym for the London International Financial Futures and Options Exchange, originally set up in 1982. It is now part of ICE following the takeover of NYSE Euronext.

ICE Futures Europe is the main exchange for trading financial derivative products in the UK, including futures and options on:

- interest rates and bonds
- equity indices (eg, FTSE)
- individual equities (eg, BP, HSBC).

It also trades derivatives on soft commodities, such as sugar, wheat and cocoa. It also runs futures and options markets in Amsterdam, Brussels, Lisbon and Paris.

Eurex

Eurex is the world's leading international derivatives exchange and is based in Frankfurt. Its principal products are German bond futures and options, the most well-known of which are contracts on the Bund (a German government bond). It also trades index products for a range of European markets.

Eurex was created by Deutsche Börse AG and the Swiss Exchange. Trading is on the fully computerised Eurex platform, that enables members from across Europe and the US to access Eurex outside Switzerland and Germany.

Intercontinental Exchange (ICE)

ICE operates an electronic global futures and OTC marketplace for trading energy commodity contracts. These contracts include crude oil and refined products, natural gas, power and emissions.

The company's regulated futures and options business, formerly known as the International Petroleum Exchange (IPE), now operates under the name ICE Futures. ICE acquired the London-based energy futures and options exchange in 2001.

ICE Futures is Europe's leading energy futures and options exchange. ICE's products include derivative contracts based on key energy commodities: crude oil and refined oil products, such as heating oil and jet fuel and other products, like natural gas and electric power.

Recently, ICE Futures introduced what has become Europe's leading emissions futures contract in conjunction with the European Climate Exchange (ECX).

ICE's other markets are centred in North America and include trading of agricultural, currency and stock index futures and options. It also took over NYSE Euronext and, as a result, by acquiring LIFFE, became the world's largest derivatives exchange operator.

London Metal Exchange (LME)

The London Metal Exchange is the world's premier non-ferrous metals market and has been operating for over 130 years. Although it is based in London, it is a global market with an international membership and with more than 95% of its business coming from overseas.

Futures and options contracts are traded on a range of metals, including aluminium, copper, nickel, tin, zinc and lead. More recently, it has also launched the world's first futures contracts for plastics.

Trading on the LME takes place in three ways: through open outcry trading in the 'ring', through an inter-office telephone market and through **LME Select**, the exchange's electronic trading platform.

4.3 Investing In Derivatives

Having looked at various types of derivatives and their main uses, we can summarise some of the main advantages and disadvantages of investing in derivatives.

Advantages

- They enable producers and consumers of goods to agree the price of a commodity today for future delivery which can remove the uncertainty of what price will be achieved for the producer and the risk of lack of supply for the consumer.

- They enable investment firms to hedge the risk associated with a portfolio or an individual stock.
- They offer the ability to speculate on a wide range of assets and markets to make large bets on price movements using the geared nature of derivatives.

Drawbacks and Risks

- Some types of derivatives investment can result in the investor losing more than their initial outlay and, in some cases, facing potentially unlimited losses.
- Derivatives markets thrive on price volatility, meaning that professional investment skills and experience are required.
- In the OTC markets, there is a risk that the counterparty may default on their obligations, and so it requires great attention to detail in terms of counterparty risk assessment, documentation and the taking of collateral.

Answers to Chapter Exercises

Exercise 1

Suppose shares in Beckenham Ventures plc are trading at 125p and an investor buys a 150p call for three months. The investor, Frank Smith, has the right to buy Beckenham Venture shares from the writer of the option (another investor – Steve Jones) at 150p if he chooses, at any stage over the next three months.

If Beckenham Ventures shares are below 150p three months later, Frank will abandon the option and Steve will keep the premium.

If they rise to, say, 200p, Frank will contact Steve and either:

- exercise the option (buy the shares at 150p and keep them, or sell them at 200p), or
- persuade Steve to give him 200–150p = 50p to settle the transaction.

1. What does Frank hope will happen to the shares in Beckenham Ventures plc in the next three months?

   Frank hopes the shares in Beckenham Ventures plc will rise and he will make a profit. Frank is speculating on Beckenham Ventures plc shares increasing in value in the next three months.

2. What does Steve hope will happen to the shares in Beckenham Ventures plc in the next three months?

   Steve has the opposite view to Frank. He is hoping that shares in Beckenham Ventures plc will not rise in value over the next three months and he is able to keep the premium received from Frank as profit.

3. If Frank paid a premium of 20p to Steve, what is Frank's maximum loss and what level does Beckenham Ventures plc have to reach for Frank to make a profit?

   The most Frank can lose is 20p, the premium he has paid. If the Beckenham Ventures plc shares rise above 150 + 20p, or 170p, then he makes a profit. If the shares rise to say 151p then Frank would exercise his right to buy – better to make a penny and cut his losses to 19p than lose the whole 20p.

Learning Objectives

Chapter Eight has covered the following Learning Objectives:

6.1.1   Know the uses and application of derivatives

6.2.1   Know the definition and function of a future

6.3.1   Know the definition and function of an option

6.3.2   Understand the following terms: calls, puts

6.4.1   Understand the following terms: long, short, holder; writing; premium

6.5.1   Know the characteristics of the derivatives and commodity markets

6.5.2   Know the advantages and disadvantages of investing in the derivatives and commodity markets

Based on what you have learned in Chapter Eight, try to answer the following end of chapter questions.

8

End of Chapter Questions

Think of an answer for each question and refer to the appropriate section for confirmation.

1. Define a derivative.

    Answer Reference: Section 1

    ....

    ....

2. What are the two trading possibilities for derivatives?

    Answer Reference: Section 1

    ....

    ....

3. What are the two primary purposes for which derivatives can be used?

    Answer Reference: Section 1

    ....

    ....

4. What are the three major forms of derivative?

    Answer Reference: Section 1

    ....

    ....

5. How does a futures contract differ from a forward?

    Answer Reference: Sections 2.1, 2.2

    ....

    ....

6. What are the 'short' and the 'long' in relation to a futures contract?

    Answer Reference: Section 2.3

    ....

    ....

7. How does an option differ from a future?

    Answer Reference: Section 3.2

    ....

    ....

8. What is the 'exercise price' in relation to an option?

    Answer Reference: Section 3.2

    ....

    ....

9. How does a call option differ from a put option?

    Answer Reference: Section 3.3

    ....

    ....

10. Explain the 'holder' and the 'writer' in relation to an option.

    Answer Reference: Section 3.3

    ....

    ....

11. What is the 'premium' in relation to options?

Answer Reference: Section 3.3

....

....

12. The physical trading of commodities is generally driven by two factors, what are they?

Answer Reference: Section 4.1

....

....

13. Where is Eurex and what is its most well-known contract?

Answer Reference: Section 4.2.1

....

....

14. Where is ICE Futures Europe and what trades there?

Answer Reference: Section 4.2.1

....

....

15. What is traded on the LME?

Answer Reference: Section 4.2.1

....

....

Chapter Nine
Investment Funds

1. Introduction

Investment management is a vital part of the financial services industry. In essence, investment managers select the most appropriate investments (mainly shares, bonds and money market instruments) for their clients. The investment managers tend to do this by creating 'funds' in which their clients can choose to invest and, since each fund includes a collection of investors, the funds are often referred to as **collective investment funds** or **collective investment schemes**.

Investment management is also referred to using alternative terms, such as 'asset management' or 'fund management' and its importance in the financial services industry is illustrated in the diagram on the following page.

As shown in the diagram on the following page, the financial services sector can be divided into two main functions – the 'sell side' and the 'buy side', and at the heart of it are the investment managers.

The sell side is involved in the selling of investment ideas, strategies, advice and services to either those with money to invest, or more likely those managing the investments on behalf of others – the investment managers. Typical sell side participants are the stockbrokers providing advice as to which are the best shares to buy and then arranging the purchase of those shares through stock exchange trading systems.

The buy side is the owners or managers of money that are paying for the sell side services with fees or commission, such as an investment manager choosing to buy a particular company's shares through a broker, and paying a commission for doing so.

Ultimately, the buy side is individuals investing their money, however much of this investment is done indirectly perhaps by a financial adviser persuading an individual to invest in a particular fund run by an investment manager, or an individual having monthly contributions deducted from his/her salary and paid into a

The UK Investment Market

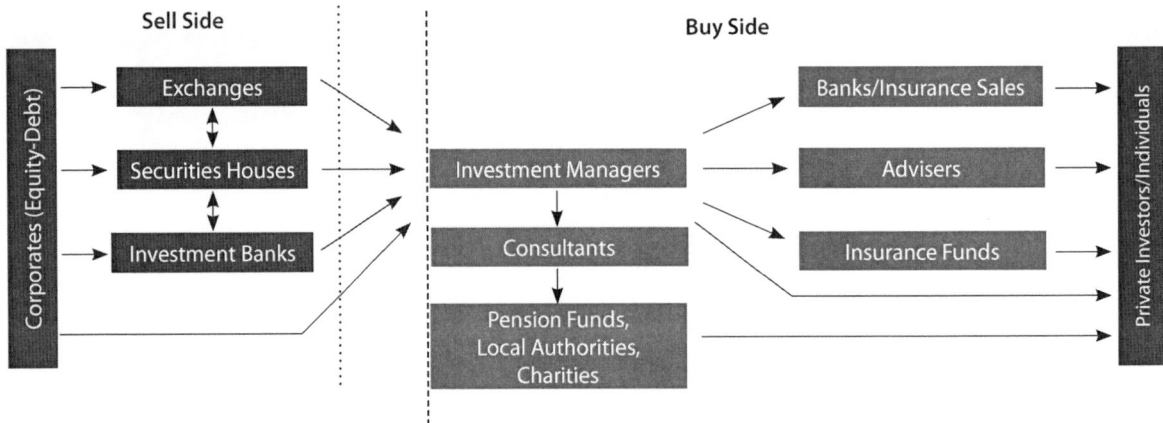

Source: Investment Association (IA)

pension fund run on behalf of the employees by an investment management company.

The size and scale of the industry can be seen in the regular reports issued by the Investment Association (IA). The IA is the trade body for the UK-based asset management industry. Its members manage a wide variety of investment vehicles, including authorised investment funds, pension funds and stocks & shares ISAs. Its role is to represent the industry, principally to government and regulators as well as the press and public, and to promote high standards.

1.1 The Benefits of Collective Investment

When investors decide to invest in a particular asset class, such as equities, there are two ways they can do it – direct investment or indirect investment.

Direct investment is when an individual personally buys shares in a company, such as BP, the oil giant. Indirect investment is when an individual buys a stake in an investment fund, such as a mutual fund that invests in the shares of a range of different types of companies, perhaps including BP.

A more formal description of a fund is that it is a collective investment scheme that pools the resources of a large number of investors, with the aim of pursuing a common investment objective. The investors could be individuals (retail investors) putting their money into a UK equity fund, run by a fund manager, that aims to make money by investing in UK company shares.

The pooling of resources into funds brings a number of benefits, including:

Economies of Scale

The fund manager will place larger orders to buy or sell investments than most retail investors, and these large investment orders will attract much more competitive dealing fees and commissions. The managers of large funds also tend to get much more attention from brokers and investment bankers, meaning that investment information can be more timely and comprehensive.

Diversification

As summarised by the phrase 'don't put all your eggs in one basket', a diversified portfolio contains a substantial number of investments and will be less risky than a portfolio with just one or two investments in it.

The value of shares and most other investments can fall as well as rise. Some might fall spectacularly, for example, shares in a company that suddenly collapses, such as Northern Rock and Lehman Brothers. However, if an investor holds a diversified pool of investments in a portfolio, the risk of single constituent investments falling spectacularly can normally be offset by outperformance on the part of other investments. In other words, risk is lessened when the investor holds a diversified portfolio of investments.

However, to create a diversified portfolio directly, an investor would require a substantial amount of money, as illustrated in the following example.

Example ——————————————

John Wiltshire has £5000 to invest. He wants to invest in top, UK company shares and is aware of the old adage of not putting all of his eggs in one basket. As a result John would like at least 50 different company shares in his portfolio.

Investing directly in shares of John's own choosing will incur stockbrokers' commission charges. Even using online brokers will probably incur a minimum commission of £12.50 per trade, irrespective of the size of the deal. So his £5,000 invested across 50 different shares would incur charges of 50 x £12.50 or £625–12.5% of the entire investment!

Alternatively, John could put his £5,000 into a UK equity fund, which is likely to be spread over comfortably more than 50 different company shares, and only incur an initial fee of 5% or less.

———————————————————————

Diversification can also come from a fund investing in a mix of different types of asset, such as a mix of cash, equities, bonds and property. A collective investment scheme could also put limited amounts of investment into bank deposits and even into other funds, when it would be termed a 'fund of funds'.

Access to Professional Investment Management

Collective investment schemes also give investors access to professional investment management and geographical areas or asset classes with which they may be unfamiliar. The great majority of private investors have very little knowledge of stock markets outside their own country and some of the best performance can be found in some of the least accessible markets around the world. Professional fund management firms usually maintain teams of fund managers who specialise in investing in specific areas of the world. They will follow their chosen markets closely and will consider carefully what to buy or sell and more importantly when to buy or sell – with timing often being the key to successful investment.

Regulatory Oversight

Another benefit of investing in funds rather than directly is the fact that many funds are carefully vetted by financial services regulators before they can be marketed to potential investors. The regulators generally ensure the fund is suitably diversified and does not take any excessive risks.

Tax Deferral

Investing in funds can be tax efficient. For example, many funds do not pay any tax on the income and gains they generate, and the investor only pays tax when she sells the investment. This is known as 'tax deferral' because the investor's requirement to pay tax is being deferred until such a time as she decides to sell her investment.

However, fund managers do not manage portfolios for nothing. As seen in the earlier example, they might charge investors fees to become involved in their funds (known as entry fees or initial charges). They also may charge investors when they leave the fund (known as exit charges), and they will charge annual management fees. Clearly, these fees are needed to cover the investment managers' salaries, technology, research, their dealing, settlement and risk management systems, and to provide them with a profit. Equally, there is no guarantee of the investment performance of the fund or of how it will perform in comparison to similar funds or benchmarks.

1.2 Investment Styles

There is a wide range of funds available with many different investment objectives and investment styles. Each of these funds has an investment portfolio managed by a fund manager according to a clearly stated set of objectives. An example of an objective might be to invest in the shares of UK companies with above-average potential for capital growth and to outperform the FTSE All Share index. Another fund's objective could be to maximise income or to achieve steady growth in capital and income.

In each case it will also be made clear what the fund manager will invest in, ie, shares and/or bonds and/or property and/or cash or money market instruments, and whether derivatives will be used to hedge currency or other market risks.

It is also important to understand the investment style the fund manager adopts. This refers to the fund manager's approach to choosing investments and meeting the fund's objectives. The investment styles can be either 'active' or 'passive'.

1.2.1 Active Management

Active management seeks to out-perform a predetermined benchmark over a specific time period. So, for example, a fund could be created

that invests in large, UK-listed company shares and aims to do better than the index for large UK-listed companies, the FTSE 100.

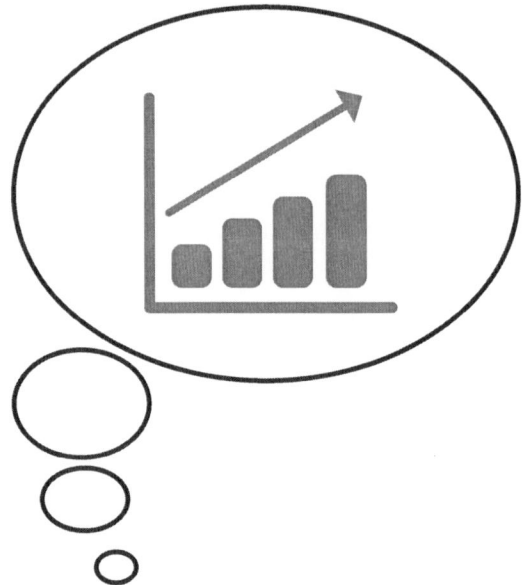

If the FTSE 100 rose by 15% in one year and the value of a fund's UK large-cap share portfolio rose by 20%, it can be said to have outperformed its benchmark. The active management has paid off for the fund's investors.

The active manager can use fundamental analysis or technical analysis to select the investments. Fundamental analysis involves forecasting what is likely to happen, and the impact that this might have on a company and its shares. So, anticipating an increase in unemployment, an active fund manager might decide to invest more heavily in retail stores selling staple goods at discount prices.

Technical analysis at its simplest involves deciding whether to buy or sell based on the past pattern of an investment's prices. For example, if a chart of a share's price over time is exhibiting a particular pattern, the technical analyst might conclude that the next movement in the share's price is likely to be upwards. He would therefore buy in anticipation of this.

Two commonly used terms in the context of active management are 'top-down' or 'bottom-up'.

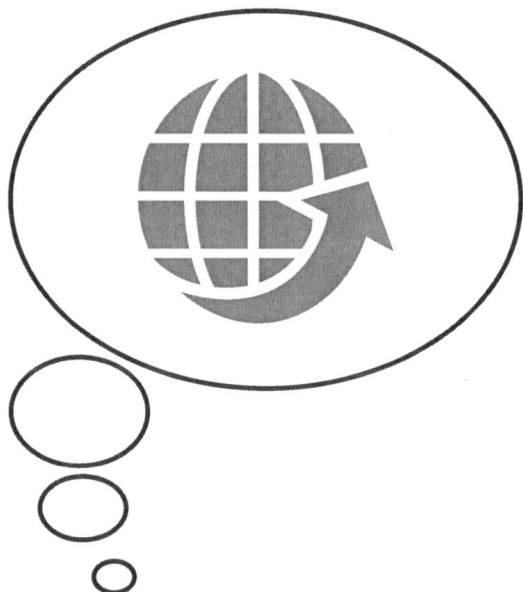

Top-down means that the manager focuses on economic and industry trends rather than the prospects of particular companies. So, a top down investment manager might decide that investment needs to be concentrated on growing economies like China, and with its growing middle class perhaps invest in luxury goods companies selling into the Chinese market.

In contrast, **bottom-up** means that the analysis of a company's financial statements, strategy and management is the priority. This might involve looking at the company's net assets, future profitability and cash flow to decide whether that company is likely to do better than its peers.

Included in the bottom-up approach is a range of investment styles:

- **Growth investing** – picking the shares of companies that are most likely to grow in the medium and long term.

- **Value investing** – picking the shares of companies that are consider cheap, in other words that are under-valued relative to their present profits or cash-flows.
- **Momentum investing** – picking those shares where the price is rising, on the assumption that this will continue.
- **Contrarian investing** – picking the shares that are out of favour and may have value the rest of the market may not have spotted.

There is also a significant range of styles used by managers of hedge funds. Hedge funds will be considered later in this chapter.

1.2.2 Passive Management

In contrast to active management that seeks to out-perform a benchmark index, passive management is seen in funds where the aim is perform in line with, or 'track' the benchmark index. As a result, passively managed funds are often described as index-tracker funds. Index-tracking, or indexation, involves constructing a portfolio in such a way that it will track, or mimic, the performance of an index, such as the FTSE 100.

The rationale of passive, index tracking funds is that relatively few active fund managers actually outperform their benchmarks. Investors in most actively managed funds would have been better off simply investing in the index, because the index actually performed better than the active fund manager's stock selections.

Passive fund management recognises this phenomenon by constructing a portfolio which simply replicates the index itself. It simply buys the index constituents which means that the performance of the portfolio is designed to 'track' the up-and-down movements of the index. The fund's charges will typically be significantly lower than actively managed funds.

No attempt is made to forecast future events and, once set up, passive portfolios are generally less expensive to run than active portfolios. This is because the ratio of staff to funds managed is lower than for actively managed portfolios and the turnover of the portfolio is lower, leading to lower dealing costs.

Passive management does have certain disadvantages such as:

- Performance is impacted by the need to rebalance the portfolio to replicate changes in the index constituent weightings and to adjust for stocks being promoted into – and being relegated from – the index. This can lead to tracking error when the performance does not match that of the underlying index.
- Most indices reflect the effect of the value of dividends from constituent equities on the ex-dividend date.
- A passively managed Index-based portfolio will clearly follow the index down in bear markets.

1.2.3 Combining Active and Passive Management

Active and passive management are not mutually exclusives. Some funds employ both styles, known as **core-satellite management**.

This is achieved by putting a large proportion of a portfolio into index tracking passive funds, say, 70% to 80% of the portfolio's value (the 'core'), so as to minimise the risk of underperformance, and then fine tuning this by investing the remainder in a number of specialist actively managed funds or individual securities. This is the 'satellite' element of the fund.

1.3 Range of Funds Available

With almost 2,500 UK-domiciled authorised investment funds available to investors, it is not surprising that a method of classifying them is needed in order to allow investors to compare funds with similar objectives.

The **IA** trade body maintains a system for classifying certain funds and a similar role is occupied by the **Association of Investment Companies (AIC)** for certain investment companies.

The IA's classification system contains over 30 sectors grouping similar funds together. Most sectors are broadly categorised between those designed to provide 'income' and those designed to provide 'growth'. Those funds that do not fall easily under these two headings are in a third category entitled 'specialist funds'.

Each of the sectors is made up of funds investing in similar asset categories, in the same stock market or in the same geographical region. So, for example, under the heading of funds principally targeting income includes sectors for UK gilts, UK corporate bonds and global bonds.

Clearly, the classification of funds into sectors is targeted at the needs of the investor, to enable the comparison of funds on a like-for-like basis. Each sector provides groups of similar funds whose performance can be fairly compared by an investor and their adviser.

An example of how the IA sectors work can be seen on the following page.

1.4 Regulation of Funds

The investment industry has many regulations that are designed to protect investors, and some of these regulations govern where and how a fund manager can invest and the documentation an investor can expect to receive.

The regulatory regime for UK funds is heavily influenced by EU directives that have been

Example

A useful example of how the IA sectors work can be seen by looking at bond funds and how the content of each differs.

UK Gilts	Funds which invest at least 95% of their assets in sterling-denominated (or hedged back to sterling) government-backed securities, with a rating the same as or higher than that of the UK, with at least 80% invested in UK government securities (gilts).
UK Index Linked Gilts	Funds which invest at least 95% of their assets in sterling-denominated (or hedged back to sterling) government-backed index-linked securities, with a rating the same as or higher than that of the UK, with at least 80% invested in UK index-linked gilts.
£ Corporate Bonds	Funds which invest at least 80% of their assets in sterling-denominated (or hedged back to sterling), triple BBB-minus or above corporate bond securities (as measured by Standard & Poor's or an equivalent external rating agency). This excludes convertibles, preference shares and permanent interest-bearing shares (PIBS).
£ Strategic Bond	Funds which invest at least 80% of their assets in sterling-denominated (or hedged back to sterling) fixed interest securities. This excludes convertibles, preference shares and permanent interest-bearing shares PIBS. At any point in time, the asset allocation of these funds could theoretically place the fund in one of the other fixed interest sectors. The funds will remain in this sector on these occasions since it is the manager's stated intention to retain the right to invest across the sterling fixed-interest credit risk spectrum.
£ High Yield	Funds which invest at least 80% of their assets in sterling-denominated (or hedged back to sterling) fixed interest securities and at least 50% of their assets in below BBB-minus fixed-interest securities (as measured by Standard & Poor's or an equivalent external rating agency), excluding convertibles, preference shares and PIBs.
Global Bonds	Funds which invest at least 80% of their assets in fixed-interest securities. All funds which contain more than 80% fixed-interest investments are to be classified under this heading regardless of the fact that they may have more than 80% in a particular geographic sector, unless that geographic area is the UK, when the fund should be classified under the relevant UK (sterling) heading.

issued in order to promote a single market in investment funds. In the UK, these are implemented by the FCA through its Collective Investment Schemes Sourcebook (COLL) and Investment Funds Sourcebook (FUND).

1.4.1 Authorised versus Unauthorised Funds

In the UK, some collective investment schemes are authorised, while others are unauthorised. Authorisation is granted by the FCA. Broadly, the FCA will only authorise those schemes that are sufficiently diversified and which invest in a range of permitted assets.

It is only authorised collective investment schemes that can be freely marketed to the general public in the UK.

Collective investment schemes that have not been authorised by the FCA cannot be marketed to the general public. These unauthorised schemes are perfectly legal, but their marketing is subject to certain restrictions which mean that the funds can only be marketed to certain types of investor such as investment professionals or sophisticated investors. Unauthorised schemes are referred to as unauthorised collective investment schemes (UCIS).

2. Unit Trusts

2.1 Introduction

A unit trust is a particular form of collective investment scheme. As its name suggests, a unit trust is established as a trust and the investors buy units in the fund. In basic terms, a trust is a particular type of entity that is often used to hold assets such as investments on behalf of another person, or group of persons. The persons who receive the benefit of the trust are known as the beneficiaries and trusts appoint one or more trustees as the legal owner of the investments, holding those investments for the benefit of the beneficiaries.

So, in a unit trust, the trustee is the legal owner of the underlying assets and the unit holders are the beneficial owners. Each unit trust may be authorised and marketable to retail investors, or unauthorised and restricted in the way it is marketed. Remember that a UK collective investment scheme such as a unit trust must be authorised by the FCA before it can be offered to the general public.

Investors pay money into the trust in exchange for units. The more people invest, the bigger the trust will grow. Unit trusts are often described as open-ended collective investment schemes because each trust can grow as more investors buy into the fund, or shrink as investors sell units back to the fund and they are cancelled.

The investors' money is invested in a diversified portfolio of assets, usually consisting of shares or bonds or a mix of the two. If the diversified portfolio increases in value, the value of the units will increase. Of course, there is a possibility that the portfolio might fall in value, in which case the units will decrease in value.

The unit trust industry started in 1931, when M&G launched the first unit trust. Today the industry manages £3 trillion in over 2,000 funds across over 30 different investment sectors.

2.2 The Function of a Unit Trust Manager

Each unit trust has a **unit trust manager** who will decide, within the rules of the trust and the various regulations, which investments are included within the unit trust to meet its investment objectives. This will include deciding what to buy and when to buy it, as well as what to sell and when to sell it. The unit trust manager may (and commonly does) outsource this decision-making to a separate investment management company.

UK Funds Under Management (2003–2013)

£m

850,000	
750,000	
650,000	
550,000	
450,000	
350,000	
250,000	
150,000	
50,000	
0	

2004   2005   2006   2007   2008   2009   2010   2011   2012   2013

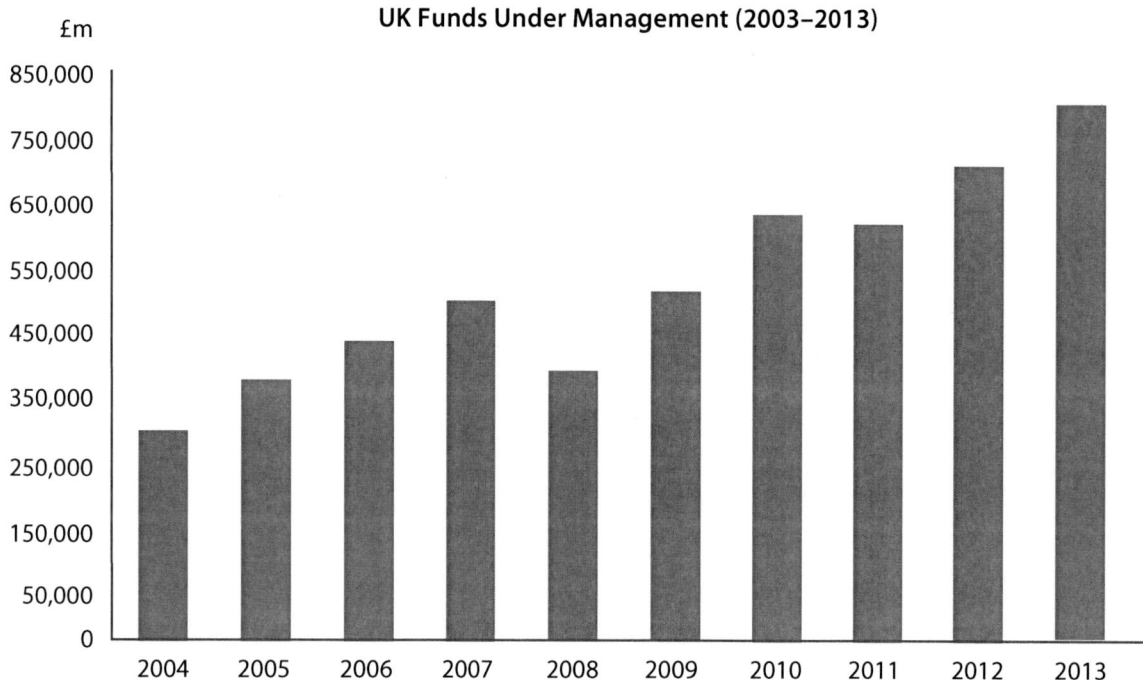

Source: Investment Association (IA)

In summary, the unit trust manager is responsible for a number of functions including the following:

- The day-to-day management of the trust fund, which will involve either deciding which investments to buy and sell in the financial markets or delegating day-to-day investment decisions to separate fund managers.
- Offering the units for sale, including valuing and fixing the price of the units. The valuation is always based on the underlying value of the investments, so if the investments were worth £1 million in total, and there were 1 million units in issue, each unit would be priced at £1. This is known as the **net asset value** or just the NAV.
- Purchasing units back from those unit holders that choose to sell. The price at which the units will be purchased (the bid price) is always lower than the price at which units will be sold to investors (the offer price). The difference between the

two prices is referred to as the spread, and is generally around 5-7%, however unit trusts are permitted to widen this gap to more than 10% if they wish to.

2.3 The Trustee

Every unit trust must also appoint a **trustee**. The trustee is the legal owner of the assets in the trust, holding the assets for the benefit of the underlying unit holders. The trustee has an important policing role, ensuring that the manager complies with the terms of the legal document that created the trust, the 'trust deed'.

So, the trustee has the responsibility of overseeing the unit trust. This will typically include:

- Holding and controlling the trust assets (the portfolio of investments).
- Collecting and distributing income from trust assets.

- Issuing unit certificates to unit trust investors.
- Approving any advertisements and marketing material.

In most cases, the role of the trustee will be carried out by either a bank, or an insurance company. These trustees are organisations that the unit holders can 'trust' with their assets because they are heavily regulated financial institutions.

3. Investment Companies with Variable Capital (ICVCs)/Open-Ended Investment Companies (OEICs)

A more modern equivalent of unit trusts are **Investment Companies with Variable Capital (ICVC)** (or **Open-Ended Investment Companies (OEICs)**). The terms ICVC and OEIC are used interchangeably within the UK finance industry.

An ICVC commonly found in Western Europe is the **Société d'Investissement à Capital Variable (SICAV)**. Like a UK OEIC, it is an investment company with variable capital. SICAVs are typically set up in Luxembourg by asset management firms so that they can be distributed to investors across Europe or further afield.

An ICVC is a form of authorised collective investment scheme, but in contrast to a unit trust, an ICVC is a collective investment scheme structured as a company, with the investors holding shares. The ICVC invests shareholders' money in a diversified pool of investments and has the ability to issue more shares or redeem shares as demanded by investors.

Although ICVCs are companies, they differ from conventional companies because they are established under special legislation that enable them to create new shares and redeem existing ones according to investor demand, unlike ordinary companies. This means they are open-ended in nature, in the same way as unit trusts.

When an ICVC is set up, it is a requirement that an **authorised corporate director (ACD)** and a depository are appointed. The ACD is responsible for the day-to-day management of the fund, including managing the investments, valuing and pricing the fund and dealing with investors. It may undertake these activities itself or delegate them to suitable third parties. Effectively, the ACD is the ICVC equivalent of the unit trust manager of an authorised unit trust (AUT).

The ICVC's investments are held by an independent depository, responsible for looking after the investments on behalf of the ICVC shareholders and overseeing the activities of the ACD. The depository occupies a similar role to that of the trustee of an authorised unit trust and is subject to similar regulatory requirements.

The register of shareholders is maintained by the ACD.

3.1 Property Authorised Investment Funds (PAIFs)

A Property Authorised Investment Fund (PAIF) is an authorised investment fund whose investment portfolio comprises predominantly real property or shares in UK real estate investment trusts and certain other similar entities. A fund has to elect to be treated under the PAIF regime and meet certain conditions before it will be treated as such by HMRC, including deriving at least 60% of its net income from property income business.

Investors are taxed in a similar way to those that invest directly in the underlying assets.

The rules surrounding PAIFs require property income received within the fund to be identified separately from other income. Other income will arise in the fund, such as interest on funds held pending investment or dividends on property company investments. This means that the fund's total income will fall into one of the following three pools:

- Property income including from UK REITS and foreign equivalents.
- Other taxable income which is primarily interest and non-UK dividends.
- UK dividend income.

The fund must make distributions to investors in a way that enables the investor to identify the amount attributable to the different types of income, and to pay tax on them accordingly. Therefore, investors will receive three different types of income and statements issued to investors should make a clear distinction between the three types.

4. Pricing, Dealing and Settlement

4.1 Pricing and Charges

The prices at which authorised unit trusts and ICVCs are bought and sold are based on the value of the fund's underlying investments – the net asset value or NAV. The authorised fund manager is, however, given certain flexibility in relation to the prices quoted to investors.

Unit trusts are traditionally dual-priced. Investors are quoted a higher offer price at which they can buy units and a lower bid price at which they can sell their units back to the manager. The difference between the two prices is known as the spread. So, for an investor to make a positive return on her investment the bid price must rise above the offer price before she sells the units.

An ICVC is single-priced and directly linked to the value of the fund's underlying investments. All shares are bought and sold at this single price, so there is no need to calculate the spread. The ICVC has been described as a 'what you see is what you get product'.

Although authorised unit trusts traditionally used **dual pricing** and ICVCs use **single pricing**, all funds now have a choice of which pricing methodology they use; whichever is chosen must be disclosed in the fund's prospectus.

When a fund is single-priced, it is important to note that an initial charge will still be charged but will be separately identified. Indeed single pricing can and generally does involve the investors paying more than the single price when they buy, due to the addition of an initial charge. Single pricing can also result in the investors getting less than the single price when they sell, because the manager can deduct a separate charge known as the **dilution levy** to make sure dealing expense are recouped. Essentially, single pricing is much more transparent about how the buying and selling prices are arrived at. Dual-pricing lacks the same transparency because it disguises the charges within the spread.

The prices of most individual funds are provided in broadsheet newspapers each day. The telephone numbers and addresses of the fund managers are normally provided alongside the prices.

4.2 Dealing and Settlement

Whether an investor wants to buy or sell units in a unit trust or shares in an ICVC, they will be either bought from, or sold back to, the authorised fund manager. There is no active secondary market in units or shares, except between the investors (or their advisers/ intermediaries) and the fund manager. The key point to note, therefore, is that units in authorised unit trusts and shares in ICVCs are bought from the managers themselves and not via a stock market.

Investors can buy or sell units in unit trusts or shares in ICVCs in a number of ways:

- direct with the fund manager (either by telephone, via the internet or by post), or
- via their broker or financial adviser, or
- through a fund supermarket or platform.

A **fund supermarket** or **platform** is an organisation that specialises in offering investors easy access to a range of unit trusts and ICVCs from different providers. They are usually based around an internet platform which takes the investor's order and processes it on their behalf, usually at reduced, or nil, commission rates. They offer online dealing, valuations, portfolio planning tools and access to key features documents and illustrations. Investors can look at their various holdings in different funds in one place, analyse their performance and easily make switches from one fund to another.

Settlement currently takes place directly with each fund group. For **purchases**, once the investment has been made and the amount invested has been received, the fund group will record ownership of the relevant number of units or shares in the fund's share register. When the investor decides to sell, he/she need to instruct the fund manager (or ask his/her adviser or the supermarket to instruct the fund manager), who then has four days from receipt of the instruction and necessary paperwork in which to settle the sale and remit the proceeds to the investor. Traditionally, this instruction had to be in writing, but since 2009 managers, supermarkets or advisers have been able to accept instruction via the internet or over the telephone, using appropriate security checks.

5. Investment Trusts

Despite its name, an investment trust is actually a company, not a trust. It is a **listed company** and, like other companies it has directors and shareholders.

However, like unit trusts and ICVCs, an investment trust invests in a diversified portfolio of investments, allowing its shareholders to diversify and lessen their risk.

When a new investment company is established and launched, it issues **shares** to new investors. Unlike an authorised unit trust or ICVC, the number of shares is likely to remain fixed for many years. As a result, these investment companies are **closed-ended**, in contrast with authorised unit trusts and ICVCs which are open-ended.

The cash from the issue of shares will be invested in a number of other investments, mainly the shares of other companies. If the value of the investments grows, then the value of the investment trust company's shares should rise too.

5.1 Real Estate Investment Trusts (REITs)

REITs are investment companies that pool investors' funds to invest in commercial and, possibly, residential property. They became available to UK investors from January 2007 and the main quoted property companies, such as Land Securities and British Land, have converted to REIT status.

One of the main features of REITs is that they provide access to property returns without the previous disadvantage of double taxation. Prior to the introduction of REITs, when an investor held property company shares, not only would the company pay corporation tax, but the investor would be liable to income tax on any dividends and capital gains tax on any growth.

Under the rules, a REIT pays no tax on property income or capital gains on property disposals, providing that at least 90% of that income (after expenses) is distributed to shareholders. These property income distributions are then taxed in the hands of the investor as if they had received that income directly themselves (ie, it is not taxed as a dividend).

REITs may also be held in both individual savings accounts (ISAs) and self-invested personal pension schemes (SIPPs).

REITs give investors access to professional property investment and provide new opportunities, such as the ability to invest in commercial property. This allows investors to diversify the risk of holding direct property investments. This type of investment trust company also removes a further risk from holding direct property, namely liquidity risk or the risk that the investment will not be able to be readily realised.

REITs are **closed-ended**; like other investment trusts, they are quoted on the LSE and other trading venues and dealt in the same way.

Some major REITs listed in the UK	
Big Yellow	Self storage
British Land	Diversified
Derwent London	Offices
Hammerson	Retail, offices
Highcroft Investments	Diversified
Land Securities	Diversified
McKay Securities	Offices
Primary Health Properties	Health care
SEGRO	Industrial
Shaftesbury	Retail
Workspace Group	Offices, Industrial

Source: REITA.org

5.2 Gearing

In contrast with ICVCs and authorised unit trusts, investment companies are allowed to borrow money on a long-term basis by taking out bank loans and/or issuing bonds. This can enable them to invest the borrowed money in more stocks and shares – a process known as 'gearing'. This approach can improve returns when markets are rising, but when markets are falling it can exacerbate losses. As a result, the greater the level of gearing used by an investment trust, the greater will be the risk.

Below are some key statistics drawn from XYZ Investment Trust showing that it has borrowed money on a long term basis. At the time, it had gross gearing of 111% (ignoring the fact that the fund also held some cash that could be used to repay some of the borrowing) and net gearing of 108% (assuming the cash is used to reduce the borrowing).

Financial make-up	
Total assets (£m):	248.4
Market capital (£m):	204.5
Number of shares:	154,643,542
Gross gearing:	111
Net gearing:	108

5.3 Pricing, Discounts and Premiums

The price of a share (except in the case of an ICVC share, where the price is based on the net asset value) is what someone is prepared to pay for it. The price of an investment trust share is no different.

The share price of an investment trust is thus arrived at in a very different way from the unit price of an authorised unit trust or the share price of an ICVC.

Remember that units in an authorised unit trust are bought and sold by its fund manager at a price that is based on the underlying value of the constituent investments. Similarly, shares in an ICVC are bought and sold by the ACD, at the value of the underlying investments.

The share price of an investment trust, however, is not necessarily the same as the value of the underlying investments. The value of the underlying investments determined on a per share basis is referred to as the **net asset value** and, because the share price is driven by supply and demand factors, it may be above or below the net asset value.

When the investment trust share price is **above the net asset value**, it is said to be trading at a premium. This is illustrated in the following example.

Example

Investment Trusts Trading at a Premium

ABC Investment Trust shares are trading at £2.30. The net asset value per share is £2.00. ABC Investment Trust shares are trading at a premium. The premium is 15% of the underlying net asset value.

At the end of 2010, Fidelity China Special Situations Trust was standing at a premium to its net asset value in response to demand for the shares. Its net asset value was 112.7p per share, but it was trading at 119.5p – a premium of 6.1%.

In contrast, when the investment trust share price is **below the net asset value**, it is said to be trading at a discount. This is illustrated in the following example.

Example

Investment Trusts Trading at a Discount

XYZ Investment Trust shares are trading at 95p. The net asset value per share is £1.00. XYZ Investment Trust shares are trading at a discount. The discount is 5% of the underlying net asset value.

Investment trust company shares generally trade at a discount to their net asset value and the extent of the discount is calculated daily and shown in the business pages of most newspapers.

A number of factors contribute to the extent of the discount and it will vary across different investment companies. The discount tends to be a function of the market's view of the quality of the management of the investment portfolio, and its choice of underlying investments.

Some investment trusts have a predetermined date at which they will be wound up, with all the investments sold and the cash distributed to the shareholders. A smaller discount tends to be displayed when investment trusts are nearing their winding-up, or where the investment trust is subject to a takeover bid by another company.

5.4 Trading in Investment Trust Shares

In the same way as other listed company shares, shares in investment trust companies are bought and sold on the LSE using the Stock Exchange Electronic Trading Service (SETS) trading system.

6. Exchange-Traded Funds (ETFs)

An ETF is an investment fund usually designed to track a particular index. This is typically a stock market index, such as the FTSE 100.

ETFs are similar to investment trusts in that the investor buys shares in the ETF that are quoted on the stock exchange. However, unlike investment trusts, ETFs are **open-ended funds**.

This means that, like ICVCs, the fund will get bigger as more people invest and smaller as people withdraw their money.

ETFs use passive investment management which is a method of managing an investment portfolio that seeks to match the performance of a broad-based market index. Its investment style is described as passive because portfolio managers do not make decisions about which securities to buy and sell; instead, they invest in the same securities that make up an index. It therefore seeks to hold a portfolio that mirrors the index it is tracking and undertakes trading only to ensure that the portfolio's performance is in line with the index.

Most index tracker funds are based on market capitalisation-weighted indices, such as the FTSE 100 or S&P 500, where the largest stocks in the index by market value have the biggest influence on the index's value. The fund will seek to track the index using either physical or synthetic replication.

Physical replication is the traditional form of index replication and is the one favoured by the largest and long-established ETF providers. It employs one of three established tracking methods:

1. **Full replication** – this method requires each constituent of the index being tracked to be held in accordance with its index weighting. Although full replication is accurate, it is also the most expensive of the three methods and so is only really suitable for large portfolios.
2. **Stratified sampling** – this method requires a representative sample of securities from each sector of the index to be held. Although this method is less expensive, the lack of statistical analysis renders it subjective and potentially encourages biases towards those stocks with the best perceived prospects.
3. **Optimisation** – this method costs less than fully replicating the index tracked, but is statistically more complex. Optimisation uses a sophisticated computer modelling technique to find a representative sample of those securities which mimic the broad characteristics of the index tracked.

Synthetic replication involves the fund manager entering into a swap (an OTC derivative) with a market counterparty to exchange the returns on the index for a payment. The advantage of this approach is that responsibility for tracking the index performance is passed on to the swap provider and costs are substantially lower. The downside is that the investor is exposed to counterparty risk, namely that the swap provider fails to meet their obligations.

ETF shares may trade at a premium or discount to the underlying investments, but the difference is usually minimal and the ETF share price essentially reflects the value of the investments in the fund. The investor's return is in the form of dividends paid by the ETF and the possibility of a capital gain (or loss) on sale.

In London, ETFs are traded on the London Stock Exchange, which has established a special subset of the Exchange for ETFs, called extraMARK. Shares in ETFs are bought and sold via stockbrokers and exhibit the following charges:

- There is a spread between the price at which investors buy the shares and the price at which they can sell them. This is usually very small, for example, just 0.1 or 0.2% for, say, an ETF tracking the FTSE 100.

- An annual management charge is deducted from the fund. Typically, this is 0.5% or less.
- The investors pay stockbroker's commission when they buy and sell. However, unlike other shares, there is no stamp duty to pay on purchases.

7. Summary: Comparison Between Investment Funds

The following table summarises the main points about each type of collective investment scheme that has been encountered in the chapter so far.

	Authorised Unit Trusts	ICVCs	Investment Trusts/REITs	Exchange-Traded Funds	Key Points
Legal Structure	Trust	Company	Company	Company	Despite the name 'investment trust', only unit trusts are truly structured as a trust.
Management	Authorised Manager (company)	Authorised Corporate Director (company)	Board of Directors	Management Company	The companies that act as manager tend to be investment management companies.
Supervision	Trustee	Depository	Board of Directors	Depository	Supervision for open-ended companies (ICVCs and ETFs) is provided by a depository.
Regulation	FCA	FCA	UK Listing Authority	FCA and UK Listing Authority	In order to be listed on the exchange, companies have to satisfy the UK Listing Authority.
Open- or closed-ended	Open	Open	Closed	Open	Only investment trust companies are closed-ended.
Pricing	Single- or dual-priced	Single- or dual-priced	Dependent on demand and supply	Largely based on net asset value	It is only investment trust companies where the price can exhibit a substantial discount or premium to NAV.
Trading	Authorised Manager	Authorised Corporate Director	Stock Market	Stock Market	Trading for unit trusts and ICVCs is with the investment manager, not on the stock market.
Settlement	Authorised Manager	Authorised Corporate Director	CREST	CREST	Stock market-traded funds are settled via CREST.

8. Hedge Funds

Hedge funds are generally unauthorised funds that cannot be marketed to retail investors. This is because there are few restrictions as to what they do with their investors' money to provide them with a return. It is not unusual for hedge funds to be heavily invested in derivatives, or to create a portfolio that is not well diversified. As a result of this, hedge funds are reputed to be high-risk. However, in some cases this perception stands at odds with reality. There are many different styles of hedge fund – some risk-averse, and some employing highly risky strategies.

One of the most obvious risks faced by investors in equities is market risk – as the broad market moves down, the investor's shares also fall in value. Traditional **absolute return** hedge funds attempt to profit regardless of the general movements of the market, by carefully selecting a combination of asset classes, including derivatives, and by holding both long positions and short positions. A long position is owning an asset, such as shares. In contrast, a short position is selling an asset that the fund does not own, in the hope of buying them asset more cheaply if the market falls.

Some of the common aspects of hedge funds are as follows:

- **High investment entry levels** – many hedge funds have high minimum initial investment levels, meaning that access is effectively restricted to wealthy investors and institutions like pension funds and insurance companies. Most hedge funds require minimum investments in excess of £50,000; some exceed £1 million. However, investors can also gain access to hedge funds through **funds of hedge funds** which can involve lower minimum investment levels.
- **Structure** – as mentioned above, most hedge funds are established as unauthorised, and therefore unregulated, collective investment schemes, meaning that they cannot be generally marketed to private individuals because they are considered too risky for the less financially sophisticated investor.
- **Investment flexibility** – subject to complying with the restrictions in their constitutional documents, the lack of regulation means that hedge funds are able to invest in whatever assets they wish. In addition to being able to take long and short positions in securities such as shares and bonds, some take positions in commodities and currencies. As seen, the investment style is generally aimed at producing 'absolute returns' – positive returns regardless of the general direction of market movements.
- **Gearing** – many hedge funds can borrow funds and use derivatives to potentially enhance their returns.
- **Prime broker** – hedge funds buy and sell investments from, borrow from and, often, entrust the safekeeping of their assets to one main wholesale broker, called their prime broker. The prime broker is commonly one of the large investment banks.
- **Liquidity** – to maximise the hedge fund manager's investment freedom, hedge funds usually impose 'lock-in' periods that prevent the investors cashing in on their investments for a minimum of say, three months.
- **Cost** – hedge funds typically charge performance-related fees which the investor pays if certain performance levels are achieved over and above the annual management fees that are comparable to the fees charged by other CISs, like unit trusts and ICVCs. These performance fees can be substantial, with 20% of the performance above certain levels (often termed 'net new highs' or the 'high water mark') being common.

9. Private Equity

Private equity is medium- to long-term finance, provided in return for an equity stake in potentially high-growth companies. It can take many forms, from providing venture capital to complete buyouts.

For a firm, attracting private equity investment is very different from raising a loan from a lender. Private equity is invested in exchange for a stake in a company and the investors' returns are dependent on the growth and profitability of the business. It, therefore, faces the risk of failure, just like the other shareholders.

The private equity firm is rewarded by the company's success, generally achieving its principal return through realising a capital gain on exit. This may involve:

- the private equity firm selling its shares back to the management of the investee company
- the private equity firm selling the shares to another investor, such as another private equity firm
- a trade sale, which is the sale of company shares to another firm
- the company achieving a stock market listing.

Private equity firms raise their capital from a variety of sources but mainly from large investing institutions. These may be happy to entrust their money to the private equity firm because of its expertise in finding businesses with good potential.

Few people or institutions can afford the risk of investing directly in individual buy-outs and, instead, use investment vehicles to achieve a diversification of risk. Traditionally this was through investment trusts, such as 3i or Electra Private Equity. With the increasing amount of funds being raised for this asset class, however, methods of raising investment have moved on. Private equity arrangements are now usually structured in different ways to more retail collective investment schemes. They are usually set up as limited partnerships, with high minimum investment levels. As with hedge funds, there are generally restrictions on when an investor can realise their investment.

9.1 Tax-Advantaged Investments

Private equity is typically used to refer to the provision of venture capital and management buyouts and buy-ins. There are a number of ways of investing in such companies, ranging from business angels to investing through tax-advantaged investment funds. The latter have to meet strict criteria to be able to offer tax advantages to investors. Some types of tax-advantaged investments are covered in the table below.

Venture Capital Trusts (VCTs)	VCTs are quoted vehicles that aim to encourage investment in smaller unlisted UK companies and companies listed on AIM by offering private investors tax incentives in return for a five-year investment commitment.
Enterprise Investment Schemes (EISs)	The EIS was set up by the government to encourage private investors or 'business angels' to invest in certain types of smaller unquoted UK companies through tax incentives on their investments, providing that the company meets certain criteria.
Seed Enterprise Investment Schemes (SEISs)	The SEIS, a tax-advantaged venture capital scheme similar to the EIS, is focused on smaller, early-stage companies carrying on, or preparing to carry on, a new business in a qualifying trade.
Social Investment Tax Relief	Social investment tax relief is the government's tax relief for social investment which encourages individuals to support social enterprises and helps them access new sources of finance.

Learning Objectives

Chapter Nine has covered the following Learning Objectives:

7.1.1   Understand the benefits of collective investment

7.1.2   Know the difference between active and passive management

7.1.3   Know the types of funds and how they are classified

7.2.1   Know the definition and legal structure of a unit trust

7.2.2   Know the roles of the manager and the trustee

7.3.1   Know the definition and legal structure of an ICVC/SICAV

7.3.2   Know the roles of the authorised corporate director and the depository

7.3.3   Know the characteristics of Property Authorised Investment Funds (PAIFs)

7.4.1   Know how unit trust units and ICVC shares are priced

7.4.2   Know how shares and units are bought and sold

7.4.3   Know how collectives are settled

7.5.1   Know the characteristics of an investment trust: gearing; real estate investment trusts (REITs)

7.5.2   Understand the factors that affect the price of an investment trust

7.5.3   Know the meaning of the discounts and premiums in relation to investment trusts

7.5.4   Know how investment trust shares are traded

7.6.1   Know the main characteristics of exchange-traded funds: trading; replication methods

7.7.1   Know the basic characteristics of hedge funds: risks; cost and liquidity; investment strategies

7.7.2   Know the basic characteristics of private equity: risks; cost and liquidity

7.8.1   Know the types of tax-advantaged investments, including: Venture Capital Trust (VCT); Enterprise Investment Scheme (EIS); Seed Enterprise Investment Scheme (SEIS); Social Investment Tax Relief

Based on what you have learned in Chapter Nine, try to answer the following end of chapter questions.

End of Chapter Questions

Think of an answer for each question and refer to the appropriate section for confirmation.

1. Give two alternative terms for investment management and detail which 'side' of the financial services industry the investment manager sits on.

    Answer Reference: Section 1

    ....

    ....

2. Give at least three benefits of pooling investment into a collective investment scheme.

    Answer Reference: Section 1.1

    ....

    ....

3. What are the two major investment styles adopted by investment managers?

    Answer Reference: Section 1.2

    ....

    ....

4. Active investment management usually uses one of two approaches. What are they?

    Answer Reference: Section 1.2.1

    ....

    ....

5. A portfolio managed in a way that combines both active and passive is commonly described as what?

    Answer Reference: Section 1.2.3

    ....

    ....

6. What are the trade bodies that represent investment managers and investment companies?
   Answer Reference: Section 1.3

   ....

   ....

7. How does an authorised fund differ from an unauthorised fund?
   Answer Reference: Section 1.4.1

   ....

   ....

8. A unit trust is what form of entity and what do investors purchase?
   Answer Reference: Section 2

   ....

   ....

9. What are the respective roles of a unit trust manager and trustee?
   Answer Reference: Sections 2.2, 2.3

   ....

   ....

10. What is an ICVC?
    Answer Reference: Section 3

    ....

    ....

11. What are the equivalents to the unit trust manager and trustee in an ICVC?
    Answer Reference: Section 3

    ....

    ....

12. ICVCs and unit trusts are generally priced on what basis?

Answer Reference: Section 4.1

....

....

13. If an investor wants to buy or sell units/shares in an existing unit trust/ICVC, with whom do they do the trade?

Answer Reference: Section 4.2

....

....

14. An investment trust is what form of entity and what do investors purchase?

Answer Reference: Section 5

....

....

15. What particular problem is removed if an investor buys shares in a REIT rather than in a conventional property company?

Answer Reference: Section 5.1

....

....

16. Can an investment trust 'gear up'?

Answer Reference: Section 5.2

....

....

17. How is it described if an investment trust's shares are trading above their net asset value?

    Answer Reference: Section 5.3

    ....

    ....

18. What is an ETF, what form of entity is it, and what do investors purchase?

    Answer Reference: Section 6

    ....

    ....

19. Are hedge funds generally authorised or unauthorised?

    Answer Reference: Section 8

    ....

    ....

20. What is 'absolute return' in the context of hedge funds?

    Answer Reference: Section 8

    ....

    ....

21. What is a prime broker?

    Answer Reference: Section 8

    ....

    ....

22. What are the usual forms of fees paid to a hedge fund manager?

Answer Reference: Section 8

....

....

Chapter Ten

Financial Services Regulation and Professional Integrity

10

1. Financial Services Regulation

1.1 The Need for Regulation

The financial services industry is all about money and investment, and things can go wrong. The risk of losing money due to sharp practice or just poor decisions in a financial transaction has meant that financial services have always needed rules and regulations to protect investors and the general public.

As markets developed, market participants began to set rules so that there were agreed standards of behaviour, and to provide a mechanism so that disputes could be settled readily. This is known as **self-regulation**, when, for example, a stock exchange would set rules for its members and police their implementation, as well as providing a secondary market for shares.

As markets, financial institutions and financial services developed further, and the potential impact that they could have on both the economy and society grew, self-regulation became increasingly untenable, and most countries moved to a statutory approach – formalising rules in law – and established their own **regulatory bodies**.

A comment by the head of the then UK regulator (the Financial Services Authority (FSA)) in 2005 captured this succinctly: *Regulation exists because of the potential economic and social effects of major financial instability, the desirability of maintaining markets which are efficient, orderly and fair and the need to protect retail consumers in their dealings with the financial services industry.*

The development of global markets and a series of crises such as the collapses of Barings Bank, Enron and WorldCom, emphasised not only the need for improved regulation and standards, but for **international co-operation** to develop a common approach in a whole range of areas. This was further exacerbated in 2008 as the global community battled against the effects of the financial crisis.

This increasing globalisation of financial markets means there is a demand from governments and investment firms for a common approach to regulation in different countries. As a result, there is a significant level of co-operation between financial services regulators worldwide and, increasingly, common standards. Anti-money laundering rules are probably the best example of this, and these will be considered in detail later in this chapter.

The main purpose and aims of financial regulation are to:

- maintain and promote the fairness, efficiency, competitiveness, transparency and orderliness of markets
- promote understanding by the public of the operation and functioning of the financial services industry
- provide protection for members of the public investing in, or holding financial products
- minimise crime and misconduct in the industry
- reduce systemic risks, and
- assist in maintaining the market's financial stability by taking appropriate steps.

1.2 UK Regulation

In the UK, the financial services sector underwent a radical change on 1 December 2001 when the **Financial Services and Markets Act of 2000 (FSMA 2000)** came into force. Before FSMA 2000, UK regulation was covered by a hotch-potch of different laws, and enforcement was carried out by a number of statutory and self-regulating organisations. This was considered to be unnecessarily complex and confusing, and it was FSMA 2000 that simplified things.

Under FSMA 2000, the government delegated overall responsibility for the regulation of the financial services industry to the Financial Services Authority (FSA). In July 2009, HM Treasury published a consultation paper titled *Reforming Financial Markets* in a response to the causes of the financial crisis. It proposed a series of sweeping policy initiatives around a number of core issues, one of which is the need to strengthen the UK's regulatory framework so that it is better equipped to deal with all firms and, in particular, globally interconnected markets and firms.

On 1 April 2013, the government transferred operational responsibility for prudential regulation from the FSA to a new subsidiary of the Bank of England, the Prudential Regulation Authority (PRA), and responsibility for market conduct to a new organisation called the Financial Conduct Authority (FCA).

Financial Policy Committee (FPC)

A committee has been established in the Bank of England, with responsibility for 'macro-prudential' regulation, or regulation of the stability and resilience of the financial system as a whole. Its role is:

Contributing to the Bank's objective to protect and enhance financial stability, through identifying and taking action to remove or reduce systemic risks, with a view to protecting and enhancing the resilience of the UK financial system.

The FPC has the power to make recommendations on a comply-or-explain basis to the PRA and the FCA; that is, to comply with the recommendation as soon as practicable, or explain to the FPC, in writing and in public, why they have not done so.

Prudential Regulation Authority (PRA)

The Prudential Regulation Authority (PRA) is responsible for prudential regulation of financial firms that manage significant risks on their balance sheets – in other words, it is responsible for the regulation and supervision of 'significant' individual firms including all deposit-taking institutions, insurers and other prudentially significant investment firms.

The latter include the supervision of central counterparties and securities settlement systems, and this responsibility sits alongside the BoE's existing responsibilities for overseeing recognised payment systems.

The PRA has a primary objective of enhancing financial stability by promoting the safety and soundness of PRA-authorised firms in a way which minimises the disruption caused by any firms which do fail. In fulfilling its objective, it will take an intrusive approach to regulation and supervision.

The PRA is responsible for prudential supervision of those firms, but their day-to-day conduct is supervised by the FCA. As a result, they are referred to as dual-regulated firms.

Financial Conduct Authority (FCA)

The FCA is responsible for the conduct of all firms and the prudential regulation of firms not supervised by the PRA. The FCA focuses on the day-to-day regulation of all firms in retail and wholesale financial markets, as well as the infrastructure that supports these markets. It has responsibility for the prudential supervision of firms that do not fall under the PRA's scope (approximately 24,000 firms).

The FCA's role includes:

- supervision of investment exchanges and monitoring firms' compliance with the Market Abuse Directive (MAD)
- powers to investigate and prosecute insider dealing
- responsibility for overseeing the Financial Ombudsman Service (FOS), the Money Advice Service (MAS) and the Financial Services Compensation Scheme (FSCS), working closely with the FPC and PRA. Its role will also include:

Under FSMA as amended by the Financial Services Act 2012, the FCA is responsible for:

- regulating standards of conduct in retail and wholesale markets
- supervising trading infrastructures that support those markets
- the prudential supervision of firms that are not PRA-regulated, and
- the functions of the UK Listing Authority (UKLA).

Its three statutory objectives are to:

- protect consumers
- enhance the integrity of the UK financial system, and
- help maintain competitive markets and promote effective competition in the interests of consumers.

These are supported by a set of principles of good regulation which the FCA must have regard to when discharging its functions. HM Treasury is responsible for oversight of how the FCA conducts its operations, and so the FCA is accountable to Treasury ministers, and through them to Parliament.

1.3 Authorisation

FSMA makes it an offence for a firm to provide financial services in the UK without being authorised to do so. There are certain exemptions from this requirement, for example, the Bank of England.

Authorisation is granted by the relevant regulator. Solo-regulated firms need to be authorised by the FCA, but, following the establishment of the FCA and the PRA on 1 April 2013, some firms, known as dual-regulated firms, are regulated by the FCA for the way they conduct their business and by the PRA for prudential requirements.

10

The regulator(s) looks at each applicant firm and determines whether it is 'fit and proper' to provide financial services. By only allowing 'fit and proper' firms to be involved in the financial services industry, the regulator begins to satisfy the statutory objectives of enhancing the integrity of the financial system and of protecting consumers.

The regulators' assessment of fitness and properness includes determining whether the firm meets certain **threshold conditions**. Before granting authorisation, the regulator considers the quality of the company's management, its financial strength and the calibre of its staff. The latter is particularly important in certain key roles, which the regulator refers to as senior management functions or controlled functions.

This is because firms are ultimately operated by individuals – the directors and employees of that firm. Particular individuals, fulfilling the key roles that are 'controlled functions' have to be approved. An individual is only permitted to perform a controlled function after they have been granted **approved person** status by the regulator. The regulator will only grant approval if it is satisfied that the candidate is a fit and proper person to perform the controlled function applied for.

1.4 Senior Managers and Approved Persons

Authorised persons are firms but, as firms, they are ultimately operated by individuals – the directors and employees. When a firm applies for authorisation (and when there are changes to key staffing roles) the regulator will assess the calibre of these individuals.

Regulating the firm, and its key individuals, is essential to ensuring that firms act in an appropriate manner; equally, ensuring that each firm has well-trained and competent staff is a vital component in the quality of the investment and financial advice given to customers.

In response to the failings that became apparent during the financial crisis and a number of financial scandals, such as LIBOR and Payment Protection Insurance (PPI), there has been a significant change to the way in which senior managers in the industry are regulated. On 7 March 2016, the Senior Managers and Certification Regime (SM&CR) was introduced to increase the accountability of senior managers within banks and, hence, to address the widely held perception that regulators have, to date, been unable to hold such individuals effectively to account.

Initially, the regime applies only to banks, building societies, credit unions and dual-regulated investment firms; similar rules are also being introduced for insurers. Firms that are regulated by the FCA only, including the majority of investment advisers and asset management firms, will not be subject to the new rules until 2018.

1.4.1 Senior Managers and Certification Regime (SM&CR)

The SM&CR consists of three key elements:

1. The Senior Managers Regime (SMR) – arrangements for senior managers, including the identification of specific senior management responsibilities and their allocation to named individuals approved by the relevant regulator.
2. The Certification Regime – certification, by the firm, of other individuals who pose material risk or the risk of inflicting significant harm on the firm or to its clients.
3. The Conduct Rules and Code of Conduct – applies to all employees.

A fundamental purpose of the SM&CR is to enhance the accountability of individual senior managers. This is achieved by making a significant shift in the way in which senior management responsibilities are defined and assigned to individuals.

Seventeen senior management functions for UK firms have been identified. Individuals who will be performing any of these functions require approval by the relevant regulator which requires the individuals to satisfy both the firm and the regulators that they are fit and proper to undertake their roles. For each of these roles, the regulators have defined a set of management responsibilities and when the firm applies for approval for an individual carrying out a senior management function, it must also provide a statement of responsibilities which details exactly what the individual will be responsible for. In addition, firms are required to produce and maintain an up-to-date management responsibilities map that includes details of the reporting lines and the lines of responsibility, reasonable details about the persons who are part of those arrangements, and the responsibilities of those persons. The intent behind these requirements is that it will now be much easier for the regulators to satisfy themselves as to who is responsible for what in the case of failures.

The SMR applies only to the most senior staff in the firm. One of the significant changes under the new regime is that, while individual senior managers will continue to be approved by the regulator, individuals carrying out other defined roles will be certified by the firm, rather than being approved by the regulator. In general terms, these are individuals who pose a material risk to the firm or its clients. The firm is responsible for assessing the 'fitness and propriety' of the individual and this assessment must be carried out, not only at the outset of an individual taking on a role, but also on at least an annual basis.

Under the new regime, a much wider group of individuals will become subject to disciplinary action as a result of falling within the scope of the new Conduct Rules. The Conduct Rules apply to senior managers, staff within the Certification Regime and all other employees except ancillary staff. The Conduct Rules are divided into two tiers – a first tier applying to all individuals, and a second tier only applying to senior managers.

The regime places three obligations on firms with regard to the new Conduct Rules:

1. Make the individuals who are subject to the rules aware that this is the case, and train them in how the rules apply to them.
2. Notify the regulators when they are aware that, or suspect that, a person has breached the Conduct Rules.
3. Notify the regulators when they have taken formal disciplinary action against a person for any reason specified by the regulator.

1.4.2 Approved Persons Regime

Individuals fulfilling key roles within a firm known as controlled functions have to be approved. An individual may be permitted to perform a controlled function only after they have been granted approved person status by the regulator. It may grant an application only if it is satisfied that the candidate is a fit and proper person to perform the controlled function stated in the application form.

In assessing the fitness and propriety of a person, the regulator will look at a number of factors against three main criteria:

1. **Honesty, integrity and reputation** – the regulator will consider such issues as any criminal record or history of regulatory misconduct.
2. **Competence and capability to fulfil the role** – including achieving success in certain regulatory examinations.

3. **Financial soundness** – the regulator will consider the capital adequacy of the applicant and their financial history; for instance, an undischarged bankrupt would be unlikely to be approved for many roles.

Controlled functions are those involved in dealing with customers or their investments, key managers in a firm including finance, compliance and risk and those exercising a measure of control over the firm as a whole.

The FCA classifies controlled functions into groups, the first of which are **significant influence functions**. The significant influence functions are:

- **Governing functions** – for example, the directors of the firm.
- **Significant management functions** – senior managers in larger firms, such as the head of equity dealing.
- **Systems and control functions** – mainly those responsible for risk management and internal audit.
- **Required functions** – specific roles, such as the director or senior manager responsible for compliance oversight.

The next group comprises:

- **Customer functions** – for example, those individuals managing investments or providing advice to customers. Customer functions are not significant influence functions.

The final group relates to functions involved with setting benchmarks, such as the London Interbank Offered Rate (LIBOR).

1.5 Conduct Risk

Since the financial crisis, conduct risk has become a major area of attention by the FCA and the boards of financial services firms. There is no agreed definition for conduct risk but in simple terms it can be thought of as how to place integrity and trust at the heart of how firms behave and how customers and investors are treated. In essence, therefore, it refers to risks attached to the way in which a firm, and its staff, conduct themselves.

A good starting point is to consider conduct risk as the latest in a series of regulatory thinking that began with treating customers fairly (TCF), which then progressed through principles-based regulation, and then on to outcomes-focused regulation, before becoming conduct risk. All of these expressions have at their heart the same basic idea, namely that regulation through the creation of rules alone is not enough to protect consumers or markets.

Compliance with rules is generally a backward-looking philosophy. The question tends to be: 'Did the firm comply?' Certainly, this was the way in which firms have operated in the past, with compliance monitoring activity devoted to uncovering incidences of historic rule breaches. The conduct risk approach, on the other hand, has a more forward-looking emphasis: 'Will the actions of the firm lead to poor outcomes for consumers or not?'

1.5.1 Treating Customers Fairly (TCF)

The requirement for firms to treat their customers fairly is firmly rooted in the Principles for Businesses. Principle 6 states that *'a firm must pay due regard to the interests of its customers and treat them fairly'*. The approach adopted to TCF has been not to define precisely what constitutes 'treating customers fairly', but rather to challenge the senior management of firms to work this out for themselves, taking into account the particular types of business they undertake. The objective is for this to be embedded into the culture of a firm at all levels, so that over time it becomes 'business as usual'.

TCF, with its focus on consumer outcomes, still underpins the delivery of the FCA's statutory consumer protection objective. It states:

We expect customers' interests to be at the heart of how firms do business. Customers can expect to get financial services and products that meet their needs from firms that they can trust. Meeting customers' fair and reasonable expectations should be the responsibility of firms, not that of the regulator.

There are six TCF outcomes:

- **Outcome 1** – consumers can be confident that they are dealing with firms where the fair treatment of customers is central to the corporate culture.
- **Outcome 2** – products and services marketed and sold in the retail market are designed to meet the needs of identified consumer groups and are targeted accordingly.
- **Outcome 3** – consumers are provided with clear information and are kept appropriately informed before, during and after the point of sale.
- **Outcome 4** – where consumers receive advice, the advice is suitable and takes account of their circumstances.
- **Outcome 5** – consumers are provided with products that perform as firms have led them to expect, and the associated service is of an acceptable standard and as they have been led to expect.
- **Outcome 6** – consumers do not face unreasonable post-sale barriers imposed by firms to change product, switch provider, submit a claim or make a complaint.

The regulator will look for evidence that firms really have incorporated TCF throughout their operations and processes. It expects to see this incorporated into a firm's systems and controls and all aspects of the business culture, including people issues, such as training and competence, remuneration, and performance management.

It also expects senior management to ensure that they have the right management information and other data to enable them to satisfy themselves that they are treating their customers fairly in practice.

2. Money Laundering

2.1 Definition and Stages of Money Laundering

Crime generates large amounts of cash and criminals like cash, particularly because it is difficult to trace. The cash could be generated through a variety of activities such as drug trafficking, arms trafficking or handling stolen goods.

However, legitimate business transactions, particularly large ones such as buying a car or a property, are not commonly done in cash. This is because cash is a security risk and has to be counted. So, for money to be really useful, it needs to be in electronic form, in a bank account. This poses a problem for criminals – how do they convert large amounts of illegal cash into legal bank account balances? The answer is to 'launder' the money and make it appear like legitimate money that is 'clean'.

So, money laundering is the process of turning money that is derived from criminal activities – **dirty money** – into money which appears to have been legitimately acquired – **clean money** – and which can therefore be more easily invested and spent.

There are three stages to a successful money laundering operation:

- **Placement** – the first stage and typically involves placing the criminally derived cash into some form of bank or building society account.
- **Layering** – the second stage and involves moving the money around in order to make it difficult for the authorities to link the placed funds with the ultimate beneficiary of the money. Disguising the original source of the funds might involve buying and selling foreign currencies, shares or bonds.

10

- **Integration** – the third and final stage. At this stage, the layering has been successful and the ultimate beneficiary appears to be holding legitimate funds ('clean' money rather than 'dirty' money). The money has been integrated back into the financial system and can be dealt with as if it were legitimate.

2.2 Legal and Regulatory Framework

The cross-border nature of money laundering has led to international co-ordination to ensure that countries have legislation and regulatory processes in place to enable the identification and prosecution of those involved. In particular the **Financial Action Task Force (FATF)** has been established as an inter-governmental body to develop and promote national and international policies to combat money laundering. It is based at the Organisation for Economic Co-operation and Development (OECD) in Paris and has issued recommendations aimed at setting minimum standards for countries to ensure that anti-money laundering efforts are consistent internationally.

At its most basic level, the requirements expect staff at firms to be able to identify suspicions of money laundering, and to report these suspicions. Initially the reporting is made to a central point within the firm, the Money Laundering Reporting Officer (MLRO), and the MLRO will then report all relevant suspicions to the appropriate authorities.

The main laws and regulations relating to money laundering in the UK are:

- Proceeds of Crime Act.
- Money Laundering Regulations.

The **Proceeds of Crime Act (POCA)** consolidated and extended existing UK legislation regarding money laundering and, as well as making money laundering a criminal offence, established three broad groups of offences related to money laundering that firms and the staff working for them need to avoid committing:

- knowingly assisting in concealing, or arranging for the acquisition, use or possession of criminal property
- failing to report knowledge or suspicions of possible money laundering
- tipping off another person that a money laundering report has been made which might prejudice the investigation or that

a money laundering investigation is being contemplated or carried out.

The Proceeds of Crime Act also made it an offence to impede any investigation, for example by destroying or disposing of any documents that are relevant to an investigation.

The maximum prison terms that can be imposed under the Proceeds of Crime Act are 14 years for the offence of money laundering, five years for failing to make a report or destroying relevant documents and two years for tipping off. In each case, the penalties can be imprisonment and/or an unlimited amount of fine.

The **Money Laundering Regulations** implemented the EU directive on money laundering, specifying the arrangements firms must have in place covering areas including record-keeping, internal controls and reporting requirements.

2.3 Action Required by Firms and Individuals

The Proceeds of Crime Act and the Money Laundering Regulations require a court to take account of industry guidance when considering whether a person or firm has committed an offence or has complied with the money laundering regulations.

This guidance is provided by the **Joint Money Laundering Steering Group (JMLSG)**, an industry body made up of 17 financial sector trade bodies.

Its guidance sets out what is expected of firms and their staff. It emphasises the responsibility of senior management to manage the firm's money laundering risks, and advises that this should be carried out using a risk-based approach. It sets out a standard approach to the identification and verification of customers, separating out basic identity from other aspects of customer due diligence measures, as well as

giving guidance on the obligation to monitor customer activity.

The following sections highlight some of the principal features of the anti-money laundering procedures a firm is expected to put in place.

2.3.1 Internal Controls

There is a requirement for firms to establish and maintain appropriate and risk-based policies and procedures in order to prevent operations related to money laundering. These controls are expected to be appropriate to the risks faced by the firm. So a small independent firm of stockbrokers in Tunbridge Wells would not be expected to maintain the same level of controls as a multi-national with branches in Latin America and the Middle East.

2.3.2 Money Laundering Reporting Officer (MLRO)

Firms are expected to appoint a director or senior manager to be the Money Laundering Reporting Officer (MLRO), who is responsible for overseeing the firm's compliance with the regulator's rules on systems and controls against money laundering.

The MLRO must receive and review the internal disclosure reports, and make external reports to the National Crime Agency (NCA) when required. The MLRO is also required to carry out regular assessments of the adequacy of the firm's systems and controls and to produce a report at least annually to senior management on its effectiveness.

The MLRO must have authority to act independently, and senior management must ensure that the MLRO has sufficient resources available to effectively carry out his or her responsibilities.

2.3.3 Risk-Based Approach

As seen, senior management are expected to ensure that they have appropriate systems and controls in place to manage the risks associated with the business and its customers.

This requires them to assess their money laundering risk and decide how they will manage it. It also means they must determine the identification and vetting procedures required to make sure that the customers of the firm are not involved in money laundering. This is referred to as appropriate customer due diligence measures, and the procedures should reflect the risk characteristics of customers, based on the type of customer and the business relationship, product or transaction.

2.3.4 Customer Due Diligence (CDD)

The Money Laundering Regulations set out a firm's obligations to conduct customer due diligence. The CDD measures that must be carried out involve:

- identifying the customer and verifying their identity, for example by seeing the customer's passport and council tax bills
- if a customer is acting for another beneficial owner, then also verifying the identity of the beneficial owner
- obtaining information of the purpose and intended nature of the business relationship.

Firms must also conduct ongoing monitoring of the business relationship with their customers to identify any unusual activity that may be suspicious.

For some particular customers, products or transactions, **simplified due diligence (SDD)** may be applied. Firms must have reasonable grounds for believing that the customer, product or transaction falls within one of the allowed categories, and be able to demonstrate this to their supervisory authority. Examples of instances where SDD may be applied include where the customer is another regulated firm in the financial sector, or a company listed on a regulated stock market, such as the London Stock Exchange.

In cases of higher risk and if the customer is not physically present when their identities are verified then **Enhanced Due Diligence (EDD)** measures must be applied on a risk-sensitive basis.

The JMLSG Guidance Notes provide extensive guidance on the customer due diligence to be applied and the above is only a very brief summary.

2.3.5 Staff Awareness and Training

The regulations require reports to be made of potential money-laundering activities. So, staff working in the financial sector are required to make reports where they know, or where they suspect, or where they have reasonable grounds for knowing or suspecting, that a person is engaged in money laundering.

Each firm is expected to provide a framework within which such suspicion reports may be raised and considered by a nominated officer, who is usually the MLRO. The nominated officer must consider each report and determine whether there are grounds for knowledge or suspicion for a report to be made to the NCA.

However, the best-designed control systems cannot operate effectively without staff who are alert to the risk of money laundering and who are trained in the identification of unusual activities or transactions which may prove to be suspicious. Firms are therefore required to:

- provide appropriate training to make staff aware of money laundering issues and how these crimes might take place through the firm
- ensure staff are aware of the law, regulations and relevant criminal offences
- consider providing case studies and examples related to the firm's business
- train employees in how to operate a risk-based approach.

2.3.6 Record-Keeping

Record-keeping is an essential component of the audit trail that the money-laundering regulations and FCA rules require to assist in any financial investigations. Firms are therefore required to maintain appropriate systems for maintaining records and making these available when required and, in particular, should retain:

- copies of the evidence obtained of a customer's identity for five years after the end of the customer relationship
- details of customer transactions for five years from the date of the transaction or five years from when the relationship with the customer ended, whichever is the later
- details of actions taken in respect of internal and external suspicion reports
- details of information considered by the nominated officer in respect of an internal report when no external report is made.

2.4   Bribery

The Bribery Act 2010 came into force in July 2011 as part of a complete reform of corruption law to provide a modern and comprehensive scheme of bribery offences that will enable courts and prosecutors to respond more effectively to bribery at home or abroad.

The Bribery Act replaces offences at common law and under legislation dating back to the early 1900s. Its key provisions are:

- Two general offences are created covering the offering, promising or giving of an advantage, and the requesting, agreeing to receive or accepting of an advantage.
- There is a discrete offence of bribery of a foreign public official to obtain or retain business or an advantage in the conduct of business.
- A new offence is created, of failure by a commercial organisation to prevent a bribe being paid for or on its behalf.

- Penalties include a maximum of ten years' imprisonment, unlimited fines, confiscation of proceeds, debarment from public sector contracts and director disqualification.

For companies, the most important point to note is that there is a new offence of failing to prevent bribery, which does not require any corrupt intent. This offence will make it easier for the Serious Fraud Office (SFO) to prosecute companies when bribery has occurred.

The only defence available to a commercial organisation charged with the corporate offence will be for the organisation to show that it had adequate procedures in place to prevent an act of bribery being committed in connection with its business. This requires firms to have an effective compliance programme that has to meet six principles:

- Develop well-designed policies, procedures and controls to ensure compliance.
- Top-level commitment is required with the board and senior management making a commitment to conduct business in a fair, honest and ethical manner.
- Risk assessments should be undertaken on an ongoing basis to identify the external and internal risks faced by the company.
- Due diligence should be undertaken on suppliers who undertake services for the company.
- Policies and procedures should be communicated internally along with training of employees and policy statements or a code of conduct published externally.
- Bribery risks should be monitored, evaluated and reassessed regularly and staff surveys undertaken. Results should be reported regularly to top management and the process independently audited.

10

2.5 Other Areas of Financial Crime

Individuals and firms may unwittingly find themselves targeted by criminals and have to be aware of this possibility. Areas that staff working in financial services need to be aware of are the theft of customer data to facilitate identity fraud, cybercrime and terrorist financing.

2.5.1 Identity Fraud

Identity fraud or identity theft is one of the fastest-growing types of fraud in the UK.

- **Identity fraud** is the use of a misappropriated identity in criminal activity, to obtain goods or services by deception. This usually involves the use of stolen or forged identity documents such as a passport or driving licence.
- **Identity theft** (also known as impersonation fraud) is the misappropriation of the identity (such as the name, date of birth, current address or previous addresses) of another person, without his or her knowledge or consent. These identity details are then used to obtain goods and services in that person's name.

A person's identity (and their ability to prove it) is central to almost all commercial activity. Organisations need to verify that the person applying for credit or investment services is who they say they are and lives where they claim to live. The procedures used by organisations to check the information supplied by customers help to detect and prevent most identity fraud. however, some fraudulent applications are accepted due to the sophisticated techniques used by the fraudsters.

When opening accounts in banks and other financial organisations, criminals will use data from legitimate persons to provide information for applications and other purposes which, when checked against normal credit reference, postal and other databases, will seem to confirm the genuine nature of the application.

Key to this is accessing what are known as 'breeder' documents – those documents that allow those who possess them to apply for or obtain other documentation and thus build up a profile or 'history' that can satisfy basic Customer Due Diligence (CDD) processes. The information may either be used quickly before the source of the data is alerted or used for example, as a facilitator for other identities so as not to alert the source.

2.5.2 Cybercrime

Cybercrime is another fast-growing area of crime. More and more criminals are exploiting the speed, convenience and anonymity of the internet to commit a diverse range of criminal activities that have no borders (either physical or virtual), cause serious harm, and pose very real threats to people worldwide.

Although there is no single universal definition of cybercrime, law enforcement generally makes a distinction between two main types of internet-related crime:

1. **Advanced cybercrime (or high-tech crime)** – sophisticated attacks against computer hardware and software.
2. **Cyber-enabled crime** – many 'traditional' crimes have taken a new turn with the advent of the internet, such as crimes against children, financial crimes and even terrorism.

In the past, cybercrime was committed mainly by individuals or small groups. Today, the authorities are seeing highly complex cybercriminal networks bring together individuals from across the globe in real time to commit crimes on an unprecedented scale. New trends in cybercrime are emerging all the time, with estimated costs to the global economy running to billions of dollars.

Criminal organisations are turning increasingly to the internet to facilitate their activities and maximise their profit in the shortest time. The crimes themselves are not necessarily new – such as theft, fraud, illegal gambling, sale of fake medicines – but they are evolving in line with the opportunities presented online and, therefore, becoming more widespread and damaging.

2.5.3 Terrorist Financing

There can be considerable similarities between the movement of terrorist funds and the laundering of criminal property. Because terrorist groups can have links with other criminal activities, there is inevitably some overlap between anti-money laundering provisions and the rules designed to prevent the financing of terrorist acts. However, there are two major differences to note between terrorist financing and other money laundering activities:

- Often, only quite small sums of money are required to commit terrorist acts, making identification and tracking more difficult.
- If legitimate funds are used to fund terrorist activities, it is difficult to identify when the funds become terrorist funds.

Terrorist organisations can, however, require significant funding, and will employ modern techniques to manage the funds and transfer them between jurisdictions, hence the similarities with money laundering.

3. Insider Dealing

When directors or employees of a listed company buy or sell shares in that company, there is a possibility that they may be committing a criminal act – that of insider dealing. The following example illustrates the possible circumstances where insider dealing might arise.

Example

Carlton Murray is the sales director of Quickdeal plc, a substantial retail company with its shares listed on the LSE. He is aware that sales have gone particularly well in the last two months, however the latest results have not yet been released to the general public. If Carlton were to buy some shares in Quickdeal for himself in order to profit from the anticipated market reaction to the positive performance he would be breaking the law. He would be 'insider dealing', using information he gained from 'inside' the company for personal gain.

Insider dealing is a criminal offence in the UK under the Criminal Justice Act 1993, and it is punishable by a fine and/or a jail term.

To be found guilty of insider dealing, the Criminal Justice Act 1993 defines who is deemed to be an insider, what is deemed to be inside information and the situations that give rise to the offence.

Inside information is information that relates to particular securities or a particular issuer of securities (and not to securities or securities issuers generally) and which:

- is specific or precise
- has not been made public, and
- if it were made public, would be likely to have a significant effect on the price of the securities.

This is generally referred to as 'unpublished price-sensitive information' and the securities are referred to as 'price-affected securities'.

Information becomes public when it is published, for example, a UK-listed company announcing its results. Furthermore, information can be treated as public even though it may be acquired only by persons exercising diligence or expertise (for example, by careful analysis of published accounts, or by scouring a library of press cuttings).

10

An **insider** is a person that has this price-sensitive information and knows that it is inside information from an inside source. The person may have:

- gained the information through being a director, employee or shareholder of the issuer of the securities
- gained access to the information by virtue of his employment, office or profession (for example, the auditors to the company)
- sourced the information from either of the above, either directly or indirectly.

The **offence of insider dealing** is committed when an insider acquires or disposes of price-affected securities while in possession of unpublished price-sensitive information. It is also an offence to encourage another person to deal in price-affected securities, or to disclose the information to another person (other than in the proper performance of employment). The acquisition or disposal must occur on a regulated market or through a professional intermediary.

The instruments covered by the insider dealing legislation in the Criminal Justice Act are described as **securities**. For the purposes of this piece of law, securities are any of the following:

- shares
- bonds (includes government bonds and others issued by a company or a public sector body)
- warrants
- depositary receipts
- options (to acquire or dispose of securities)
- futures (to acquire or dispose of securities)
- contracts for differences (based on securities, interest rates or share indices).

Note that the definition of 'securities' does not embrace commodities (like oil or aluminium) or derivatives on commodities (such as options and futures on agricultural products, metals or energy products). Units/shares in open-ended collective investment schemes (such as OEICs, unit trusts and SICAVs) are also excluded from the definition of securities for insider dealing purposes.

4.   Market Abuse

Market abuse may arise in circumstances where financial investors have been unreasonably disadvantaged, directly or indirectly, by others who behave unlawfully. Certain types of behaviour, such as insider dealing and market manipulation, can amount to market abuse.

Market abuse is a civil offence and can be subject to fines and sanctions by the regulator. Insider dealing and market manipulation may also be a criminal offence and offences are prosecuted in the courts.

Market abuse was introduced by FSMA 2000, but concerns about market distortion led the EU to introduce the Market Abuse Regulations (MAR) in 2016 which apply unchanged across all EU countries. MAR builds on the existing regime but is wider in scope as it covers more financial instruments and more trading venues, extends market manipulation to include attempted market manipulation and prohibits abusive behaviour in respect of benchmarks.

There are three market abuse behaviours specified in MAR – insider dealing, unlawful disclosure of inside information and market manipulation. These behaviours are specifically prohibited, subject to certain exemptions.

Insider dealing

- Insider dealing arises when a person in possession of inside information uses it to deal, or to attempt to deal or to recommend or induce another to do so.
- Dealing includes acquiring or disposing of financial instruments to which the inside information relates, as well as to cancelling or amending an order that was made before having inside information in relation to that instrument.

- A person using the recommendation or inducement will also be insider-dealing where they know or ought to know that the recommendation or inducement is based on inside information.
- In the UK, the FCA judges what a reasonable person knows, or ought to know, in such circumstances.

Public disclosure requirements

- The general disclosure obligation requires issuers to inform the public as soon as possible about inside information which directly concerns them. Where their securities are admitted to trading on a regulated market, disclosure must also be made to the officially appointed central storage mechanism.
- There is an obligation to prepare and maintain insider lists of any person with access to inside information.
- Directors and senior executives (and their closely associated persons) who have regular access to inside information must notify both the issuer and the FCA of every account transaction relating to the issuer's shares, debt instruments, derivatives or other linked financial instruments.

Market manipulation

- Market manipulation is committed if a person carries out any of the specified activities or behaviours in Article 12 of MAR. These include:
  - giving false or misleading signals about the supply of, demand for or price of a financial instrument
  - using fictitious devices or other deception or contrivance that is likely to affect the price of financial instruments
  - disseminating information which gives, or is likely to give, false or misleading signals as to supply, demand or price of financial instruments; or secures, or is likely to secure, their price at an abnormal or artificial level, including circulating rumours knowing the information was false or misleading

  - certain other behaviours including collaborating to secure a dominant position over the supply or demand for a financial instrument or creating other unfair trading conditions including by algorithmic and high-frequency trading.

5. Data Protection

Customers routinely entrust financial firms with important personal data; if this falls into criminal hands, fraudsters can attempt to undertake financial transactions in the customer's name. Firms must take special care of their customers' personal data and comply with the data protection principles.

The Data Protection Act 1988 details how personal data should be dealt with to protect its integrity and to protect the rights of the persons concerned.

In order to comply with the Act, firms have a number of legal responsibilities, including:

- notifying the Information Commissioner that they are processing information
- processing personal information in accordance with the eight principles of the Data Protection Act
- answering subject access requests received from individuals.

Any firm that is holding and processing personal data must be registered with the Information Commissioner. The firm is described as a **data controller**, and is required to comply with the Data Protection Act.

The Data Protection Act lays down eight data protection principles:

- Personal data shall be processed fairly and lawfully.
- Personal data shall be obtained for one or more specified and lawful purposes, and shall not be further processed in any

manner that is incompatible with those purposes.

- Personal data shall be adequate, relevant and not excessive in relation to the purpose or purposes for which it is processed.
- Personal data shall be accurate and, where necessary, kept up-to-date.
- Personal data shall not be kept for longer than is necessary for its purpose or purposes.
- Personal data shall be processed in accordance with the rights of the subject under the Act.
- Appropriate technical and organisational measures shall be taken against unauthorised or unlawful processing of personal data, and against accidental loss or destruction of, or damage to, the personal data.
- Personal data shall not be transferred to a country or territory outside the European Economic Area (EEA) unless that country or territory ensures an adequate level of protection in relation to the processing of personal data.

Under these principles, firms are therefore required to take particular care where financial or medical information is held on a laptop or other portable device. Data held on portable devices should be encrypted and organisations must have policies on the appropriate use and security of portable devices and ensuring their staff are properly trained in these policies.

Other steps that can be taken to keep data safe include the following regulatory recommendations:

- Employees should not have access to data beyond that which is necessary for them to perform their job. When possible, data should be segregated and information such as passport numbers, bank details and social security numbers should be blanked out.
- The firm should look to monitor and control all flows of information into and out of the company.

- All forms of removable media should be disabled, except when there is a genuine business need. There should be no physical means available for unauthorised staff to remove information undetected.
- When laptops or other portable devices are in use, these should be encrypted and wiped afterwards. Usage of such devices should be logged and monitored under the authority of an appropriate individual. Watertight policies on using such devices should be in place.
- Software that tracks all activities, as well as web surfing and email traffic, should be installed on every single terminal on the firm's network, and staff should be aware of this.
- The firm should completely block access to all internet content that allows web-based communication. This includes all web-based email, messaging facilities on social networking sites, external instant messaging and 'peer-to-peer' file sharing software.
- The firm should conduct due diligence of data security standards of its third party suppliers before contracts are agreed. This should also be reviewed periodically. If the firm chooses to outsource its IT, conduct checks should be made on the outsource provider's staff as well as the firm's own staff, since they have access to the firm's network.
- All visitors to the firm's premises should be logged in and out, and be supervised while on site. Logs should be kept for a minimum of 12 months.

If a firm outsources at all, there are data protection implications. Firms must assess that the organisation can carry out the work in a secure way, check that they are doing so and take proper security measures. The firm must also have a written contract with the organisation that lays down how it can use and disclose the information entrusted to it.

A new EU Data Protection Directive comes into effect in 2018 – the General Data Protection Regulation (GDPR). The GDPR will replace the Data Protection Act 1988 and the new data privacy laws will govern the use and privacy of EU citizens' data, including the governing of the use of this data by law enforcement. The new rules give:

- easier access to your own data
- a right to data portability
- a clarified right to be forgotten, and
- the right to know when your own data has been hacked.

6. Complaints and Compensation

6.1 Complaints

It is almost inevitable that customers will raise complaints against a firm providing financial services. Sometimes these complaints will be valid and sometimes not. The FCA requires authorised firms to deal with complaints from **eligible complainants** promptly and fairly. Eligible complainants are, broadly, individuals and small businesses.

In essence, the firm needs to have written procedures that the staff must follow in the event of a complaint. These procedures require the firm to provide a definitive response to the complaint within a reasonable timescale, and to also make the complainant aware that, should he or she be unhappy with the response, there is a possibility of obtaining an independent view from the **Financial Ombudsman Service (FOS)**.

So, the FCA requires firms to have appropriate written procedures for handling expressions of dissatisfaction from eligible complainants. These procedures should be followed regardless of whether the complaint is oral or written and whether the complaint is justified

or not, as long as it relates to the firm's provision of or failure to provide a financial service. If the complaint came from an 'ineligible' complainant, such as a large business client, the firm is still able to apply these procedures, if it so chooses.

These internal complaints-handling procedures should provide for the receiving of complaints, acknowledgement of complaints in a timely manner, responding to those complaints, appropriately investigating the complaints and notifying the complainants of their right to go to the FOS when relevant. Among other requirements, the complaints-handling procedures must require the firm to issue its final response to the complainant. This **final response** must follow within **eight weeks** of the date of the original complaint and the complainant must be notified of his/her right to refer their complaint to the FOS if dissatisfied with the firm's response.

Under the internal complaints-handling procedures, the complaints must be investigated by an employee of sufficient competence who was not directly involved in the matter that is the subject of the complaint. The person charged with responding to the complaints must have the authority to settle the complaint, including offering redress when appropriate, or should have access to someone with the necessary authority.

The responses should adequately address the subject matter of the complaint and, when a complaint is upheld, to offer appropriate redress. When the firm decides that redress is appropriate, the firm must provide the complainant with fair compensation for any acts or omissions for which it was responsible and comply with any offer of redress the complainant accepts. Any redress for financial loss should include consequential or prospective loss, in addition to actual loss.

The firm must take reasonable steps to ensure that all relevant employees are aware of the firm's complaints-handling procedures and endeavour to act in accordance with these. This includes anyone that is not directly employed by the firm but is acting as an appointed representative to the firm.

6.2 The Financial Ombudsman Service (FOS)

Under the provisions of the FSMA, the FSA (now FCA) was given the power to make rules relating to the handling of complaints, and the FOS was established as an independent body to administer and operate a dispute resolution scheme. It is funded by compulsory contributions from authorised firms.

The Financial Ombudsman Service is designed to resolve complaints about financial services firms quickly and with minimum formality. Eligible complainants are able to refer complaints to the FOS if they are not satisfied with the response of the financial services firm. The decision of the FOS is binding on firms, although not binding on the person making the complaint.

The Financial Ombudsman can require the firm to pay over money as a result of a complaint. This money award against the firm will be of such amount that the Ombudsman considers to be fair compensation; however, the sum cannot exceed £150,000. If the decision is made to make a money award, the Ombudsman can award compensation for financial loss, pain and suffering, damage to reputation and distress or inconvenience.

6.3 The Financial Services Compensation Scheme (FSCS)

Imagine a bank, authorised by the FCA and serving retail customers, were to collapse and its retail customers were unable to recover any of their deposited money. It would create uproar and undermine confidence in the financial system – depositors would begin to consider keeping cash under the mattress to be a more viable alternative! Thankfully, the Financial Services Compensation Scheme (FSCS) has been established to pay compensation or arrange continuing cover to eligible claimants in the event of a default by an authorised person or firm. Default is, typically, the firm suffering insolvency. It is funded by compulsory financial services industry contributions.

Eligible claimants are, broadly speaking, the less knowledgeable clients of the firm, such as individuals and small organisations. These less knowledgeable clients are generally the firm's 'private customers' and exclude the more knowledgeable 'professional customers'. The scheme is similar to an insurance policy that is paid for by all authorised firms and provides protection to some clients in the event of a firm collapsing. The claims could come from money on deposit with a bank, or claims in connection with investment business, such as the collapse of a fund manager or stockbroker.

The maximum level of compensation for claims against firms declared in default is 100% of the first £50,000 per person per firm for investments, and £85,000 for bank deposits.

Slightly different limits apply where an investment firm or insurer goes into default.

- For investments, the maximum level of compensation is £50,000 per person per firm.
- For insurance, the maximum level of compensation is 100% of the benefits for long-term insurance and certain types of compulsory insurance and 90% for other types of claims.

Learning Objectives

Chapter Ten has covered the following Learning Objectives:

8.1.1   Understand the need for regulation

8.1.2   Know the function of UK regulators in the financial services industry

8.1.3   Understand the reasons for authorisation of firms

8.1.4   Know the requirements of the Senior Managers and Certification Regime and the approved persons regime

8.1.5   Know the outcomes arising from the FCA's approach to managing conduct risk within firms, including Treating Customers Fairly

8.2.1   Know what money laundering is the stages involved and the related criminal offences

8.2.2   Know the purpose and the main provisions of the Proceeds of Crime Act and the Money Laundering Regulations

8.2.3   Know the action to be taken by those employed in financial services if money laundering activity is suspected and what constitutes unsatisfactory evidence of identity

8.2.4   Know the purpose of the Bribery Act

8.2.5   Know how firms and individuals can be exploited as a vehicle for financial crime: theft of customer data to facilitate identity fraud; cybercrime; terrorist financing

8.3.1   Know the offences that constitute insider dealing and the instruments covered

8.3.2   Know the offences that constitute market abuse and the instruments covered

8.4.1   Understand the basic steps firms should take to comply with the Data Protection Act

8.5.1   Know the requirements for handling customer complaints, including the role of the Financial Ombudsman Service

8.5.2   Know the circumstances under which the Financial Services Compensation Scheme pays compensation

Based on what you have learned in Chapter Ten, try to answer the following end of chapter questions.

End of Chapter Questions

Think of an answer for each question and refer to the appropriate section for confirmation.

1. What is the global approach to regulating financial services?
    Answer Reference: Section 1.1

    ....

    ....

2. Name the three statutory objectives of the FCA.
    Answer Reference: Section 1.2

    ....

    ....

3. What must be satisfied before a UK firm can become authorised?
    Answer Reference: Section 1.3

    ....

    ....

4. Broadly, what is a 'controlled function' and what is expected of persons fulfilling such functions?
    Answer Reference: Section 1.4

    ....

    ....

5. What five groups of functions are 'controlled'?
    Answer Reference: Section 1.4.2

    ....

    ....

6. What are the three stages of a successful money laundering operation?

    Answer Reference: Sections 2.1

    ....

    ....

7. What is FATF?

    Answer Reference: Section 2.2

    ....

    ....

8. What are the three groups of offences laid down in the Proceeds of Crime Act?

    Answer Reference: Section 2.2

    ....

    ....

9. What is the maximum prison sentence under the Proceeds of Crime Act?

    Answer Reference: Section 2.2

    ....

    ....

10. What is the JMLSG?

    Answer Reference: Section 2.3

    ....

    ....

11. What is the role of the MLRO?

    Answer Reference: Section 2.3.2

    ....

    ....

10

12. Due diligence could be any one of three possibilities in relation to anti-money laundering procedures – what are they?

Answer Reference: Section 2.3.4

....

....

13. Insider dealing covers price-affected securities – what are securities in this context?

Answer Reference: Section 3

....

....

14. Market abuse must satisfy one or more of three conditions – what are they?

Answer Reference: Section 4

....

....

15. The Data Protection Act requires firms holding personal data to be registered with whom?

Answer Reference: Section 5

....

....

16. What are the FOS and the FSCS, and what are their roles?

Answer Reference: Sections 6.2, 6.3

....

....

Chapter Eleven

Taxation, Investment Wrappers and Trusts

1. Introduction

The old proverb says that 'nothing is certain but death and taxes', highlighting the fact that, in the developed world, taxes are as inevitable as death! This chapter starts by outlining the main types of tax and how the tax to be paid is calculated.

Generally taxes need to be paid, however there are certain schemes which government has introduced to encourage people to save and invest by reducing the tax burden. These are often in the form of 'investment wrappers', a little like parcelling away certain investments and freeing them from tax.

The chapter details the major wrappers – individual savings accounts (ISAs) – and then how the government encourages people to save for their retirement by giving tax incentives on pension contributions. After considering investment bonds, the chapter concludes with a review of trusts. Trusts are often used to achieve certain ends, like transferring ownership to others in as tax efficient a manner as possible.

2. Taxation

This section reviews the main taxes that affect individuals, with particular focus on the impact of tax on the money made from investments. The main taxes are income tax, capital gains tax, stamp duty and inheritance tax.

2.1 Income Tax

Individuals have to pay income tax on the money they earn from their work and also on any interest or dividends that arise from their savings and investments.

The UK tax authority – Her Majesty's Revenue & Customs or simply HMRC – classifies income into three types:

- **Non-savings income** – this category includes earnings from work and pension income.
- **Savings income** – this includes interest from bank accounts and bonds.
- **Dividend income** – this final category includes dividends paid by companies and investment funds.

As stated above, individual, private investors are liable to pay tax on the income generated from their savings and investments. In this context, taxable income includes interest on bank deposits, the dividends from shares, income distributed by unit trusts and the interest on government and corporate bonds.

In simple terms, the calculation of the tax payable by each individual is done in the following three steps:

Step 1

All of the income from the three categories is added up for the year, first non-savings income (such as wages) and then savings income (interest) and finally dividend income.

Step 2

Deduct the annual personal allowance from the bottom of the 'pile' of income in step 1. All individuals have an **annual personal allowance** on which no tax is due, and the remaining income is grouped into bands and taxed at different rates. The personal allowance applies up to an earnings limit of £100,000, after which it is gradually reduced.

Dividends are treated as the 'top slice' of taxable income, savings as the next slice and other non-savings income as the lowest slice. This means that the personal allowance will always be deducted first from the other (eg, earned) income, and, if there is any remaining, then from savings income, and finally from dividend income.

Step 3

Calculate the tax due on the remaining income after deducting the personal allowance and any other deductions using the published bands and rates.

There are a number of other deductions that an individual is allowed to make from gross income before tax is payable; for example, subject to certain limitations, contributions made to a personal or corporate pension scheme; and charitable donations made by individuals on or after 6 April 2000.

Some income is tax-free, including Premium Bond prizes; interest on national savings certificates; income from Individual Savings Accounts (ISAs); gambling and National Lottery wins; compensation for loss of employment of up to £30,000 and statutory redundancy payments; and dividends on ordinary shares of a venture capital trust (VCT).

2.1.1 Savings Interest

Interest income is referred to by HMRC as **non-dividend savings income** and, as seen above, it is treated as the second slice and taxed **after** earned income.

Technically, non-dividend savings income applies to UK and overseas savings income from the following sources:

- interest from banks and building societies
- interest from gilts and corporate bonds
- the income component from purchased life annuities
- the taxable amount on deep-discounted securities (eg, zero coupon bonds)
- some distributions from unit trusts.

From 6 April 2016, a new personal savings allowance was introduced to remove tax on up to £1,000 of savings income for basic rate taxpayers and up to £500 for higher rate taxpayers. Additional rate taxpayers will not receive an allowance. As part of this change, from April 2016, banks and building societies stopped automatically taking 20% in income tax from the interest earned on non-ISA savings and this removed the need for non-taxpayers to complete a form R85.

The starting rate for savings band (£0–£5,000) which was introduced in April 2015 also remains in place, but is restricted depending on the amount of non-savings income an individual has. For example, someone with non-savings income greater than £16,000 (personal allowance plus starting rate for savings band) will not have access to the starting rate band for their savings income, but will still be entitled to use the new personal savings allowance if they are a basic rate or higher rate taxpayer. Anyone with non-savings income of less than £16,000 may be able to access some of the starting rate band, as well as the new personal savings allowance.

Any tax due is calculated by reference to the following income tax rates and tax bands for the 2017–18 tax year.

Savings rate: 0%	£0–£5,000
Basic rate: 20%	£0–£33,500
Higher rate: 40%	£33,501–150,000
Additional rate: 45%	£150,001 and over

The following examples highlight the way tax is calculated for individuals in a little more detail.

Example

Claire is a UK taxpayer who is less than 65 years old. She receives earned income of £12,500 and savings income of £3,000 in the year. The personal allowance is first applied against the earned income, which leaves £1,000 taxable. The starting rate band for savings of £5,000 is then reduced by £1000, leaving £4,000 of savings interest that can be earned tax free.

Income Tax Calculation for 2017–18	£
Earned income	12,500
Non-dividend savings income	3,000
Pension contribution	0
Statutory total income	15,500
Personal allowance	(11,500)
Starting rate for savings band	(4,000)
Personal savings allowance	(1,000)
Taxable non-dividend savings income	0
Taxable earned income	1,000
Basic rate tax on earned income	200
Total tax	200

11

Example

Barry has gross savings income of £13,500 and no earned income during the year. Even though Barry's income is in excess of the personal allowance of £11,500, the starting rate allowance of £5,000 is also available, meaning that Barry pays no tax on his income.

Income Tax Calculation for 2017–18	£
Earned income	0
Non-dividend savings income	13,500
Pension contribution	0
Statutory total income	13,500
Personal allowance	(11,500)
Starting rate for savings band	(5,000)
Personal savings allowance	(1,000)
Taxable non-dividend savings income	0
Taxable earned income	0
Basic rate tax on non-dividend savings income	0
Basic rate tax on earned income	0
Total tax liability	0

Example

Carlos is self-employed and has earned income of £60,500 and non-dividend savings income of £5,000. As his earned income exceeds £16,500 (personal allowance of £11,500 plus starting rate for savings band of £5,000) the starting rate for savings band is not available, and only the personal allowance and personal savings allowance remain.

After deducting the personal allowance, the first £33,500 of taxable income is taxed at the 20% rate, and the balance is taxed at the higher rate of 40%. Therefore, as Carlos is a higher rate taxpayer, only £500 of the personal savings allowance is available to deduct against his non-dividend savings income of £5,000.

Income Tax Calculation for 2017–18	£
Earned income	60,500
Non-dividend savings income	5,000
Pension contribution	0
Statutory total income	65,500
Personal allowance	(11,500)
Starting rate for savings band	0
Taxable earned income	49,000
Personal savings allowance	(500)
Taxable non-dividend savings income	4,500
Basic rate tax on the first £33,500 @ 20%	6,700
Higher rate tax on the balance of £20,000 @ 40%	8,000
Total tax liability	14,700

2.1.2 Dividend Income

The taxation of dividends changed significantly as of April 2016, with the first £5,000 of dividend income in each tax year now tax-exempt. Sums above that amount will be taxed at 7.5% for basic rate taxpayers, 32.5% for higher rate taxpayers and 38.1% for additional rate taxpayers. The spring 2017 Budget announced that the dividend allowance will be reduced to £2,000 from April 2018.

2.2 Capital Gains Tax (CGT)

Capital gains tax (CGT) is a tax charged on the increase in the capital value of an asset, normally only paid when the asset is disposed of. So, if an individual bought shares for £2,000 and later sold them for £17,000, then that individual has made a capital gain of £15,000.

CGT may be payable when an asset is sold or otherwise disposed of which includes when a person:

- sells, gives away, exchanges, or transfers – 'dispose of' – all or part of an asset
- receives a capital sum, such as an insurance payout for a damaged asset.

Most types of assets are liable to CGT and include items such as:

- shares
- unit trusts
- certain bonds
- property (except the person's main home, or principal private residence, see below).

As you can see from the list above, nearly all types of assets are caught by CGT.

There are, however, a number of notable **exemptions**:

- Although property is chargeable to CGT, any gain on the sale of the person's main home is exempt. For CGT purposes, the main home is referred to as the 'principal private residence'.

- Your car, and other personal possessions worth up to £6,000 each, such as jewellery or paintings.
- Gains on gilts and certain other sterling bonds, called 'qualifying corporate bonds'.
- Gains on assets held in accounts that benefit from tax exemptions, such as a Individual Savings Account (ISA), Junior ISA or approved pension.
- Betting, lottery or pools winnings.
- Transfers between spouses.

In addition, individuals have an annual tax-free allowance which is known as the **annual exempt amount** and which allows them to make a certain amount of gains tax-free each year.

Any net gains in excess are chargeable as follows:

- 10% and 20% for individuals (the rate used will depend on the amount of their total taxable income and gains)
- 18% and 28% for gains on the sale of residential properties
- 20% for trustees or personal representatives
- 10% for gains qualifying for Entrepreneurs' Relief.

2.3 Inheritance Tax (IHT)

Inheritance tax (IHT) is usually paid on the assets (known as the estate) that someone leaves when they die. It is also sometimes payable on trusts or gifts made during someone's lifetime.

IHT is based on the value of assets that are transferred during the individual's lifetime or that are remaining at death, known as the estate of the deceased.

Each individual has a nil rate band which is currently set at £325,000; and any transfers in excess of the **nil-rate band** are then charged at 40%.

Inheritance tax is a complex area but some of the major **exemptions** are:

- assets left to the deceased person's spouse
- assets left to registered charities
- gifts made more than seven years before death can be exempt if certain conditions are met.

Since October 2007, it has also been possible to transfer any unused nil-rate band from a late spouse or civil partner to the second spouse or civil partner when they die. The percentage that is unused on the first death can then be used to reduce the IHT liability on the second death and can increase the inheritance tax threshold of the second partner from £325,000 to as much as £650,000 depending on the circumstances.

The Finance Act 2012 introduced a reduction in the rate of IHT from 40% to 36% where 10% or more of a deceased person's net estate (after deducting IHT exemptions, reliefs and the nil-rate band) is left to charity. The measure applies to deaths on or after 6 April 2012.

2.4 Stamp Duty and Stamp Duty Reserve Tax (SDRT)

Stamp duty is a tax paid on the purchase of shares when a stock transfer form is used. Stamp duty reserve tax (SDRT) is payable when shares are purchased electronically and no stock transfer form is used. The rate is 0.5% of the purchase price and is paid only by the purchaser.

There is no stamp duty payable on the purchase of most foreign shares, bonds, investment companies with variable capital (ICVCs) or unit trusts or on exchange-traded funds (ETFs).

You must pay Stamp Duty Land Tax (SDLT) if you buy a property or land over a certain price in England, Wales and Northern Ireland. (SDLT no longer applies in Scotland. Instead you pay Land and Buildings Transaction Tax when you buy a property). The current SDLT threshold is £125,000 for residential properties and £150,000 for non-residential land and properties. How much you pay depends on whether the land or property is residential or is non-residential.

2.5 Value Added Tax (VAT)

VAT is chargeable by firms and individuals whose turnover exceeds a certain amount, when they supply what are known as taxable goods or services. Although this affects all firms except those below the VAT threshold, they are allowed to deduct tax they have paid on purchases, so reducing their liability.

The standard rate of VAT is currently 20%. It is relevant to a number of investment services. For example, fees charged for providing an investment management service to an authorised unit trust would be VAT-exempt, while those charged to clients (eg, private individuals) would be VATable. There are also exceptions when no VAT is payable, such as with broker's commission for the execution of a stock market trade.

3. Investment Wrappers

As part of their economic policies, many governments wish to encourage both savings and share ownership. One of the ways this is achieved in the UK is by giving tax advantages to make certain savings and investment products attractive to savers and investors alike. Some of the principal schemes available are known as investment 'wrappers': the term includes products such as Individual Savings Accounts (ISAs) and pensions.

As a result of their attractiveness, they are subject to a range of rules prescribing areas such as, who can invest, the amount of annual contributions that can be made and what are permissible investments. These rules are made by HMRC.

3.1 Individual Savings Accounts (ISAs)

Individual Savings Accounts (ISAs) were set up by the government to encourage individual investment. They were introduced in 1999 and have since been the main vehicle for saving and investing tax-efficiently. The particular incentive for investment is that the investments held within an ISA are free of income tax and CGT.

The ISA itself is often referred to as an investment wrapper because it is essentially an account that holds other savings and investments, such as deposits, shares, open-ended investment companies (OEICs) and unit trusts, and allows them to be invested in a tax-efficient manner.

The ISA acts as a wrapper, shielding the return on savings and investments held in it from tax. Firms offering investments in ISAs, such as banks, building societies and fund management companies, must be approved by HMRC. The approved entity is known as the ISA manager. HMRC is also responsible for setting the detailed rules applicable to ISAs.

Significant changes were made to ISAs in recent budgets in order to introduce greater flexibility and increase their use and attraction as a savings vehicle. As a result, many changes are being introduced and more can be expected.

3.1.1 Types of ISA

From April 2017, there are four types of ISA:

- **Cash ISA**
  - This is the most common ISA which includes deposits with banks and building societies and some cash-type products.
  - Cash ISAs are the tax-free equivalent of traditional savings accounts.
- **Stocks and Shares ISA**
  - These can hold most fixed-interest securities, equities and virtually all unit trusts, investment trusts and OEICs, except cash-like and limited redemption funds.
  - They also include life assurance policies (but not pensions) which, before 2005–06, formed a separate component.
- **Innovative Finance ISA**
  - From April 2016, a third type of ISA was introduced – the Innovative Finance ISA.
  - This ISA covers peer-to-peer (P2P) lending, where lenders are matched with borrowers so each enjoys better rates and will mean those lending through P2P platforms will be able to get their interest tax-free.
- **Lifetime ISA**
  - The Lifetime ISA became available in April 2017 and is designed to help young people save flexibly for the long term throughout their lives.
  - They are available to adults under the age of 40 and contributions can be made up to the age of 50. The government will add a bonus to the contributions made.

In addition, there is the Help to Buy ISA and Junior ISA (JISA).

3.1.2 Characteristics and Benefits

ISAs offer a range of tax benefits:

- There is no additional income tax liability on UK dividends for taxpayers.
- All gains are free of CGT.
- Interest on fixed-interest securities in the stocks and shares component and on deposits in the cash component is free of income tax.
- An individual does not need to report details of their ISAs to HMRC.

Stocks and Shares ISAs can usefully shelter capital gains and can be attractive for higher rate taxpayers.

Other key features of ISAs are as follows:

- Investors can only open one Cash ISA, one Stocks and Shares ISA and one Innovative Finance ISA each year. Once open, transfers can be made to other providers.
- There is a maximum amount that can be subscribed each year into ISAs and it is up to the investor whether they invest in a Cash ISA, a Stocks and Shares ISA, an Innovative Finance ISA or a combination of both providing that the maximum subscription limit is not exceeded.
- An investor can hold their cash funds within a Stocks and Shares ISA if they wish and if the provider allows it, but many prefer to have separate accounts for their cash savings and their investments.
- It is up to providers to determine which type of ISA they will offer.

3.1.3 Eligibility

To be able to apply for an ISA, an investor must be able to meet eligibility rules on age and residence.

The age rules are as follows:

- To open a Cash ISA, an individual must be aged 16.

- The investor must be aged at least 18 for a Stocks and Shares ISA, an Innovative Finance ISA or a Lifetime ISA.
- For a Lifetime ISA other age rules apply to subscriptions; for example the individual may only open a Lifetime ISA under the age of 40 but they may subscribe to that ISA until they reach 50.

To be eligible, an investor must also meet a residence qualification. The investor must be either of the following:

- A UK resident for tax purposes, or a non-resident UK Crown servant (or their spouse/civil partner), subject to UK income tax on their overseas earnings.
- If an ISA holder ceases to be resident in the UK, they can keep the ISA and retain the tax benefits, but cannot pay in any further money.

ISAs cannot be assigned, put into trust or arranged on a joint basis. Investments must be made with the investor's own cash.

3.1.4 Subscriptions

Investors can subscribe in each tax year to:

- one Cash ISA
- one Stocks and Shares ISA
- one Innovative Finance ISA, and
- one Lifetime ISA.

They cannot subscribe to two (or more) Cash ISAs, two (or more) Stocks and Shares ISAs, two (or more) Innovative Finance ISAs, or two or more Lifetime ISAs in the same tax year. This is known as the 'one ISA of each type per tax year' rule.

Subscription limits are set annually and are usually increased by the rate of inflation unless the Chancellor announces a different rate at the budget. For the tax year 2017–18, the ISA subscription limit is £20,000.

- The whole allowance can be invested in a Cash ISA or a Stocks and Shares ISA, or an Innovative Finance ISA or any combination of these.
- Up to £4,000 of the annual subscription limit can be subscribed to a Lifetime ISA.
- An investor can invest in any combination of ISAs providing that the total subscriptions are within the limits and the one ISA of each type per tax year rule is met.

Investors are also allowed to transfer shares they have received from approved profit sharing schemes, share incentive plans or Save As You Earn (SAYE) share options. Investors have to transfer such shares within 90 days of receipt at market value. The value of these transfers will reduce the remaining ISA subscription balance available for that year.

3.1.5 Lifetime ISA

A new type of ISA became available from April 2017 – the Lifetime ISA. Its key features are:

- It is available to individuals aged between 18 and 40.
- From April 2017, people under the age of 40 will be able to open a Lifetime ISA and contribute up to £4,000 in each tax year. The government will then provide a 25% bonus on these contributions at the end of the tax year. Any contributions to a Lifetime ISA will sit within the overall ISA contribution limit.
- Individuals will be able to open more than one Lifetime ISA during their lives, but will only be able to pay into one Lifetime ISA in each tax year.
- The savings and the bonus can be used towards a deposit on a first home worth up to £450,000. If the investor has a Help to Buy ISA, they can transfer those savings into the Lifetime ISA in 2017, or continue saving into both – but they will only be able to use the bonus from one to buy a house.
- Individuals will be able to contribute to their Lifetime ISA and will receive a government bonus on contributions up until the point they reach 50.

After an investor's 60th birthday, they can take out all the savings tax-free. Withdrawals can be made before they become 60, but they will lose the government bonus (and any interest or growth on this). They will also have to pay a 5% charge.

3.1.6 Help to Buy ISA

A Help to Buy ISA for first-time buyers became available from 1 December 2015 and offers a government bonus when investors use their savings to purchase their first home. They count as a type of Cash ISA and if used, investors forgo their right to subscribe to a Cash ISA.

- For every £200 that a first-time buyer saves, there will be a £50 bonus payment up to a maximum of £3,000 on £12,000 of savings. The maximum initial deposit will be £1,000 and the maximum monthly saving thereafter will be £200.
- The bonus will be available for purchases of homes of up to £450,000 in London and up to £250,000 elsewhere. The bonus will only apply for home purchase.
- Savers will have access to their own money and will be able to withdraw funds from their account if they need them for any purpose.

The Help to Buy ISA will be open for new savers until 30 November 2019, and open to new contributions until 2029.

3.1.7 Transfers

It is possible to transfer between ISA providers, and between a Cash ISA and a Stocks and Shares ISA, or vice versa. Individuals are also able to transfer savings from other ISAs as one way of funding their Lifetime ISA.

Although it is a legal requirement for ISA providers to permit transfers out, there is no corresponding rule for accepting transfers.

When an investor wants to transfer an ISA or transfer from one type to the other, it is important they do not withdraw the funds themselves and then redeposit into a new account. If they do, the funds are treated as having been withdrawn and any new deposit counts towards the annual subscription limits. Instead, they should approach the new ISA manager who will arrange for the transfer.

If an investor wishes to transfer the current year's subscription to a new provider, all of that current year's contribution must be transferred. For earlier years' contributions, partial transfers are permitted.

Since April 2015 spouses and civil partners have been able to inherit their partner's ISA assets when they die. Previously, when someone died the savings in their ISA lost the tax-free status and, although these may have passed to their spouse under their will or intestacy, that partner would then pay tax on any income or gains that subsequently arose.

This change is about the surviving spouse gaining an additional ISA allowance. They can open an ISA into which they can pay up to the value of the deceased's account on date of death. This change does not impact the individual's ability to subscribe to their normal annual ISA allowance of £20,000 for 2017–18.

3.1.8 Withdrawals

An investor has the right to withdraw all or part of the cash and investments held in an ISA, and the terms and conditions for the account make clear that the investor retains beneficial ownership. Any withdrawal will be subject to the terms and conditions for the account, such as satisfying notice periods. Furthermore, withdrawal rights in relation to non-cash Innovative Finance ISA investments are available only as set out in the terms and conditions of the account.

Money contributed to an ISA cannot normally be withdrawn and then replaced without it counting again towards the annual subscription limit. However, from April 2016, individuals are now able to withdraw money from their Cash or Stocks and Shares ISA and replace it in the same year without it counting towards their annual ISA subscriptions limit

Since April 2016, investors have been able to withdraw money from their Cash ISAs and replace it in the same tax year without it counting towards their annual subscription limit (a Flexible ISA).

- A Flexible ISA is an ISA whose terms and conditions allow the investor to replace cash they have withdrawn, without the replacement counting towards their annual subscription limit.
- Where a withdrawal is made, any subsequent subscriptions in the same tax year that would otherwise count towards the subscription limit will do so only to the extent that previously withdrawn amounts have been fully replaced.
- Flexibility can be offered in respect of cash only. It can be offered for Cash ISAs and also in respect of any cash held in a Stocks and Shares or an Innovative Finance ISA (including from the sale of investments).
- Offering flexibility is optional for ISA managers. It is not available for Junior ISAs (JISAs), Help to Buy ISAs or Lifetime ISAs.

3.1.9 Junior ISAs (JISAs)

Junior ISAs (JISAs) were introduced in 2011 as a new tax-free children's savings account to replace the Child Trust Fund (CTF). JISAs offer a simple and tax-free way to save for a child's future.

Key Features

- **Eligibility**
  - All UK-resident children (aged under 18) who do not have a CTF are eligible.

- **Types of account**
  - Both Cash and Stocks and Shares JISAs are available.
  - The qualifying investments for each of these are the same as for existing ISAs and children are able to hold up to one Cash and one Stocks and Shares JISA at a time.
- **Annual subscription limit**
  - Each eligible child is able to receive contributions of up to a fixed amount each year (£4,128 in 2017–18) into their JISA.
  - The subscription limit is indexed by the Consumer Prices Index (CPI).
- **Account opening**
  - Anyone with parental responsibility for an eligible child is able to open a JISA on their behalf.
  - Eligible children over the age of 16 are also able to open a JISA for themselves.
- **Account operation**
  - Until the child reaches 16, accounts will be managed on their behalf by a person who has parental responsibility for that child.
  - At age 16, the child assumes management responsibility for their account.
  - Withdrawals are not permitted until the child reaches 18 except in cases of terminal illness or death.
- **Transfers**
  - It is possible to transfer accounts between providers, but it is not possible to hold more than one Cash or Stocks and Shares JISA at any time.
  - It had previously not been possible to transfer CTFs into JISAs, but this changed in April 2015.
- **Maturity**
  - At the age of 18, the JISA will automatically become a normal adult ISA.
  - The funds will then be accessible to the child.

Having a JISA does not affect an individual's entitlement to adult ISAs. It will be possible for JISA account holders to open adult Cash ISAs from the age of 16, and JISA contributions will not impact upon their adult ISA subscription limits.

Example

A person aged between 16 and 18 years of age can hold a Cash ISA but cannot open a Stocks and Shares ISA. They will be able to pay in the maximum subscription into a Cash ISA in addition to any amounts that they pay into a JISA that they hold. So, in 2017–18, they could pay £4,128 into a JISA and £20,000 into a Cash ISA.

3.2 Pensions

3.2.1 Retirement Planning

For many people their pension and their house are their main assets.

Pensions are becoming increasingly important as people live longer and commentators speak of a 'pensions time bomb', when the pension provided by the state, the individuals and their employers will be inadequate to meet needs in retirement. As an example, it is predicted that by 2040 over 50% of the people in the UK will be over 65. When the state pension was introduced in the UK, the initial need was funding for the rare event of people living beyond the age of 65. Today this is very common.

3.2.2 Benefits

A pension is an investment fund where contributions are made, usually during the individual's working life, to provide a lump sum on retirement plus an annual pension payable thereafter. Pension contributions are tax-effective, as tax relief is given on contributions. In other words, the contributions to a pension made by an individual reduce the total on which income tax in charged in each tax year.

Some of the main tax incentives of pensions include:

- Tax relief on contributions made.
- Pension funds are not subject to income tax and CGT and so the pension fund can grow tax-free.
- The ability to take a pension from age 55.
- An option to take a tax-free lump sum at retirement.
- The option to include death benefits as part of the scheme.

These tax advantages were put in place by the government to encourage people to provide for their own old age. Pensions are subject to income tax when they are received.

3.2.3 State Pension Scheme

The state pension currently comes in two parts:

- basic state pension
- additional state pension or state second pension (S2P).

The government pays state pensions from current National Insurance contributions, and makes no investment for future needs. This is a problem as dependency ratios (the proportion of working people to retired people) are forecast to fall from 4:1 in 2002 to 3:1 by 2030 and 2.5:1 by 2050. This means that by 2050 either each worker will have to support almost twice as many retired people, or the support per head will need to fall substantially, or some combination of these changes.

As a result of these cost pressures, major changes are underway to the state pension scheme:

- The age at which the state pension is payable is rising such that the pension age for both men and women will be 65 from 6 April 2018, ie, everyone will draw their pensions at the same age. Those born after 6 October 1954, but before 6 April 1968,

however, will not draw their pensions until the age of 66. For those born after 1968, the pension age will increase from 66 to 67 and then to 68. It may subsequently rise even further.
- The current state pension is being replaced by a flat rate pension, although the amount payable will depend on whether the individual has made sufficient national insurance contributions during their working life.

3.2.4 Occupational Pension Schemes

One of the earliest kinds of scheme supplementing state funding was the occupational pension scheme.

Occupational pension schemes are run by companies for their employees. In an occupational pension scheme, the employer makes pension contributions on behalf of its workers. The occupational pension scheme could take the form of a defined benefit scheme, also known as a 'final salary scheme', where the pension received is related to the number of years of service and the individual's final salary. For example, an occupational pension scheme might provide an employee with 1/60th of their final salary for every year of service; the employee could then retire with an annual pension the size of which was related to the number of years' service.

The advantages of occupational pension schemes are:

- Employers generally contribute to the fund (some pension schemes do not involve any contributions from the employee – these are called **non-contributory** schemes).
- Running costs are often lower than for personal schemes and the costs are often met by the employer.
- The employer must ensure the fund is well run and for **defined benefit schemes** must make up any shortfall in funding.

Employers have generally stopped providing defined benefit schemes to new employees because of rising life expectancies and volatile investment returns, and the implications these factors have on the funding requirement for defined benefit schemes.

Instead, occupational pension schemes are now typically provided to new employees on a **defined contribution** basis – when the size of the pension is driven by the contributions paid and the investment performance of the fund. Under this type of scheme, an investment fund is built up and the amount of pension that will be received at retirement will be determined by the value of the fund and the amount of pension it can generate.

In April 2015, the tax rules were changed to give people greater access to their pensions and members of defined contribution schemes can now access their pension pot in different ways. People are no longer required to buy an annuity, although this option may still be the best route for many. Instead, it is now possible for an individual to take their entire pension as a lump sum at retirement age although they will pay tax on the money. Alternatively, they can select to take an adjustable income, take cash out in lumps or a mix of the options.

The higher cost of providing a defined benefit scheme is part of the reason why many companies have closed their defined benefit schemes to new joiners and make only defined contribution schemes available to staff.

A key advantage of defined contribution schemes for employers over defined benefit schemes is that poor performance is not the employer's problem; it is the employee who will end up with a smaller pension.

Occupational pension schemes are structured as **trusts**, with the investment portfolio managed by professional asset managers. The asset managers are appointed by, and report

to, the trustees of the scheme. The trustees will typically include representatives from the company (eg, company directors) as well as employee representatives.

3.2.5 Private Pensions or Personal Pensions

Private pensions or personal pensions are individual pension plans. They are **defined contribution** schemes that might be used by employees of companies that do not run their own scheme or when employees opt out of the company scheme or in addition to an existing pension scheme. They are also used by the self-employed.

Many employers actually organise **group personal pension schemes** for their employees, by arranging the administration of these schemes with an insurance company or an asset management firm. Such employers may also contribute to the personal pension schemes of their employees.

Employees and the self-employed who wish to provide for their pension and do not have access to occupational schemes or employer-arranged personal pensions have to organise their own personal pension schemes. These will often be arranged through an insurance company or an asset manager, where the individual can choose from the variety of investment funds offered.

Individuals also have the facility to run a **self-invested personal pension (SIPP)**, commonly administered by a stockbroker or IFA on their behalf. In a SIPP, it is the individual who decides which investments are included in the scheme, subject to HMRC guidelines.

The schemes are approved by HMRC which means that they are **tax-exempt**. The contributions are tax-deductible and there is no tax either on investment income or capital gains.

In a private scheme, the key responsibility that lies with the individual is that the individual chooses the investment fund in a scheme administered by an insurance company or asset manager, or the actual investments in a SIPP. It is then up to the individual to monitor the performance of his investments and assess whether it will be sufficient for his retirement needs.

3.2.6 Stakeholder Pensions

A stakeholder pension is simply a type of personal pension that incurs low charges. Stakeholder pensions are available from a range of financial services companies, such as banks, insurance companies and building societies.

Stakeholder pensions must satisfy a number of minimum government standards to ensure that they offer value for money and flexibility, including:

- **Low charges** – for people who joined a stakeholder pension scheme on or after 6 April 2005, the cap is an annual management charge of 1.5% for the first ten years, which will reduce to 1% from ten years onwards if these members remain in the scheme.
- **Low and flexible contributions** – the minimum contribution cannot be greater than £20, and there cannot be a requirement for regular monthly contribution.
- **Transferability** – there must be no charges for transfer to another scheme.
- **Default option** – pension funds can allocate funds between different kinds of investment. A stakeholder scheme must provide a default for those unwilling to choose their own allocation between, say, UK shares, overseas shares or bond funds.

3.2.7 NEST and Auto-enrolment

Government estimates suggest that around seven million people are not saving enough to give them the retirement income they will want or expect. The Pensions Act 2008 is aimed at tackling this challenge. The Act imposes new duties on employers to provide access to a workplace pension scheme for most workers, which started to be introduced in 2012. Employers have to enrol some or all of their workers into a pension scheme that meets or exceeds certain legal standards, and may need to make a minimum contribution.

Employers need to automatically enrol workers aged at least 22 but under state pension age who earn more than £10,000 in a year. These people are known as eligible jobholders and their employers will have to make a minimum contribution into the pension scheme on their behalf.

From the date they are automatically enrolled, they will have a month to choose not to join, or 'opt out'. If they do nothing, they will be enrolled in the scheme. They will make contributions to their retirement pot from their pay for as long as they are employed or until they take their money out.

Workers and employers can both contribute into NEST to build a retirement pot that is invested on behalf of the worker. Workers who earn over a certain amount are entitled to a minimum contribution into their pot when they are paid.

Minimum contributions are based on 'qualifying earnings' and are a section of a worker's pay. For the 2017–18 tax year, this is everything over £5,876 and up to £45,000. The qualifying earnings band is reviewed by the government each year. The rate itself only applies to a worker's qualifying earnings. So in the 2017–18 tax year, a worker's minimum contribution will be 2% of everything they earn over £5,876 but not of anything they earn over £45,000.

The minimum contribution is made up of money from a worker's pay, money from their employer and tax relief from the government.

4. Trusts

4.1 What is a Trust?

A trust is the legal means by which one person gives property to another person to look after on behalf of another individual or a set of individuals.

Starting with the individuals involved, the person who creates the trust is known as the **settlor**. The person they give the property to, to look after on behalf of others, is called the **trustee**, and the individuals for whom it is intended are known as the **beneficiaries**.

4.2 Uses of Trusts

Trusts are widely used in estate and tax planning for high net worth individuals and some of their main uses include:

- providing funds for a specific purpose, such as the maintenance of young children
- setting aside funds for disabled or incapacitated children in order to protect and provide for their financial maintenance
- reducing future inheritance tax liabilities by transferring assets into a trust and so out of the settlor's ownership
- separating out rights to income and capital so that, for example, the spouse of a second marriage receives the income from an asset during their life and the capital passes on that person's death to the settlor's children.

Trusts are also the underlying structure for many major investment vehicles, such as pension funds, charities and unit trusts.

11

Learning Objectives

Chapter Eleven has covered the following Learning Objectives:

9.1.1   Know the direct and indirect taxes as they apply to individuals: income tax; capital gains tax; inheritance tax; stamp duty, stamp duty reserve tax and stamp duty land tax; VAT

9.1.2   Know the main exemptions in respect of the main personal taxes

9.2.1   Know the definition of and aim of ISAs

9.2.2   Know the tax incentives provided by ISAs

9.2.3   Know the types of ISA available: Cash; Stocks and Shares; Junior ISA; Help to Buy; Innovative Finance; Lifetime

9.2.4   Know the eligibility conditions for investors

9.2.5   Know the following aspects of investing in ISAs: subscriptions; transfers; withdrawals; eligibility conditions

9.3.1   Know the benefits provided by pensions

9.3.2   Know the basic characteristics of the following: state pension scheme; occupational pension schemes; personal pensions including self-invested personal pensions (SIPPs); stakeholder pensions; NEST/auto enrolment

9.4.1   Know the definition of the following terms: trustee; settlor; beneficiary

9.4.2   Know the main reasons for creating trusts

Based on what you have learned in Chapter Eleven, try to answer the following end of chapter questions.

End of Chapter Questions

Think of an answer for each question and refer to the appropriate section for confirmation.

1. What are the various rates of income tax?
    Answer Reference: Section 2.1

    ....

    ....

2. What is the personal allowance?
    Answer Reference: Section 2.1

    ....

    ....

3. Since April 2016, how much dividend income in each tax year is now tax-exempt?
    Answer Reference: Section 2.1.2

    ....

    ....

4. What assets are exempt from Capital Gains Tax?
    Answer Reference: Section 2.2

    ....

    ....

5. What is the rate of Inheritance Tax?
    Answer Reference: Section 2.3

    ....

    ....

6. How does Stamp Duty differ from Stamp Duty Reserve Tax (SDRT)?
    Answer Reference: Section 2.4

    ....

    ....

7. What are the four main types of ISA?
    Answer Reference: Section 3.1.1

    ....

    ....

8. How much can be invested in an ISA?
    Answer Reference: Section 3.1.4

    ....

    ....

9. What is the key difference between a defined benefit pension scheme and a defined contribution
    pension scheme?
    Answer Reference: Section 3.2.4

    ....

    ....

10. Who are the three parties that are typically involved in a trust?
    Answer Reference: Section 4

    ....

    ....

Glossary and Abbreviations

Active Management

A type of investment approach employed to generate returns in excess of the market.

Additional Rate (of Income Tax)

Tax on top band of income, currently 45%.

Alternative Investment Market (AIM)

Established by the London Stock Exchange. It is the junior market for smaller company shares.

Annual General Meeting (AGM)

Yearly meeting of shareholders. Mainly used to vote on dividends, appoint directors and approve financial statements.

Approved Persons

Employees in controlled functions, who must be approved by the regulator.

Articles of Association

The legal document which sets out the internal constitution of a company. Included within the Articles will be details of shareholder voting rights and company borrowing powers.

Asset

Any item of economic or financial value owned by someone or a company.

Auction

Sales system used by the Debt Management Office (DMO) when it issues gilts. Successful applicants pay the price they bid.

Authorisation

Required status under FSMA 2000 for firms that wish to provide financial services.

Authorised Corporate Director (ACD)

Fund manager for an OEIC.

Authorised Unit Trust (AUT)

Unit trust which is freely marketable. Authorised by the FCA.

Balance of Payments

A summary of all the transactions between a country and the rest of the world. The difference between a country's imports and exports.

Bank of England (BoE)

The UK's central bank. Implements economic policy decided by the Treasury and determines interest rates.

Base Currency

The first currency quoted in a currency pair.

Basic Rate (of Income Tax)

Rate of tax charged on income that is below the higher rate tax threshold.

Bearer Securities

Those whose ownership is evidenced by the mere possession of a certificate. Ownership can therefore pass from hand to hand without any formalities.

Beneficiaries

The beneficial owners of trust property, or those who inherit under a will.

Bid Price

Price at which dealers buy stock. It is also the price quoted by unit trusts that are dual-priced for sales of units.

Bonds

Interest bearing securities which entitle holders to annual interest and repayment at maturity. Commonly issued by both companies and governments.

Bonus Issue

A free issue of shares to existing shareholders. No money is paid. The share price falls pro rata. Also known as a Capitalisation or Scrip Issue.

Broker

An individual who handles orders to buy and sell from its investors or clients. Brokers often charge a commission for the work they perform. A broker who specialises in stocks, bonds or options acts as an agent and must be registered with the exchange where the securities are traded.

CAC 40

Index of the prices of 40 major French company shares.

Call Option

Option giving its buyer the right to buy an asset at an agreed price.

Capital

Cash and assets used to generate income or make an investment.

Capital Gains Tax (CGT)

Tax payable by individuals on profit made on the disposal of certain assets.

Central Bank

Central banks typically have responsibility for setting a nation's or a region's short-term interest rate, controlling the money supply, acting as banker and lender of last resort to the banking system and managing the national debt.

Certificated

Ownership designated by certificate.

Certificates of Deposit (CDs)

Certificates issued by a bank as evidence that interest-bearing funds have been deposited with it. CDs are traded within the money market.

Clean Price

The quoted price of a gilt. The price quoted for a gilt excludes any interest that has accrued from the last interest payment date and is known as the 'clean' price. Accrued interest is added on afterwards and the price is then known as the 'dirty' price.

Closed-Ended

Organisations such as companies which are a fixed size as determined by their share capital. Commonly used to distinguish investment trusts (closed-ended) from unit trusts and OEICs (open-ended).

Commercial Paper (CP)

Money market instrument issued by large corporates.

Commission

Charges for acting as agent or broker.

Commodity

Items including sugar, wheat, oil and copper. Derivatives of commodities are traded on exchanges (eg, oil futures on ICE Futures).

Contract

A standard unit of trading in derivatives.

Controlled Functions

Job roles which require the employee to be approved by the FCA. There are groups of controlled functions, including significant influence functions, customer functions and LIBOR functions.

Coupon

Amount of interest paid on a bond.

Credit Creation

Expansion of loans which increases the money supply.

CREST

Electronic settlement system used to hold stock and settle transactions for UK shares.

Currency

Any form of money that circulates in an economy as an accepted means of exchange for goods and services.

Data Protection Act

Legislation regulating the use of client data.

Dealer

An individual or firm acting in order to buy or sell a security for its own account and risk.

Debt Management Office (DMO)

The agency responsible for issuing gilts on behalf of the Treasury.

Dematerialised (Form)

System where securities are held electronically without certificates.

Deposit

A deposit is a sum of money held at a financial institution on behalf of an account holder for safekeeping.

Derivatives

Options and futures. Their price is derived from an underlying asset.

Dilution Levy

An additional charge levied on investors buying or selling units in a single-priced fund to offset any potential effect that large purchases or sales can have on the value of the fund.

Diversification

Investment strategy of spreading risk by investing in a range of investments.

Dividend

Distribution of profits by a company.

Dividend Yield

Most recent dividend expressed as a percentage of current share price.

Dow Jones Industrial Average (DJIA)

Major share index in the USA, based on the prices of 30 major company shares.

Dual Pricing

Involves using the market's bid and offer prices of the underlying assets to produce separate prices for buying and selling of shares/units in the fund.

Economic Cycle

The course an economy conventionally takes as economic growth fluctuates over time. Also known as the Business Cycle.

Economic Growth

The growth of GDP or GNP expressed in real terms, usually over the course of a calendar year. Often used as a barometer of an economy's health.

Effective Annual Rate

The annualised compound rate of interest applied to a cash deposit or loan. Also known as the Annual Equivalent Rate (AER).

Equity

Another name for shares. It can also be used to refer to the amount by which the value of a house exceeds any mortgage or borrowings secured on it.

Eurobond

An interest-bearing security issued internationally.

Euronext

European stock exchange network formed by the merger of the Paris, Brussels, Amsterdam and (later) Lisbon exchanges.

Exchange

Marketplace for trading investments.

Exchange Rate

Rate at which one currency can be exchanged for another.

Exchange-Traded Fund (ETF)

Type of collective investment scheme that is open-ended but traded on an investment exchange, rather than directly with the fund's managers.

Ex-Dividend (xd)

The period during which the purchase of shares or bonds (on which a dividend or coupon payment has been declared) does not entitle the new holder to this next dividend or interest payment.

Exercise Price

The price at which the right conferred by an option can be exercised by the holder against the writer.

Financial Conduct Authority (FCA)

One of the bodies that replaced the FSA in 2013 and which is responsible for regulation of conduct in retail, as well as wholesale, financial markets and the infrastructure that supports those markets.

Financial Services and Markets Act 2000 (FSMA 2000)

Legislation which provides the framework for regulating financial services.

Fiscal Policy

The use of government spending, taxation and borrowing policies to either boost or restrain domestic demand in the economy so as to maintain full employment and price stability.

Fit and Proper

FSMA 2000 requires that every firm conducting financial services business must be 'fit and proper'.

Floating Rate Notes (FRNs)

Debt securities issued with a coupon periodically referenced to a benchmark interest rate, such as LIBOR.

Foreign Exchange Market

A market for the trading of foreign currencies.

Forward

A derivatives contract that creates a legally binding obligation between two parties for one to buy and the other to sell a prespecified amount of an asset at a prespecified price on a prespecified future date. As individually negotiated contracts, forwards are not traded on a derivatives exchange.

Forward Exchange Rate

An exchange rate set today, embodied in a forward contract, that will apply to a foreign exchange transaction at some prespecified point in the future.

FTSE 100

Main UK share index of 100 leading shares ('Footsie').

FTSE 250

UK share index based on the 250 shares immediately below the top 100.

FTSE 350

Index combining the FTSE 100 and FTSE 250 indices.

FTSE All Share Index

Index comprising around 98% of UK-listed shares by value.

Full Listing

Those public limited companies (plcs) admitted to the London Stock Exchange's (LSE) official list. Companies seeking a full listing on the LSE must satisfy the UK Listing Authority's (UKLA) stringent listing requirements and continuing obligations once listed.

Fund

A collective investment scheme where money is combined and invested in a portfolio of shares with a common investment purpose.

Fund Manager

Firm that invests money on behalf of clients.

Fund Supermarket

An internet-based service that provides a convenient way of investing in collective investment funds by allowing a variety of funds to be purchased from a number of different management groups in one place.

Future

An agreement to buy or sell an item at a future date, at a price agreed today. Differs from a forward in that it is a standardised amount and therefore the contract can be traded on an exchange.

Gross

Total amount before deductions (ie, taxes).

Gross Domestic Product (GDP)

A measure of a country's output.

Harmonised Index of Consumer Prices (HICP)

Standard measurement of inflation throughout the European Union.

Hedge Fund

A high-risk investment vehicle which uses advanced and aggressive investment financial techniques in order to make maximum gains.

Hedging

A technique employed to reduce the impact of adverse price movements in financial assets held. Often uses derivatives to achieve this aim.

Higher Rate (of Income Tax)

Tax on the band of income above the basic rate and below the additional rate, currently 40%.

HM Treasury

Her Majesty's Treasury. The UK government department responsible for the country's taxes, finance and economy.

Holder

Investor who buys put or call options.

Independent Financial Adviser (IFA)

A financial adviser who is not tied to the products of any one product provider and is duty-bound to give clients best advice and offer them the option of paying for advice. IFAs must establish the financial planning needs of their clients through a personal fact-find, and satisfy these needs with the most appropriate products offered in the marketplace.

Index

A statistical measure of the changes in a selection of stocks representing a portion of the overall market.

Individual Savings Account (ISA)

Savings scheme introduced in 1999 which provided a wrapper in which cash, stocks and shares can benefit from tax concessions.

Inflation

An increase in the general level of prices.

Inheritance Tax (IHT)

Tax on the value of an estate when a person dies.

Initial Public Offering (IPO)

A new issue of ordinary shares, whether made by an offer for sale, an offer for subscription or a placing. Also known as a new issue.

Insider Dealing

Criminal offence by people with unpublished price-sensitive information who deal, advise others to deal or pass the information on.

Integration

Third stage of money laundering.

Intercontinental Exchange (ICE)

ICE operates regulated global futures exchanges and over-the-counter (OTC) markets for agricultural, energy, equity index and currency contracts, as well as credit derivatives. ICE conducts its energy futures markets through ICE Futures Europe, which is based in London.

Interest

The price paid for borrowing money. Generally, interest is expressed as a percentage rate over a period of time, such as 5% per annum.

Investment Bank

Business that specialises in raising debt and equity for companies.

Investment Company with Variable Capital (ICVC)

Collective investment vehicle similar to a unit trust. Alternatively described as an Open-Ended Investment Company (OEIC).

Investment Trust (Company)

A company, not a trust, which invests in a diversified range of investments.

Layering

Second stage in money laundering.

Liability

An obligation that legally binds an individual or company to settle a debt or a payment.

LIFFE

The UK's principal derivatives exchange for trading financial and soft commodity derivatives products. Owned by ICE.

Limited Company (ltd)

A privately owned company with limited liability among its owners.

Liquidity

The ease with which an item can be traded on the market. Liquid markets are described as deep.

Liquidity Risk

The risk that shares may be difficult to sell at a reasonable price.

Listing

Companies whose securities are listed on the London Stock Exchange and available to be traded.

Loan Stock

A corporate bond issued in the domestic bond market without any underlying collateral, or security.

London InterBank Offered Rate (LIBOR)

A benchmark money market interest rate.

London Metal Exchange (LME)

Market for trading in derivatives of certain metals, such as copper, zinc and aluminium.

London Stock Exchange (LSE)

Main UK market for securities.

Long Position

The position following the purchase of a security or buying a derivative.

Market

All exchanges are markets – electronic or physical meeting place where assets are bought or sold.

Market Capitalisation

Total market value of a company's shares. The share price multiplied by the number of shares in issue.

Market Maker

An LSE member firm which is obliged to offer to buy and sell securities in which it is registered throughout the mandatory quote period. In return for providing this liquidity to the market, it can make its profits through the differences at which it buys and sells.

Market Price

Price of a share as quoted on the exchange.

Maturity

Date when the capital on a bond is repaid.

Memorandum of Association

The legal document that principally defines a company's powers, or objects, and its relationship with the outside world. The Memorandum also details the number and nominal value of shares the company is authorised to issue and has issued.

Merger

The combining of two or more companies into one new entity.

Mixed Economy

Economy which works through a combination of market forces and government involvement.

Monetary Policy

The setting of short-term interest rates by a central bank in order to manage domestic demand and achieve price stability in the economy.

Monetary Policy Committee (MPC)

Committee run by the Bank of England which sets interest rates.

Mortgages

A mortgage, or more precisely a mortgage loan, is a long-term loan used to finance the purchase of real estate (eg, a house). Under the Mortgage Agreement, the borrower agrees to make a series of payments back to the lender. The money lent by the bank (or building society) is secured against the value of the property: if the payments are not made by the borrower, the lender can take back the property.

Mutual Fund

A type of collective investment scheme found in the US.

NASDAQ

National Association of Securities Dealers Automated Quotations. US market specialising in the shares of technology companies.

NASDAQ Composite

NASDAQ stock index.

National Debt

A government's total outstanding borrowing resulting from financing successive budget deficits, mainly through the issue of government-backed securities.

National Savings and Investments (NS&I)

Government agency that provides investment products for the retail market.

Nikkei 225

Main Japanese share index.

Nominal Value

The amount of a bond that will be repaid on maturity. Also known as face or par value.

Nominated Adviser (NOMAD)

Firm which advises AIM companies on their regulatory responsibilities.

Offer Price

Price at which dealers sell stock. It is also the price quoted by unit trusts that are dual-priced for purchases of units.

Open Economy

Country with no restrictions on trading with other countries.

Open-Ended

Type of investment such as OEICs or unit trusts which can expand without limit.

Open-Ended Investment Company (OEIC)

Collective investment vehicle similar to a unit trust. Alternatively described as an Investment Company with Variable Capital (ICVC).

Open Outcry

Trading system used by some derivatives exchanges. Participants stand on the floor of the exchange and call out transactions they would like to undertake.

Option

A derivative giving the buyer the right, but not the obligation, to buy or sell an asset.

Ordinary Shares

Most common form of share. Holders may receive dividends if the company is profitable.

Over-the-Counter (OTC) Derivatives

Derivatives that are not traded on a derivatives exchange, owing to their non-standardised contract specifications.

Panel on Takeovers and Mergers (POTAM or PTM)

A self-regulatory body that produces the City Code regulating takeovers.

Passive Management

An investment approach that aims to track the performance of a stock market index. Employed in those securities markets that are believed to be price-efficient.

Pension Fund

A fund set up by a company or government to invest the pension contributions of members and employees to be paid out at retirement age.

Personal Allowance

Amount of income that each person can earn each year tax-free.

Placement

First stage of money laundering.

Platform

Platforms are online services such as fund supermarkets and wraps that are used by intermediaries to view and administer their investment clients' portfolios.

Portfolio

A selection of investments.

Preference Share

Shares which pay fixed dividends. Do not have voting rights, but do have priority over ordinary shares in default situations.

Premium

The amount of cash paid by the holder of an option to the writer in exchange for conferring a right.

Premium Bond

National Savings & Investments bonds that pay prizes each month. Winnings are tax-free.

Primary Market

The function of a stock exchange in bringing new securities to the market and raising funds.

Protectionism

The economic policy of restraining trade between countries by imposing methods such as tariffs and quotas on imported goods.

Proxy

Appointee who votes on a shareholder's behalf at company meetings.

Prudential Regulation Authority (PRA)

The UK body that is responsible for prudential regulation of all deposit-taking institutions, insurers and investment banks.

Public Limited Company (plc)

A company whose shares can be owned by the general public and are usually bought and sold, through a regulated stock exchange (eg, London Stock Exchange).

Public Sector Net Cash Requirement (PSNCR)

Shortfall of government revenue compared to government expenditure.

Put Option

Option when buyer has the right to sell an asset.

Quote-Driven

Dealing system driven by securities firms who quote buying and selling prices.

Real Estate Investment Trust (REIT)

An investment trust that specialises in investing in commercial property.

Redemption

The repayment of principal to the holder of a redeemable security.

Redemption Yield

A measure that incorporates both the income and capital return – assuming the investor holds the bond until its maturity – into one figure.

Registrar

An official of a company who maintains the share register.

Resolution

Proposal on which shareholders vote.

Retail Bank

Organisation that provides banking facilities to individuals and small/medium businesses.

Retail Prices Index (RPI)

Index that measures the movement of prices.

Rights Issue

The issue of new ordinary shares to a company's shareholders in proportion to each shareholder's existing shareholding, usually at a price deeply discounted to that prevailing in the market.

RPIX

Index that shows the underlying rate of inflation, excluding the impact of mortgage payments.

Secondary Market

Market place for trading in existing securities.

Securities

Bonds and equities.

Settlor

The creator of a trust.

Shareholders

Those who own the shares of the company. Essentially, they are the owners of the company.

Short Position

The position following the sale of a security not owned, or selling a derivative.

Société d'Investissement à Capital Variable (SICAV)

Type of European collective investment scheme that is open-ended.

Single Pricing

Refers to the use of the mid-market prices of the underlying assets to produce a single price.

Special Resolution

Proposal put to shareholders requiring 75% of the votes cast.

Spread

Difference between a buying (bid) and selling (ask or offer) price.

Stamp Duty

Tax at ½% on the purchase of certain assets including certificated securities.

Stamp Duty Land Tax (SDLT)

Tax charged on the purchase of properties and land above a certain value.

Stamp Duty Reserve Tax (SDRT)

Stamp duty levied at ½% on purchase of dematerialised equities.

State-Controlled Economy

Country where all economic activity is controlled by the state.

Stock Exchange Automated Quotations (SEAQ)

LSE screen display system where market makers display the prices at which they are willing to deal. Used mainly for fixed-income stocks and small cap shares.

Stock Exchange Electronic Trading Service (SETS)

LSE's electronic order-driven trading system.

STRIPS

The principal and interest payments of those designated gilts that can be separately traded as zero coupon bonds (ZCBs). STRIPS is the acronym for Separate Trading of Registered Interest and Principal of Securities.

Swap

An over-the-counter (OTC) derivative whereby two parties exchange a series of periodic payments based on a notional principal amount over an agreed term. Swaps can take the form of interest rate swaps, currency swaps and equity swaps.

T+2

The two-day rolling settlement period over which all certificated deals executed on the London Stock Exchange's (LSE) SETS are settled.

Takeover

When one company buys more than 50% of the shares of another.

Tracker Fund

A fund that tries to mirror the performance of a chosen share index.

Treasury

Government department ultimately responsible for the regulation of the financial services industry.

Treasury Bills

Short-term (usually 90-day) borrowings of the UK government. Issued at a discount to the nominal value at which they will mature. Traded in the money market.

Trustees

The legal owners of trust property who owe a duty of skill and care to the trust's beneficiaries.

Two-Way Price

Prices quoted by a market maker at which they are willing to buy (bid) and sell (offer).

Underlying

Asset from which a derivative is derived.

Unit Trust

A system whereby money from investors is pooled together and invested collectively on their behalf into an open-ended trust.

Wraps

A type of fund platform that enables advisers to take a holistic view of the various assets that a client has in a variety of accounts.

Writer

Party selling an option. The writers receive premiums in exchange for taking the risk of being exercised against.

Xetra Dax

German shares index, comprising 30 shares.

Yield

Income from an investment as a percentage of the current price.

Zero Coupon Bonds (ZCBs)

Bonds issued at a discount to their nominal value that do not pay a coupon but which are redeemed at par on a prespecified future date.

ACD	Authorised Corporate Director	**EU**	European Union
AER	Annual Effective (or Equivalent) Rate	**FATF**	Financial Action Task Force
AGM	Annual General Meeting	**FCA**	Financial Conduct Authority
AIC	Association of Investment Companies	**FED**	Federal Reserve
		FIA Europe	Futures Industry Association
AIM	Alternative Investment Market	**FOS**	Financial Ombudsman Service
APR	Annual Percentage Rate	**FPC**	Financial Policy Committee
AUT	Authorised Unit Trust	**FSCS**	Financial Services Compensation Scheme
BBA	British Bankers' Association		
BIS	Bank for International Settlements	**FRN**	Floating Rate Note
BoE	Bank of England	**FSMA**	Financial Services and Markets Act (2000)
CBOE	Chicago Board Options Exchange	**FX**	Foreign Exchange
CD	Certificate of Deposit	**GDP**	Gross Domestic Product
CDD	Customer Due Diligence	**HICP**	Harmonised Index of Consumer Prices
CGT	Capital Gains Tax		
CP	Commercial Paper	**HMRC**	Her Majesty's Revenue & Customs
CPI	Consumer Prices Index	**ICE**	Intercontinental Exchange
CTF	Child Trust Fund	**ICMA**	International Capital Market Association
DMO	Debt Management Office	**ICVC**	Investment Company with Variable Capital
DJIA	Dow Jones Industrial Average		
ECB	European Central Bank	**IFA**	Independent Financial Adviser
ECX	European Climate Exchange	**IHT**	Inheritance Tax
ESMA	European Securities and Markets Authority	**IPO**	Initial Public Offer
		ISA	Individual Savings Account
ETD	Exchange-Traded Derivative	**JISA**	Junior Individual Savings Account
ETF	Exchange-Traded Fund		

JMLSG	Joint Money Laundering Steering Group	**SDLT**	Stamp Duty Land Tax
LIBOR	London InterBank Offered Rate	**SDRT**	Stamp Duty Reserve Tax
LME	London Metal Exchange	**SEAQ**	Stock Exchange Automated Quotation system
LSE	London Stock Exchange	**SETS**	Stock Exchange Electronic Trading Service
MAS	Money Advice Service	**SETSqx**	Stock Exchange Electronic Trading Service – Quotes and Crosses
MLRO	Money Laundering Reporting Officer	**SICAV**	Société D'Investissement à Capital Variable
MPC	Monetary Policy Committee		
MTS	An electronic exchange for trading European government bonds	**SIPP**	Self-Invested Personal Pension
		SM&CR	Senior Managers and Certification Regime
NAV	Net Asset Value	**SMR**	Senior Managers Regime
NYSE	New York Stock Exchange	**STRIPS**	Separate Trading of Registered Interest and Principal of Securities
OEIC	Open-Ended Investment Company		
OTC	Over-the-Counter	**SWIFT**	Society of Worldwide Interbank Financial Telecommunication
P2P	Peer-to-Peer		
PIBS	Permanent Interest-Bearing Shares	**TISA**	Tax Incentivised Savings Association
Plc	Public Limited Company		
POCA	Proceeds of Crime Act	**TSE**	Tokyo Stock Exchange
PRA	Prudential Regulation Authority	**UCITS**	Undertakings for Collective Investment in Transferable Securities
PSNCR	Public Sector Net Cash Requirement		
REIT	Real Estate Investment Trust	**UKLA**	United Kingdom Listing Authority
RPI	Retail Price Index	**VAT**	Value Added Tax
RPIX	Retail Prices Index (excluding mortgages)	**VCT**	Venture Capital Trust
		WMA	Wealth Management Association
S2P	State Second Pension		
SDD	Simplified Due Diligence		

Multiple Choice
Questions

The following questions have been compiled to reflect as closely as possible the standard you will experience in your examination. Please note, however, they are not the CISI examination questions themselves.

Tick one answer for each question. When you have completed all questions, refer to the end of this section for the answers.

1. Which of the following is a wholesale market activity associated with an investment bank?

   A. Execution-only stockbroking
   B. Life assurance
   C. Mergers and acquisitions
   D. Private banking

2. Holding assets in safekeeping is one of the principal activities of:

   A. A custodian bank
   B. An international bank
   C. An investment bank
   D. A retail bank

3. An economy that is characterised by an absence of barriers to trade and controls over foreign exchange is known as:

   A. A market economy
   B. A mixed economy
   C. A state-controlled economy
   D. An open economy

4. For those on a fixed income, high levels of inflation would normally:

   A. Allow them to save more
   B. Reduce their tax allowances
   C. Allow them to invest for longer periods
   D. Reduce the amount of goods they can buy

5. What is the definition of a country's invisible trade balance?

   A. International transactions related to the purchase and sale of domestic and foreign investment assets
   B. The difference between the value of imported and exported goods
   C. The total value of goods and services that flow in and out of the country
   D. The difference between the value of imported and exported services

6. Which organisation provides compensation in the event that a bank goes bust?

    A. FCA
    B. FOS
    C. FSCS
    D. PRA

7. Which of the following instruments is zero coupon?

    A. Certificates of deposit
    B. Cash ISAs
    C. Bank current accounts
    D. Treasury bills

8. Which type of foreign exchange transaction would normally settle two days later?

    A. Forward
    B. Future
    C. Spot
    D. Swap

9. Energy commodity futures contracts are traded on which market?

    A. LIFFE
    B. Eurex
    C. ICE Futures Europe
    D. LME

10. Which of the following markets would normally trade aluminium and tin derivatives?

    A. LIFFE
    B. ICE
    C. LME
    D. LSE

11. Which stock market index provides the widest view of the US stock market?

    A. Dow Jones Industrial Average
    B. NASDAQ Composite
    C. Nikkei 225
    D. S&P 500

12. The key difference between the primary market and the secondary market is that:

    A. The primary market relates to equities and the secondary market relates to bonds
    B. The primary market covers regulated and protected activities and the secondary market covers unregulated and unprotected activities
    C. The primary market is where new shares are first marketed and the secondary market is where existing shares are subsequently traded
    D. The primary market involves domestic trading and the secondary market involves overseas trading

13. In the event of a company going into liquidation, who would normally have the lowest priority for payment?

    A. Banks
    B. Bondholders
    C. Ordinary shareholders
    D. Preference shareholders

14. What type of corporate action would have taken place if an existing shareholder purchased new shares in the company, thereby increasing the total shares issued?

    A. Bonus issue
    B. Capitalisation issue
    C. Rights issue
    D. Scrip issue

15. The passing of a special resolution at a company meeting requires what MINIMUM percentage of votes in favour?

    A. 50
    B. 75
    C. 90
    D. 100

16. What is the corporate equivalent of Treasury bills known as?

    A. Supranational bonds
    B. Commercial paper
    C. Structured products
    D. Certificates of deposit

17. Which of the following is a mandatory corporate action with options?

    A. Bonus issue
    B. Merger
    C. Rights issue
    D. Takeover

18. Which types of instrument would you expect to see traded on SETS?

    A. Options
    B. Futures
    C. Unit trusts
    D. FTSE 350 shares

19. A UK company has issued a fixed coupon bond into the Japanese market denominated in yen to make it attractive to Japanese investors. What type of bond is this known as?

    A. Asset-backed bond
    B. Eurobond
    C. Foreign bond
    D. Covered bond

20. Which of the following defines a future?

    A. An agreement to buy or sell an item at a future date at a price to be specified at a future date
    B. An agreement to buy or sell an item now at a price to be specified in the future
    C. An agreement to buy or sell an item at a future date at a price specified now
    D. An agreement to buy or sell an item now at a price specified now

21. You have a holding of £10,000 5% Treasury Gilt 2018 which is currently priced at 112 and on which you receive half-yearly interest of £250. What is its flat yield?

    A. 5.0%
    B. 4.46%
    C. 2.50%
    D. 2.23%

22. If interest rates increase, what will be the effect on a 5% government bond?

    A. Price will rise
    B. Price will fall
    C. Coupon will rise
    D. Coupon will fall

23. Which of the following statements concerning call and put options is true?

    A. The buyer of a call has the right to sell an asset
    B. The buyer of a put has the right to buy an asset
    C. The seller of a call has the right to sell an asset
    D. The buyer of a call has the right to buy an asset

24. An investor who has entered into a contract which commits him to buying the underlying asset at a future date is described as?

    A. Holder
    B. Long
    C. Short
    D. Writer

25. Which of the following is a common measure of a country's output?

    A. GDP
    B. Balance of Payments
    C. PSNCR
    D. RPI

26. Which type of collective investment scheme would you expect to trade at a discount or premium to its net asset value?

    A. Unit trust
    B. ETF
    C. Investment trust
    D. OEIC

27. Which of the following types of collective investment scheme has traditionally been dual-priced, but may now also use single pricing?

    A. ETF
    B. REIT
    C. Investment trust
    D. Unit trust

28. A fund that aims to mimic the performance of an index deploys which type of investment style?

    A. Contrarian
    B. Growth
    C. Passive
    D. Momentum

29. Under which of the following types of mortgage does the monthly payment normally comprise a combination of interest and capital?

    A. Endowment
    B. ISA
    C. Pension-linked
    D. Repayment

CISI
CHARTERED INSTITUTE FOR
SECURITIES & INVESTMENT

30. The standard settlement period for the sale of a unit trust is which of the following?

   A. T+1
   B. T+3
   C. T+4
   D. T+5

31. What minimum percentage of profits, after expenses, must be distributed for a real estate investment trust (REIT) to retain its tax status?

   A. 90
   B. 85
   C. 75
   D. 60

32. What type of investment vehicle would you expect to have the highest minimum investment limit?

   A. ETF
   B. Hedge fund
   C. Investment trust
   D. SICAV

33. From 2013, which UK regulatory body is responsible for the supervision of investment exchanges?

   A. Financial Conduct Authority
   B. Financial Policy Committee
   C. Financial Services Authority
   D. Prudential Regulatory Authority

34. A money launderer is actively switching monies between investment products. The stage of money laundering relevant to these activities is known as:

   A. Investment
   B. Integration
   C. Layering
   D. Placement

35. The type of customer due diligence necessary when individuals are not physically present when their identites are verified is known as:

   A. Sensitive
   B. Enhanced
   C. Simplified
   D. Non-standard

246

36. Insider dealing rules apply to which of the following securities?

    A. Commodity derivatives
    B. OEIC shares
    C. Government bonds
    D. Unit trusts

37. What is the maximum payout that can be awarded by the Financial Ombudsman Service?

    A. £30,000
    B. £50,000
    C. £100,000
    D. £150,000

38. Behaviour likely to give a false or misleading impression of the supply, demand or value of the investments deemed under the legislation to be qualifying, is most likely to constitute which of the following offences?

    A. Front running
    B. Money laundering
    C. Market abuse
    D. Insider dealing

39. Which of the following assets is exempt from capital gains tax?

    A. Buy-to-let properties
    B. Shares
    C. UK government bonds
    D. Unit trusts

40. What income tax will an additional rate taxpayer with an overall income of £250,000 per annum pay on a UK dividend?

    A. 7.5%
    B. 32.5%
    C. 38.1%
    D. 45%

41. What is the minimum age for holding a Stocks and Shares ISA?

    A. 16
    B. 18
    C. 25
    D. There is no minimum age

42. Sue, a higher rate taxpayer aged 43, receives £10,000 in dividend income. What rate of income tax will she pay?

    A. 7.5%
    B. 20%
    C. 32.5%
    D. 37.5%

43. At what age can a child withdraw money from their Junior ISA?

    A. 15
    B. 16
    C. 18
    D. 21

44. If an individual investor wishes to be able to manage the investments in a pension themselves, which type of pension would be the most suitable?

    A. SSAS
    B. SIPP
    C. Occupational pension
    D. Stakeholder pension

45. The Data Protection Principles place what particular responsibility on firms retaining personal data?

    A. To keep it indefinitely
    B. To keep it for a minimum of six years
    C. To not keep it for longer than is necessary for its purpose
    D. To not keep it for longer than 12 months

46. The individual charged with looking after the assets of a trust is known as the:

    A. Beneficiary
    B. Executor
    C. Settlor
    D. Trustee

47. You have a loan where interest is charged quarterly at 20% pa. What is the effective annual rate of borrowing?

    A. 21%
    B. 21.18%
    C. 21.35%
    D. 21.55%

48. If you expect interest rates to rise over the next few years, which type of mortgage payment would you expect to be most attractive?

    A. Tracker
    B. Discounted
    C. Fixed
    D. Variable

49. A policy that only pays out if death occurs during the term of the policy is:

    A. An endowment plan
    B. A term assurance
    C. An income replacement plan
    D. A whole-of-life assurance

50. Which of the following types of investment fund is most likely to utilise gearing?

    A. ETF
    B. Investment trust
    C. ICVC
    D. Unit trust

42/50

Answers to Multiple Choice Questions

1.   C   Chapter 2, Section 5.1

Advice on mergers and acquisitions is a wholesale market activity provided by investment banks.

2.   A   Chapter 2, Section 5.8

The primary role of a custodian is the safekeeping of assets.

3.   D   Chapter 7, Section 2.5

In an open economy there are few barriers to trade or controls over foreign exchange.

4.   D   Chapter 7, Section 4.2

High levels of inflation mean that prices rise and so someone on a fixed income would be able to buy fewer goods.

5.   D   Chapter 7, Section 5.2.2

The invisible trade balance is the difference between the value of imported and exported services. B is known as the visible trade balance, C is the country's current account, and A is the capital account.

6.   C   Chapter 2, Section 3.4

The Financial Services Compensation Scheme (FSCS) provides protection in the event of a deposit-taking institution going bust.

7.   D   Chapter 6, Section 2

Treasury bills do not pay interest but instead are issued at a discount to par.

8.   C   Chapter 6, Section 3

The 'spot rate' is the rate quoted by a bank for the exchange of one currency for another with immediate effect; however, spot trades are settled two business days after the transaction date.

9.   C   Chapter 8, Section 4.2.1

ICE Futures Europe operates the electronic global futures and OTC marketplace for trading energy commodity contracts. These contracts include crude oil and refined products, natural gas, power and emissions.

10.   C   Chapter 8, Section 4.2.1

A range of metals including aluminium, copper, nickel, tin, zinc and lead are traded on the London Metal Exchange (LME).

11.   **D**   **Chapter 4, Section 3.2**

The S&P 500 is generally regarded as providing the widest view of the US market compared to the Dow Jones and the NASDAQ Composite.

12.   **C**   **Chapter 3, Section 3.1**

The primary market is where new shares in a company are marketed for the first time. When these shares are subsequently resold, this is normally done on the secondary market.

13.   **C**   **Chapter 3, Section 4.1**

If the company closes down, often described as the company being 'wound up', the ordinary shareholders are paid after everybody else.

14.   **C**   **Chapter 3, Section 7.2**

Under a rights issue, a shareholder is offered the right to subscribe for further 'new' shares at a fixed price per share.

15.   **B**   **Chapter 3, Section 2.3**

Matters of major importance, such as a proposed change to the company's constitution, require a 'special resolution' and at least 75% to vote in favour.

16.   **B**   **Chapter 6, Section 2**

Commercial paper is issued by companies and is effectively the corporate equivalent of a Treasury bill.

17.   **C**   **Chapter 3, Section 7.2**

A rights issue is a mandatory with options type of corporate action.

18.   **D**   **Chapter 4, Section 4**

SETS is used to trade equity shares.

19.   **C**   **Chapter 5, Section 4.3**

A foreign bond is one issued by an overseas entity into a domestic market and is denominated in the domestic currency.

20.   **C**   **Chapter 8, Section 2.2**

The definition of a future is an agreement to buy or sell an item at a future date at a price agreed now.

21.   **B**   **Chapter 5, Section 5.2**

The flat yield is calculated by taking the annual coupon and dividing by the bond's price, and then multiplying by 100 to obtain a percentage. So the calculation is 5/112 x 100 = 4.46%.

22.   **B**   **Chapter 5, Section 5.1**

Bonds have an inverse relationship with interest rates so if interest rates rise, then bond prices will fall.

23.   **D**   **Chapter 8, Section 3.3**

A call option is when the buyer has the right to buy the asset at the exercise price, if he chooses to. The seller is obliged to deliver if the buyer exercises the option.

24.   **B**   **Chapter 8, Section 2.3**

A contract to buy an underlying asset at a future date is a future and the buyer is referred to as long.

25.   **A**   **Chapter 7, Section 5.2.1**

GDP is used as a measure of a country's output. It is the total of consumer spending, investment and government spending plus the value of exports minus the value of imports.

26.   **C**   **Chapter 9, Section 5.3**

Investment trusts are structured and listed on a stock market as with any other type of share and able to borrow money to gear up the portfolio. The share price, however, is not necessarily the same as the value of the underlying investments (determined on a per share basis and referred to as the net asset value). The share price could therefore trade at a premium or discount to the net asset value.

27.   **D**   **Chapter 9, Section 4.1**

Unit trusts have traditionally been dual-priced, that is, quoting separate prices for buying and selling the units. They now have a choice whether to use dual or single pricing.

28.   **C**   **Chapter 9, Section 1.2.2**

A passive fund aims to generate returns in line with a chosen index or benchmark.

29.   **D**   **Chapter 6, Section 5.2.1**

Monthly payments on repayment mortgages are a combination of capital and interest. The monthly payments on ISA and endowment mortgages are interest-only payments with the capital repayment provided by the investments within the ISA or endowment fund. Pension-linked mortgages are interest-only mortgages and the capital is repaid from the cash sum provided by the pension policy.

30.   **C**   **Chapter 9, Section 4.2**

Fund groups are required to settle sales within four days of the receipt of all required documentation.

31.   **A**   **Chapter 9, Section 5.1**

At least 90% of profits, after expenses, must be distributed to shareholders for a REIT to retain its tax status.

32.   **B**   **Chapter 9, Section 8**

Hedge funds typically have high minimum investment levels, ranging from £50,000 to over £1 million in some cases.

33.   **A**   **Chapter 10, Section 1.2**

The Financial Conduct Authority is responsible for the regulation of all firms in retail and wholesale financial markets, as well as the infrastructure that supports these markets. This includes supervision of investment exchanges.

34.   **C**   **Chapter 10, Section 2.1**

Layering is the second stage and involves moving the money around in order to make it difficult for the authorities to link the placed funds with the ultimate beneficiary of the money.

35.   **B**   **Chapter 10, Section 2.3.4**

JMLSG guidance requires enhanced due diligence to take account of the greater potential for money laundering in higher risk cases, specifically when the customer is not physically present when being identified.

36.   **C**   **Chapter 10, Section 3**

The instruments (securities) covered by the insider dealing legislation in the Criminal Justice Act include government bonds, but does not embrace commodity derivatives, shares in OEICs or unit trusts.

37.   **D**   **Chapter 10, Section 6.2**

The FOS can make an award against what it considers to be fair compensation; however, the sum cannot exceed £150,000.

38.   **C**   **Chapter 10, Section 4**

Market abuse includes behaviour likely to give a false or misleading impression of the supply, demand or value of qualifying investments.

39.   **C**   **Chapter 11, Section 2.2**

UK government bonds (gilts) are exempt from CGT.

40.   **C**   **Chapter 11, Section 2.1.2**

From April 2016, dividends are taxed at 7.5% for basic rate taxpayers, 32.5% for higher rate taxpayers and 38.1% for additional rate taxpayers.

41.   **B**   **Chapter 11, Section 3.1.3**

Stocks & Shares ISAs are available only to residents of the UK over the age of 18. Cash ISAs are available to UK residents aged 16 and over.

42.   **C**   **Chapter 11, Section 2.1.2**

The first £5,000 of dividend income in each tax year is tax-free, and sums above that will be taxed at 7.5% for basic rate taxpayers, 32.5% for higher rate taxpayers and 38.1% for additional rate taxpayers.

43.   **C**   **Chapter 11, Section 3.1.9**

At the age of 16, a child assumes management responsibility for their Junior ISA, but they cannot withdraw funds until the age of 18, except in the case of terminal illness or death.

44.   **B**   **Chapter 11, Section 3.2.5**

Individuals can manage the investments held within a self-invested personal pension (SIPP) subject to HMRC guidelines.

45.   **C**   **Chapter 10, Section 5**

One of the eight Data Protection Principles states that personal data shall not be kept for longer than is necessary for its purpose or purposes..

46.   **D**   **Chapter 11, Section 4.1**

A settlor creates the trust and the person he gives the property to, to look after for the beneficiaries is the trustee.

47.   **D**   **Chapter 2, Section 4.4**

Interest will be charged on the outstanding balance at 5% per quarter so the effective annual rate is $[(1.05 \times 1.05 \times 1.05 \times 1.05)] - 1 \times 100 = 21.55\%$.

48.   **C**   **Chapter 6, Section 5.1**

A fixed rate mortgage should be the most attractive if interest rates are expected to rise over the next few years.

49.   **B**   **Chapter 6, Section 6.1.1**

Term assurance is designed to pay out only if death occurs within a specified period.

50.   **B**   **Chapter 9, Section 5.2**

One of the distinguishing features of an investment trust is its ability to borrow funds for investment, in other words, to use gearing.

Syllabus Learning Map

Syllabus Unit/ Element		Chapter/ Section
Element 1	**Introduction**	
1.1	**The Financial Services Industry** On completion the candidate should:	
1.1.1	know the role of the following within the financial services industry: • retail banks • building societies • investment banks • pension funds • insurance companies • fund managers • platforms • stockbrokers • custodians • industry trade and professional bodies • peer-to-peer/crowdfunding	Chapter 2 Sections 2 and 5–5.11
1.1.2	know the function of and differences between retail and professional business and who the main customers are in each case: • retail clients and professional clients	Chapter 2 Section 5.11
1.1.3	know the role of the following investment distribution channels: • independent financial adviser • restricted advice • execution-only • robo-advice	Chapter 2 Sections 6.1–6.4

Syllabus Unit/ Element		Chapter/ Section
Element 2	**The Economic Environment**	
2.1	**The Economic Environment** On completion, the candidate should:	
2.1.1	know the factors which determine the level of economic activity: • state-controlled economies • market economies • mixed economies • open economies	Chapter 7 Sections 2.1–2.5
2.1.2	know the function of central banks: • the Bank of England • the Federal Reserve • the European Central Bank	Chapter 7 Sections 3–3.4
2.1.3	know the functions of the Monetary Policy Committee	Chapter 7 Section 3.2
2.1.4	know how goods and services are paid for and how credit is created	Chapter 7 Section 4.1

Syllabus Unit/ Element		Chapter/ Section
2.1.5	understand the impact of inflation/deflation on economic behaviour	Chapter 7 Section 4.2
2.1.6	know the meaning of the following measures of inflation: • Retail Prices Index • Consumer Prices Index	Chapter 7 Section 5.1
2.1.7	understand the impact of the following economic data: • gross domestic product (GDP) • balance of payments • budget deficit/surplus • level of unemployment • exchange rates	Chapter 7 Sections 5.2–5.2.4

Element 3	Financial Assets and Markets	
3.1	**Cash** On completion, the candidate should:	
3.1.1	know the characteristics of fixed term and instant access deposit accounts	Chapter 2 Sections 3–3.2
3.1.2	understand the distinction between gross and net interest payments	
3.1.3	know the characteristics of Bitcoin	
3.2	**Money Market Instruments** On completion, the candidate should:	
3.2.1	know the difference between a capital market instrument and a money market instrument	
3.2.2	know the definition and features of the following: • Treasury bill • Commercial paper • Certificate of deposit • money market funds	Chapter 6 Section 2
3.2.3	know the advantages and disadvantages of investing in money market instruments	
3.3	**Property** On completion, the candidate should:	
3.3.1	know the characteristics of property investment: • commercial/residential property • direct/indirect investment	Chapter 6 Section 4
3.3.2	know the advantages and disadvantages of investing in property	
3.4	**Foreign Exchange Market** On completion, the candidate should:	
3.4.1	know the basic structure of the foreign exchange market including: • currency quotes • settlement • spot/forward	Chapter 6 Section 3

Syllabus Unit/ Element		Chapter/ Section
Element 4	**Equities**	
4.1	**Equities** On completion, the candidate should:	
4.1.1	know how a company is formed and the differences between private and public companies	Chapter 3 Sections 2.1 and 2.2
4.1.2	know the features and benefits of ordinary and preference shares: • dividend • capital gain • share benefits	Chapter 3 Sections 4–5.4
	• right to subscribe for new shares • right to vote	Chapter 3 Sections 5.4–5.4.2
4.1.3	be able to calculate the share dividend yield	Chapter 3 Section 5.1
4.1.4	understand the advantages, disadvantages and risks associated with owning shares: • price risk • liquidity risk • issuer risk	Chapter 3 Sections 6–6.3
4.1.5	know the definition of a corporate action and the difference between mandatory, voluntary and mandatory with options	Chapter 3 Section 7
4.1.6	understand the following terms: • bonus/scrip/capitalisation issues • rights issues • dividend payments • takeover/merger	Chapter 3 Sections 7–7.5
4.1.7	know the purpose and format of annual general meetings	Chapter 3 Section 2.3
4.1.8	know the function of a stock exchange: • primary/secondary market • listing	Chapter 3 Sections 3.1–3.2
4.1.9	know the types and uses of a stock exchange index	Chapter 4 Sections 3–3.2
4.1.10	know to which markets and exchanges the following indices relate: • FTSE • Dow Jones Industrial Average • S&P 500 • Nikkei 225 • CAC40 • XETRA Dax • NASDAQ Composite • Hang Seng	Chapter 4 Sections 3.1–3.2

Syllabus Unit/ Element		Chapter/ Section
4.1.11	know how shares are traded: • order-driven/quote-driven	Chapter 4 Section 4
4.1.12	know the method of holding title – registered/bearer/immobilised/ dematerialised	Chapter 4 Sections 5–5.2
4.1.13	understand how settlement takes place and the key participants within the settlement process	

Element 5	Bonds	
5.1	**Characteristics** On completion, the candidate should:	
5.1.1	understand the characteristics and terminology of bonds: • coupon • redemption • nominal value	Chapter 5 Section 2
5.2	**Government Bonds** On completion, the candidate should:	
5.2.1	know the definition and features of government bonds: • types • yields	Chapter 5 Sections 3–3.1.2
5.3	**Corporate Bonds** On completion, the candidate should:	
5.3.1	know the definitions and features of the following types of bond: • domestic • foreign • eurobond	Chapter 5 Sections 4–4.4
5.4	**Bonds** On completion, the candidate should:	
5.4.1	know the advantages and disadvantages of investing in different types of bonds	Chapter 5 Section 5.1
5.4.2	be able to calculate the flat yield of a bond	Chapter 5 Section 5.2
5.4.3	understand the role of credit rating agencies and the differences between investment and non-investment grades	Chapter 5 Section 5.3

Element 6	Derivatives	
6.1	**Derivatives Uses** On completion, the candidate should:	
6.1.1	know the uses and application of derivatives	Chapter 8 Sections 1–2.1
6.2	**Futures** On completion, the candidate should:	
6.2.1	know the definition and function of a future	Chapter 8 Section 2.2

Syllabus Unit/ Element		Chapter/ Section
6.3	**Options** On completion, the candidate should:	
6.3.1	know the definition and function of an option	Chapter 8 Section 3.2
6.3.2	understand the following terms: • calls • puts	Chapter 8 Section 3.3
6.4	**Terminology** On completion a candidate should:	
6.4.1	understand the following terms: • long • short • holder • writing • premium	Chapter 8 Sections 1, 2.3 and 3.3
6.5	**Derivatives/Commodity Markets** On completion, the candidate should:	
6.5.1	know the characteristics of the derivatives and commodity markets	Chapter 8
6.5.2	know the advantages and disadvantages of investing in the derivatives and commodity markets	Sections 4–4.3

Element 7	Investment Funds	
7.1	**Introduction** On completion, the candidate should:	
7.1.1	understand the benefits of collective investment	Chapter 9 Section 1.1
7.1.2	know the difference between active and passive management	Chapter 9 Sections 1.2–1.2.2
7.1.3	know the types of funds and how they are classified	Chapter 9 Sections 1.3–1.4.1
7.2	**Unit Trusts** On completion, the candidate should:	
7.2.1	know the definition and legal structure of a unit trust	Chapter 9 Sections 2.1–2.3
7.2.2	know the roles of the manager and the trustee	Chapter 9 Sections 2.2–2.3
7.3	**Investment Companies with Variable Capital (ICVCs)** On completion, the candidate should:	
7.3.1	know the definition and legal structure of an ICVC/SICAV	Chapter 9
7.3.2	know the roles of the authorised corporate director and the depositary	Section 3

Syllabus Unit/ Element		Chapter/ Section
7.3.3	know the characteristics of Property Authorised Investment Funds (PAIFs)	Chapter 9 Section 3.1
7.4	**Pricing, Dealing and Settling** On completion, the candidate should:	
7.4.1	know how unit trust units and ICVC shares are priced	Chapter 9 Section 4.1
7.4.2	know how shares and units are bought and sold	Chapter 9
7.4.3	know how collectives are settled	Section 4.2
7.5	**Investment Trusts** On completion, the candidate should:	
7.5.1	know the characteristics of an investment trust: • gearing • real estate investment trusts (REITs)	Chapter 9 Sections 5–5.4
7.5.2	understand the factors that affect the price of an investment trust	
7.5.3	know the meaning of the discounts and premiums in relation to investment trusts	
7.5.4	know how investment trust shares are traded	
7.6	**Exchange-Traded Funds (ETFs)** On completion, the candidate should:	
7.6.1	know the main characteristics of exchange-traded funds: • trading • replication methods	Chapter 9 Section 6
7.7	**Alternative Investments** On completion, the candidate should:	
7.7.1	know the basic characteristics of hedge funds: • risks • cost and liquidity • investment strategies	Chapter 9 Section 8
7.7.2	know the basic characteristics of private equity: • risks • cost and liquidity	Chapter 9 Section 9
7.8	**Tax Advantaged Investments** On completion, the candidate should:	
7.8.1	know the types of tax-advantaged investments, including: • Venture Capital Trust (VCT) • Enterprise Investment Scheme (EIS) • Seed Enterprise Investment Scheme (SEIS) • Social Investment Tax Relief	Chapter 9 Section 9.1

Syllabus Unit/ Element		Chapter/ Section
Element 8	**Financial Services Regulation**	
8.1	**Introduction** On completion, the candidate should:	
8.1.1	understand the need for regulation	Chapter 10 Section 1.1
8.1.2	know the function and impact of UK regulators in the financial services industry	Chapter 10 Sections 1.2–1.3
8.1.3	understand the reasons for authorisation of firms	Chapter 10 Section 1.3
8.1.4	know the requirements of the Senior Managers and Certification Regime and the approved persons regime	Chapter 10 Section 1.4
8.1.5	know the outcomes arising from the FCA's approach to managing conduct risk within firms including Treating Customers Fairly	Chapter 10 Section 1.5
8.2	**Financial Crime** On completion, the candidate should:	
8.2.1	know what money laundering is, the stages involved and the related criminal offences	Chapter 10 Section 2.1
8.2.2	know the purpose and the main provisions of the Proceeds of Crime Act and the Money Laundering Regulations	Chapter 10 Section 2.2
8.2.3	know the action to be taken by those employed in financial services if money laundering activity is suspected and what constitutes satisfactory evidence of identity	Chapter 10 Sections 2.3–2.5
8.2.4	know the purpose of the Bribery Act	
8.2.5	know how firms and individuals can be exploited as a vehicle for financial crime: • theft of customer data to facilitate identity fraud • cybercrime • terrorist financing	
8.3	**Insider Dealing and Market Abuse** On completion, the candidate should:	
8.3.1	know the offences that constitute insider dealing and the instruments covered	Chapter 10 Section 3
8.3.2	know the offences that constitute market abuse and the instruments covered	Chapter 10 Section 4
8.4	**Data Protection** On completion, the candidate should:	
8.4.1	understand the basic steps firms should take to comply with the Data Protection Act	Chapter 10 Section 5

Syllabus Unit/ Element		Chapter/ Section
8.5	**Complaints and Compensation** On completion, the candidate should:	
8.5.1	know the requirements for handling customer complaints including the role of the Financial Ombudsman Service	Chapter 10 Sections 6.1–6.2
8.5.2	know the circumstances under which the Financial Services Compensation Scheme pays compensation	Chapter 10 Section 6.3

Element 9	Taxation, Investment Wrappers and Trusts	
9.1	**Tax** On completion, the candidate should:	
9.1.1	know the direct and indirect taxes as they apply to individuals: • income tax • capital gains tax • inheritance tax • stamp duty, stamp duty reserve tax and stamp duty land tax • VAT	Chapter 11 Sections 2–2.5
9.1.2	know the main exemptions in respect of the main personal taxes	
9.2	**Investment Wrappers** On completion, the candidate should:	
9.2.1	know the definition of and aim of ISAs	Chapter 11 Sections 3–3.2
9.2.2	know the tax incentives provided by ISAs	
9.2.3	know the types of ISA available: • Cash • Stocks and Shares • Junior ISAs • Help to Buy • Innovative Finance • Lifetime	
9.2.4	know the eligibility conditions for investors	
9.2.5	know the following aspects of investing in ISAs: • subscriptions • transfers • withdrawals • eligibility conditions	
9.3	**Pensions** On completion, the candidate should:	
9.3.1	know the benefits provided by pensions	Chapter 11 Sections 3.3.1–3.3.7
9.3.2	know the basic characteristics of the following: • state pension scheme • occupational pension schemes • personal pensions, including self-invested personal pensions (SIPPs) • stakeholder pensions • NEST/auto-enrolment	

Syllabus Unit/ Element		Chapter/ Section
9.4	**Trusts** On completion, the candidate should:	
9.4.1	know the definition of the following terms: • trustee • settlor • beneficiary	Chapter 11 Sections 4.1–4.2
9.4.2	know the main reasons for creating trusts	

Element 10	Other Financial Products	
10.1	**Loans** On completion, the candidate should:	
10.1.1	know the differences between bank loans, overdrafts, credit card borrowing and payday loans	Chapter 2 Sections 4–4.3
10.1.2	know the difference between the quoted interest rate on borrowing and the effective annual rate of borrowing	Chapter 2 Section 4.4
10.1.3	be able to calculate the effective annual rate of borrowing, given the quoted interest rate and frequency of payment	
10.1.4	know the difference between secured and unsecured borrowing	Chapter 2 Section 4.3
10.2	**Mortgages** On completion, the candidate should:	
10.2.1	understand the characteristics of the mortgage market: • interest rates • loan to value	Chapter 6 Sections 5–5.1
10.2.2	know the definition of and types of mortgage: • repayment • interest-only • offset	Chapter 6 Sections 5.2.1–5.2.3
10.2.3	know the fees applicable	Chapter 6 Section 5.3
10.3	**Life Assurance** On completion, the candidate should:	
10.3.1	understand the basic principles of life assurance	Chapter 6 Sections 6–6.1.2
10.3.2	know the definition of the following types of life policy: • term assurance • whole-of-life	
10.4	**Protection Insurance** On completion, the candidate should:	
10.4.1	understand the main areas in need of protection: • family and personal • mortgage • long-term care • business protection	Chapter 6 Section 6.2

Syllabus Unit/ Element		Chapter/ Section
10.4.2	know the definition of the following types of protection insurance: • critical illness insurance • income protection • mortgage protection • accident and sickness cover • household cover • medical insurance • long-term care insurance	Chapter 6 Sections 6.3–6.3.7

Examination Specification

Each examination paper is constructed from a specification that determines the weightings that will be given to each element. The specification is given below and should be used in conjuction with the Syllabus Learning Map.

It is important to note that the numbers quoted may vary slightly from examination to examination as there is some flexibility to ensure that each examination has a consistent level of difficulty. However, the number of questions tested in each syllabus element should not change by more than plus or minus 2.

Element Number	Element	Questions
1	Introduction	2
2	Economic Environment	3
3	Financial Assets and Markets	5
4	Equities	8
5	Bonds	5
6	Derivatives	4
7	Investment Funds	7
8	Financial Services Regulation	6
9	Taxation, Investment Wrappers and Trusts	6
10	Other Financial Products	4
Total		50

CISI Associate (ACSI) Membership can work for you...

Studying for a CISI qualification is hard work and we're sure you're putting in plenty of hours, but don't lose sight of your goal!

This is just the first step in your career; there is much more to achieve!

The securities and investments industry attracts ambitious and driven individuals. You're probably one yourself and that's great, but on the other hand you're almost certainly surrounded by lots of other people with similar ambitions.

So how can you stay one step ahead during these uncertain times?

Entry Criteria:
Pass in either:
- Investment Operations Certificate (IOC), IFQ, ICWIM, Capital Markets in, eg, Securities, Derivatives, Advanced Certificates; or
- one CISI Diploma/Masters in Wealth Management paper

Joining Fee: £25 or free if applying via prefilled application form   **Annual Subscription (pro rata):** £125

Using your new CISI qualification* to become an Associate (ACSI) member of the Chartered Institute for Securities & Investment could well be the next important career move you make this year, and help you maintain your competence.

Join our global network of over 40,000 financial services professionals and start enjoying both the professional and personal benefits that CISI membership offers. Once you become a member you can use the prestigious ACSI designation after your name and even work towards becoming personally chartered.

* ie, Investment Operations Certificate (IOC), IFQ, ICWIM, Capital Markets

Benefits in Summary...
- Use of the CISI CPD Scheme
- Unlimited free CPD seminars, webcasts, podcasts and online training tools
- Highly recognised designatory letters
- Unlimited free attendance at CISI Professional Forums
- CISI publications including *S&I Review* and *Change – The Regulatory Update*
- 20% discount on all CISI conferences and training courses
- Invitation to CISI Annual Lecture
- Select Benefits – our exclusive personal benefits portfolio

The ACSI designation will provide you with access to a range of member benefits, including Professional Refresher where there are currently over 60 modules available on subjects including Behavioural Finance, Cybercrime and Conduct Risk. CISI TV is also available to members, allowing you to catch up on the latest CISI events, whilst earning valuable CPD hours.

Plus many other networking opportunities which could be invaluable for your career.

Revision Express

You've bought the workbook... now test your knowledge before your exam.

Revision Express is an engaging online study tool to be used in conjunction with CISI workbooks. It contains exercises and revision questions.

Key Features of Revision Express:
- Examination-focused – the content of Revision Express covers the key points of the syllabus
- Questions throughout to reaffirm understanding of the subject
- Special end-of-module practice exam to reflect as closely as possible the standard you will experience in your exam (please note, however, they are not the CISI exam questions themselves)
- Exercises throughout
- Extensive glossary of terms
- Useful associated website links
- Allows you to study whenever you like

IMPORTANT: The questions contained in Revision Express elearning products are designed as aids to revision, and should not be seen in any way as mock exams.

Price per elearning module: £35
Price when purchased with the CISI workbook: £105

To purchase Revision Express:

call our Customer Support Centre on:
+44 20 7645 0777

or visit CISI Online Bookshop at:
cisi.org/bookshop

For more information on our elearning products, contact our Customer Support Centre on +44 20 7645 0777, or visit our website at cisi.org/elearning

Professional Refresher

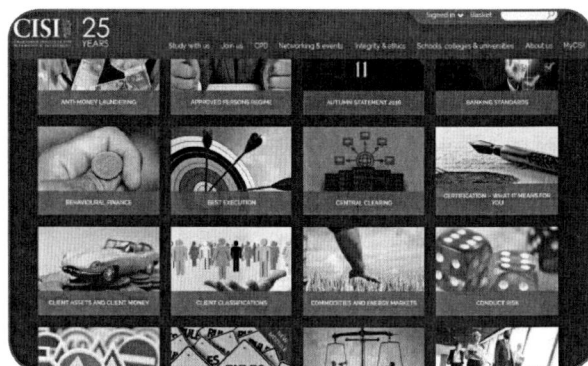

Self-testing elearning modules to refresh your knowledge, meet regulatory and firm requirements, and earn CPD hours.

Professional Refresher is a training solution to help you remain up-to-date with industry developments, maintain regulatory compliance and demonstrate continuing learning.

This popular online learning tool allows self-administered refresher testing on a variety of topics, including the latest regulatory changes.

There are currently over 90 modules available which address UK and international issues. Modules are reviewed by practitioners frequently and new topics are added to the suite on a regular basis.

Benefits to firms:
- Learning and tests can form part of business T&C programme
- Learning and tests kept up-to-date and accurate by the CISI
- Relevant and useful – devised by industry practitioners
- Access to individual results available as part of management overview facility, 'Super User'
- Records of staff training can be produced for internal use and external audits
- Cost-effective – no additional charge for CISI members
- Available to non-members

Benefits to individuals:
- Comprehensive selection of topics across industry sectors
- Modules are frequently reviewed and updated by industry experts
- New topics introduced regularly
- Free for members
- Successfully passed modules are recorded in your CPD log as Active Learning
- Counts as structured learning for RDR purposes
- On completion of a module, a certificate can be printed out for your own records

The full suite of Professional Refresher modules is free to CISI members or £250 for non-members. Modules are also available individually. To view a full list of Professional Refresher modules visit:

cisi.org/refresher

If you or your firm would like to find out more contact our Client Relationship Management team:

+ 44 20 7645 0670
crm@cisi.org

For more information on our elearning products, contact our Customer Support Centre on +44 20 7645 0777, or visit our website at cisi.org/refresher

Feedback to the CISI

Have you found this workbook to be a valuable aid to your studies? We would like your views, so please email us at learningresources@cisi.org with any thoughts, ideas or comments.

Accredited Training Partners

Support for examination students studying for the Chartered Institute for Securities & Investment (CISI) Qualifications is provided by several Accredited Training Partners (ATPs), including Fitch Learning and BPP. The CISI's ATPs offer a range of face-to-face training courses, distance learning programmes, their own learning resources and study packs which have been accredited by the CISI. The CISI works in close collaboration with its ATPs to ensure they are kept informed of changes to CISI examinations so they can build them into their own courses and study packs.

CISI Workbook Specialists Wanted

Workbook Authors

Experienced freelance authors with finance experience, and who have published work in their area of specialism, are sought. Responsibilities include:
- Updating workbooks in line with new syllabuses and any industry developments
- Ensuring that the syllabus is fully covered

Workbook Reviewers

Individuals with a high-level knowledge of the subject area are sought. Responsibilities include:
- Highlighting any inconsistencies against the syllabus
- Assessing the author's interpretation of the workbook

Workbook Technical Reviewers

Technical reviewers provide a detailed review of the workbook and bring the review comments to the panel. Responsibilities include:
- Cross-checking the workbook against the syllabus
- Ensuring sufficient coverage of each learning objective

Workbook Proofreaders

Proofreaders are needed to proof workbooks both grammatically and also in terms of the format and layout. Responsibilities include:
- Checking for spelling and grammar mistakes
- Checking for formatting inconsistencies

If you are interested in becoming a CISI external specialist call:
+44 20 7645 0609

or email:
externalspecialists@cisi.org

For bookings, orders, membership and general enquiries please contact our Customer Support Centre on +44 20 7645 0777, or visit our website at cisi.org